10632204

A24

i ana, 1951

PU
Pu

ALSO BY TATYANA TOLSTAYA

On the Golden Porch

Sleepwalker in a Fog

The Slynx

PUSHKIN'S CHILDREN

Writings on Russia and Russians

Tatyana Tolstaya

TRANSLATED BY JAMEY GAMBRELL

A Mariner Original
Houghton Mifflin Company
BOSTON ◆ NEW YORK ◆

Copyright © 2003 by Tatyana Tolstaya
English translation copyright © 1991, 1992, 1993, 1994, 1995,
1996, 1997, 1998, 2000 by Jamey Gambrell
All rights reserved

For information about permission to reproduce
selections from this book, write to Permissions,
Houghton Mifflin Company, 215 Park Avenue South,
New York, New York 10003.

Library of Congress Cataloging-in-Publication Data
is available.
ISBN 0-618-12500-0

Book design by Melissa Lotfy
Typefaces: Adobe Garamond and Baker Signet

Printed in the United States of America
QUM 10 9 8 7 6 5 4 3 2

Portions of this book previously appeared in *The New
York Review of Books, The New Republic, Wilson Quarterly,
The New Yorker,* and *The New York Times Magazine.*

Excerpt from *The Struggle for Russia* by Boris Yeltsin,
copyright © 1994 by Boris Yeltsin. Used by permission of
Times Books, a division of Random House, Inc.

CONTENTS

INTRODUCTION

IF THE REALLY LUCKY WRITERS are the ones who survive the hideous misadventures of history, then Tatyana Tolstaya is fortunate beyond telling. Consider the devastating events she and her countrymen have lived through in the half-century her lifetime spans: hunger, persecution, treachery and corruption, highly convoluted inducements to fear, brainwashing (and, sometimes, in the face of it, the most heroic adherence to the liberty of the mind), scarcity and demeaning—not ennobling—poverty, decades of spiritual stagnation and disgust. And then consider the stage on which these tragedies of the Soviet Union played themselves out: Great Russia itself, the chill white motherland, endless, magnificent, all-consuming. Oh, to be born in the proximity of such material!

Even better luck, the author who claims this rich inheritance came of age as a writer sometime around the middle of the 1980s, just in time to record the death by putrefaction of Soviet socialism, the collapse of its vast empire, and the subsequent lurching advance of the post-Soviet state. These events took place beginning in 1985, with the designation of Mikhail Gorbachev as general secretary of the Communist Party of the Union of Soviet Socialist Republics. His momentous years in power were followed by the adventures in government of President Boris Yeltsin. Under the pallid leader Vladimir Putin, Russia now struggles with its past and future. Tolstaya has written about all of it and so presents the happy reader with the twenty essays in this book, a brilliant writer's ongoing account of the most transcendent political event of the second half of the twentieth century.

Tolstaya has published three other books in English translation: two short works of fiction written in a delicate, richly meditative register, and her latest novel, *The Slynx*. As a writer of fact Tolstaya takes on a very different voice. In fact, she writes as a participant in her country's lamentable history, and she is a spinning fury, emitting words like sparks, enraged, saved from choking on the absurdities she has been called to witness only by the irresistible need to laugh at them. Indignation is her creative fuel, and her only relief is a related mordant tenderness for the sorry protagonists of so much stupidity. She does beautifully when she has to wave farewell to the poet Joseph Brodsky, dead so long before his time. She does even better, though, when she takes on the lumbering Boris Yeltsin and slaps him around in print, calling him a great Russian dolt, upbraiding him for doing this and failing to do the other, then stops in her tracks to observe him, deathly tired of so much responsibility, as he asks his helicopter pilot to land by a river and just linger a while. And what of her description of the epic, pathetic, and maligned Russian Everyman, grimy from centuries of poverty and self-neglect, without so much as a radish to bite on before he gulps down a shot of vodka, sniffing instead at the filthy sleeve of his greatcoat in order to get, at least, a good whiff of its many spicy odors?

Tolstaya is the offspring of a deeply literary family (although, she has said, she was well into adulthood before she started writing, in response to "steady and gentle pressure" from her father). Lev Tolstoy is among her forebears. Her paternal grandfather, Alexei Tolstoy, was a famous writer of the Soviet era. Her father was a brilliant scholar. Her mother's father, Mikhail Lozinsky, produced definitive translations of Shakespeare, Dante, and Lope de Vega. Tolstaya was born while Joseph Stalin was still alive, but the near-sacred family name shielded its members from terror, and Tatyana grew up in relative comfort in a book-filled apartment—all of which placed her rather outside the Soviet norm and granted her precocious observer status. She learned early to tell stories and quarrel with words, and would suffer when she was not able to find the inner words to describe her feelings, she later recalled. At university she studied the classics. She worked in a publishing house. At last, she started writing. She made a short trip to the United States and then, in the company of her husband, moved there in 1989. She learned English, and when she realized she was learning too much of it she fled back to her native country, before her Russian suffered any damage. (She retains enough English, however, to work closely with Jamey Gambrell on the latter's beautiful, muscular translations.)

The author's childhood, glowing and privileged in so many ways, nevertheless coincided with the cold war's years of frozen panic, and also with the long interregnum in which the Soviet leadership relaxed in power, believing itself eternal. Growing up surrounded by the bad faith and false language of that particular stage of socialism, Tolstaya learned to take rhetoric seriously. This lucky accident—yet another!—gives her enormous range, as rhetoric permeated every aspect of Soviet life. Lenin's tomb was a rhetorical exercise, and so was urban design, as Tolstaya reminds us when she writes about the heirs to Field Marshal Potemkin: the scruffy bureaucrats who ordered all the houses on Richard Nixon's route to the Kremlin painted and refurbished in preparation for his visit. But most of all, of course, rhetoric dominated language, and language dominated thought. "The Party is our Helmsman!" "You are walking the true path, comrades!" (rhetoric loves exclamation points) and "The Party is the Mind, Honor, and Conscience of the People!" (rhetoric loves capital letters, too) are among the deadly avalanche of slogans the young Tatyana's love of words survived.

The author's swift, skillful weaving between false words and the reality they hit at a slant allows her readers to become intimate with the eerie unnaturalness of Soviet existence. On the surface, the coarse fabric of everyday life could not have been more stultifying and commonplace. But because it was shot through with the glinting thread of so many wild, extravagant, preposterous lies, it acquired a dreaminess, a mythical quality, that serves Tolstaya's literary purposes well. Memorably, she tells how, as a child playing in the courtyard, she helped defeat U.S. imperialism and the omnipresent network of spies and infiltrators she had been warned against: "Who knows, they might be anywhere, disguised as Soviet citizens in regular clothes. They would reveal all our mysteries, steal the secrets of our might, and, God forbid, become just as strong and unconquerable as we were." These enemy agents must be deceived at all costs. When on a spring day an aged, wheezing couple shuffles towards her to ask directions, she understands her duty and sends them tottering away in the opposite direction from the botanical gardens they wish to visit.

Early guilt can carve an entire life into a different shape. Age eight, watching the elderly couple make their painful progress in the wrong direction, she is overwhelmed by the knowledge that they are not spies. "I heard the scrape and clank of the cogs in the state propaganda machine, a machine that had forgotten why it was turning," she writes. She understands something basic about how the lies her elders told her have twisted her soul. Who knows but that her nonfiction writing career has been one long effort to make things right with the two pathetic strangers she betrayed as a child?

Be that as it may, any writer's struggle to survive a regime that dictates thought is a remarkable moral journey. Alice, making her way through the looking-glass world, passive and bemused and so easily conned into apologizing for mistakes she has not made, acquires great moral power when she at last succumbs to rage. "I can't stand this any longer!" she yells, sick of the insanity, sick of the Red Queen and her threats. Then she picks up the pathetic, flailing queen and shakes her and shakes her and shakes her . . . until at last she wakes up. So Tolstaya.

In Tolstaya's writing, we get a first-person Alice, clear-eyed and back from mirror land. There is a luminous directness to Tolstaya's discussion of Russian intellectuals, who have struggled for two centuries to understand whether it is morally tolerable to write as Pushkin did, without political engagement. Curiously, although Tolstaya comes down squarely on the side of creative freedom, it is as a chronicler of political events that her own words catch fire. Her opinions are passionate, changeable, arguable, and sometimes even questionable—she is not, praise heaven, that most tedious of media creatures, a pundit—and every one carries the full force of the lived moment. She is not a reporter with a tape recorder in her hand, but a Russian writer with a unique voice and an urge to communicate the state of things.

Emerging from these pages, we can imagine Tolstaya and her world with such intensity that it would be difficult to persuade us of any difference between our imagination and her reality: the prerevolutionary kitchens with their pheasant consommés, their ovens like furnaces, and the miserable servant sleeping in the cupboard; Stalin and his handy eraser, with which he cheerfully removed his enemies not only from the world of the living but from the pages of photographed history too; Solzhenitsyn, once our moral guide, now the dreary geezer mouthing tedious, endless nostrums in the wasteland of the television screen. It's all so appalling, so hopeless, so ridiculous. If one could only stop laughing, it might be possible to give in to a spell of moral anguish. "Oh, but you know, I heard the most amazing thing today. Let me tell you . . ." Tolstaya exclaims, and we listen entranced to her latest story.

ALMA GUILLERMOPRIETO

PUSHKIN'S CHILDREN

Women's Lives

Review of *Soviet Women: Walking the Tightrope,* by Francine du Plessix Gray (Doubleday, 1990)

URING THE TWO WEEKS I spent in the United States, at least forty people asked me: "And what do you think about this book?" The person asking the question would simply point at it, without mentioning the author or title—the assumption seemed to be that it was obviously the book worth talking about at the moment. It was given to me twice during my stay.

The most important thing about *Soviet Women* for me is that it rings true. It consists of numerous stories, portraits of living people—women and men whom I recognize as though I actually knew them. Each is present as a person, with his or her own point of view and taste. The opinion of any of these Soviet citizens can easily be argued with, and one can often object that a highly personal point of view is being given, and that the person talking is simply wrong and doesn't understand anything—but the sum of these opinions of Russian women and men will, I believe, shake up the view of Soviet society that has formed in the West.

Francine du Plessix Gray traveled with a tape recorder from

the Baltic states to Siberia, asking women of many nationalities and cultures about their lives, in order to form a general picture of the situation of Soviet women. She was drawn to make this visit by affection for and curiosity about the country of her mother's and her grandparents' birth, and those of us who met her sensed the warmth of her involvement; but this did not hinder the sharpness of her observations. Her sense of humor must have helped her out more than once in situations that would have driven mad anyone who expected to make a quick, businesslike compilation of information on a country where—just imagine—the entire female population vigorously repudiates feminism.

Once or twice a year the doorbell of every Soviet apartment rings and a stern middle-aged woman with a list of residents in hand appears on the threshold. With no introduction, she curtly and glumly inquires: "Bothered by rats? Hear any mice? Bedbugs, cockroaches?" The mistress of the house, caught unawares, or perhaps gotten out of bed, mutters hurriedly in her confusion: "No . . . no . . . not yet," whether or not any of the above-mentioned animals have paid a visit: everyone knows it's useless to fight them anyway. The stern visitor nods, makes a notation in her book, and, without so much as a word of farewell, turns and rings the next apartment. For years, women from Western countries who call themselves feminists have interviewed us in the same cold, rigid manner: "How do your men oppress you? Why don't they wash the dishes? Why don't they prepare meals? Why don't they allow women into politics? Why don't women rebel against the phallocracy?"

Soviet women are dumbfounded. Not only do they not want to be involved in the depressing, nauseating activity called Soviet "politics"—which for years amounted to sitting for hours on end in a stuffy room amid piles of paper and pronouncing officially authorized sentences—they would much rather not work at all. In bewilderment, they ask themselves: What do we need this ridiculous feminism for anyway? In order to do the work of two people? So men can lie on the sofa? For as soon as a Soviet man sees that someone is doing his work for him, he quickly lies down on the sofa and falls into a reverie with a feeling of relief.

Russian men have been recumbent for many centuries. Emel, the hero of Russian fairy tales, lies on the stove, and a fish—a pike—brings everything to him, from daily sustenance to a princess, upon marriage to whom he will be able to do nothing at all with complete justification. Ilya Muromets, the knight—hero of Russian folk epics—lies quite still without lifting a finger for thirty-three years, until some sorcerers chance to pass by and endow him with heroic powers. Oblomov, the famous protagonist of the nineteenth-century writer Goncharov's novel, remains in repose his entire life—too lazy even to write a letter to put his finances in order.

With laughter and regret, all Russia recognized itself in the person of Oblomov. The heroes of Russian folklore and literature set their affairs straight thanks to magical wives and fiancées who sew, weave, spin, cook, bake, heal, cast spells, come to their rescue in dangerous situations, and save them from inevitable doom. Men in Russian folklore are often fools and idlers; women are sorceresses, terrifying or gentle, cannibals or beauties; they are beings that deftly transform themselves into swans and frogs at just the right moment. When the silly hero, unschooled in the mysteries of female magic, tries to approach things rationally by burning the mysterious and dangerous frog skin or stealing the swan's feathers, women abandon him, fly off to distant kingdoms beyond the dark blue forest, to grass mountains or lost islands. In short, as Francine Gray says, quoting a Soviet proverb, "Women can do everything, and men do all the rest."

Russian men may have been lying down for hundreds of years, and Russian women may have been bemoaning this state of affairs, but there are exceptions among men. And even the exceptions seem to come straight out of Russian literature. Once one of my friends, Irina, a music teacher with three children, got a phone call from an unknown man. "Hello," he said. "I want to be your slave."

"Where do you know me from?" said Irina, surprised.

"I don't know you," responded the man. "I simply dialed your phone number by chance. But it doesn't matter. I feel terribly sorry for all women on earth. Poor souls! They do the work of three people, these gentle, unfortunate creatures. And no one helps! I decided to dedicate my life to a woman — all of you are equally wonderful. Please allow me to come to your home and do the heaviest work."

The man began to cry, and Irina agreed that he could come that evening, when her husband was at home.

"I want to wash the floors," he said. "I'll take out the garbage, cook, take the children for walks."

We can't trust him with the children — he's probably some kind of maniac, thought the couple. "Well, here, return these empty bottles for starters," they told him, figuring that the slave would steal the deposit money and that would be the last they'd see of him, thank heavens. But the slave turned in the bottles and came back with the money.

Then he began to work at housecleaning. When everything was done, the slave masters invited their new acquisition for a cup of tea. A completely Dostoyevskian conversation ensued — a long, philosophical, Russian sort of conversation about morality, about whether or not one would inevitably experience a fall if one raised oneself above other people, and about how while they had been exploiting him, they had been overwhelmed by proprietary instincts and negative feelings of superiority, and their souls had recognized the sin of pride. So they asked him to finish his tea and leave.

"What do you mean, leave?" the slave protested. "I'm yours now. You don't have the right to get rid of me. You can only sell me. For the time being, I'm going to sleep in the hall on the rug. You're depressing me!"

It was with a great deal of difficulty that Irina and her husband sold the slave to a sick woman, Elena, who needed constant help because she was an invalid and bedridden. From time to time, Irina would phone the slave, "Well, how's it going?"

"Wonderful," he'd reply. "I'm working around the house and I finally feel useful."

"How's it going?" Irina asked the slave a week later.

"Not bad," said the slave, "only she demands that I buy her French perfume with my own money. What impudence. I've liberated her from this work, and she tyrannizes me."

"Well, how's it going?" Irina asked the slave a month later.

"It's awful, awful," complained the slave. "It's not enough that I wash her, dress her, comb her hair, take her out for walks, tell her interesting stories, buy her everything she wants. She also wants me to enter the university, and makes me read Pushkin and write compositions. Of course, I'm a slave, but what right does she have to interfere in my inner life?"

Finally he himself called Irina. "Congratulate me, I'm a free man! Finally! I won't have anything to do with another woman ever again!"

And he disappeared forever into the sea of life from which he had so unexpectedly surfaced.

Happily free of the dry, rigid rationalism of many of her Western colleagues, Francine Gray did not force herself on Russian women with ready-made, one-size-fits-all stereotypes; she didn't wave preconceived formulas for the reorganizing of Russian women's lives at them and didn't exclaim, "Horrors! Shame!" as have—in all sincerity—many of her more simple-minded compatriots.

She noticed—and was herself surprised to find—that Russian, even Soviet, society is matriarchal. The term *matriarchy* is of course too weighty a term to apply without caution to the complex, motley, and paradoxical society that arose (and is apparently fast disintegrating) in a huge country stretching from ocean to ocean and comprising hundreds of peoples who speak virtually all imaginable languages and pray to all imaginable gods. But if we don't insist on a strict, overly scholarly approach, and if, dimming the sharp, surgical light of rationalism, we allow ourselves to relax, listen, observe, absorb, and *feel*—that is, do exactly what Russian people do almost professionally—then it is possible to speak about the matriarchal qualities of many features of the Russian consciousness. And the Russian mentality has to some degree penetrated all corners of the empire—often not for the best.

Sensitivity, reverie, imagination, an inclination to tears, compassion, submission mingled with stubbornness, patience that permits survival in what would seem to be unbearable circumstances, poetry, mysticism, fatalism, a penchant for walking the dark, humid back streets of consciousness, introspection, sudden, unmotivated cruelty, mistrust of rational thought, fascination with the word—the list could go on and on—all these are qualities that have frequently been attributed to the "Slavic soul." When one puts them all together, one forms the impression that the description is of a woman. (These qualities, however, also equally fit the male Russian literary and folk heroes mentioned above.) Russian writers and thinkers have often called the "Russian soul" female, contrasting it to the rational, clear, dry, active, well-defined soul of the Western man. The West, in fact, often refuses to speak about the "soul" at all, insofar as it applies to a people or a culture. The West refuses to use such an unscientific concept: you can't hold the "soul" in your hand, therefore it's impossible—and unnecessary—to study it. Logical categories are inapplicable to the soul. But Russian sensitivity, permeating the whole culture, doesn't want to use logic —logic is seen as dry and evil, logic comes from the devil. The most important thing is sensation, smell, emotion, tears, mist, dreams, and enigma.

In Russian culture, emotion is assigned an entirely positive value, and thus the culture's sexual stereotypes differ from those of the Protestant, Enlightenment West. The more a person expresses his emotions, the better, more sincere, and more "open" he is. When Russians speak of the soul, what is meant is this developed subculture of emotion. You don't have to explain what the soul is; any Russian is capable of expounding upon the subject at length and with deep feeling. Within this subculture, women are seen as stronger: that is, they appear to feel more, express things more openly, display their emotions more clearly — they are, in effect, "more Russian."

Russian literature is not intellectual, but emotional. In Russia, the people who are committed to insane asylums are not those who have lost their reason, but those who have suddenly acquired it. At the very least, he who attempts to reason logically is declared a dangerous eccentric. In Griboedov's play *Woe from Wit,* written at the very beginning of the nineteenth century, the hero arrives in Moscow after spending several years in the West. The absurdity of Moscow life horrifies him and casts him into despair. He tries to appeal to reason, to logic — a waste of time and effort. He is immediately declared insane — in a matter of five minutes this becomes clear to everyone. Despairing, the hero runs away. Where to? To the West, of course. The philosopher and writer Chaadaev, one of the most brilliant men of the same period, was likewise declared insane. Truly mad people — *iurodivye,* as they are called in Russian — are thought of as "God's people"; they are holy, and their incoherence, absurd pronouncements, and strange behavior are considered a genuine sign of a special, mystical link with God.

I do not presume to give even an outline of the Russian worldview — at the very least that would be immodest. But my Russian *feeling* tells me how accurately Francine du Plessix Gray understood (or felt?) the powerful female principle that suffuses the Russian universe. Home, hearth, household, children, birth, family ties, the close relationship of mothers, grandmothers, and daughters; the attention to all details, control over everything, power, at times extending to tyranny—all this is Russian woman, who both frightens and attracts, enchants and oppresses. To imagine that Russian women are subservient to men and that they must therefore struggle psychologically or otherwise to assert their individuality vis-à-vis men is, at the very least, naive.

Of course, social inequities exist: many traditionally female occupations (including that of doctor) are among the lowest paid in the country; many women in the Soviet Union break their backs at excessively hard physical labor (women do a great deal of the road construction work, for instance); many work around the clock without a chance to rest. There are women who are beaten or brutalized by their husbands; there are women alcoholics, women who would sell their children for a bottle of vodka. There is a bit of everything, as is true everywhere in the world. But most Russian women—"normal" women—are, as a rule, far from weak creatures.

Russian women often exude such a strong, psychologically overpowering aura that men, floundering helplessly like moths in the wind, are only to be pitied. A Russian woman is most definitely mistress of her household; the children belong to her and to her alone; the family often doesn't even ask for male advice, or only consults men to clarify a situation: women will do things their way in any event.

When, a few years ago, *Literaturnaya gazeta* began a discussion about "who is master in the house," the publication was bombarded with a stream of male complaints—thousands of unhappy representatives of the "stronger sex" complained about all manner of oppression. The most common was the situation of divorce. If there are children in the family, they inevitably stay with the mother when the couple divorces, although theoretically the law recognizes the equal rights of each parent. But no one would ever think of awarding custody of children to the father; the organizations that supervise the treatment of children consist entirely of women, and the very idea of entrusting a child to a man would seem absurd to them. Dozens of complaining letters from men merged in a common, miserable howl. This was perhaps the first time that men had received the right to express themselves on the theme of the family in the Soviet press, and the results astounded many people.

The letters from women in this polemic were fairly unanimous as well: "The creep got what he deserved." "What good are men?" "All men are pigs" — alas, a common female refrain. Of course, there's an ongoing fight over these "pigs," since every woman wants to have her own "creep" at home. The feeling of property — as opposed to companionship or partnership in marriage, for instance — is a very Russian characteristic.

Men are the property of women; if this property betrays, or runs away, or decides to lay down its own law — it will receive its just deserts. Francine Gray, having spoken with dozens of women, noted with surprise that almost all of them talked about men as they would about furniture or other inanimate objects. A group of women doctors kept a few men in their group "for a tonic." You can always find this kind of "Schweppes" in female collectives: among doctors, teachers, in publishing houses, in the many research institutes that exist in the Soviet Union where women are in the majority. The "tonifying" man is usually spoiled, receives a great deal of attention; women try to dress up for him (our women tend to dress for work as if for the theater), they like to bring him homemade meat pies and salads, they even pretend that they are happy to submit. But if he should try to boss them around — woe to him. If women aren't the death of him, then at least they are always capable of arranging some quiet, legally unassailable sabotage, and it is impossible to force a woman to work if she doesn't want to. Women will quickly unify and attack the accusing man with reproaches of callousness, oppression, cruelty, and lack of understanding of a woman's hard fate.

It is difficult — especially in a short article — to speak of problems whose roots go back in history. But the events of the last decades are available for observation: the October revolution; a lengthy civil war; the almost complete destruction of the intelligentsia in Russia; the coming of new classes to power; the mixing of all layers of the population and all nationalities who live in the Russian empire; the many years of Stalinist terror, with tens of millions of prisoners and deaths; then the war, which destroyed at least twenty million men (according to some estimates, as many as thirty-six million people altogether).

During the four years of war there was only one sex in Russia —women. The men had gone to war. Not only did the country have to be fed, but weapons had to be manufactured—and this was done by women and small children. And after the war, sometimes only one man would return alive to a Russian village full of women—and even he was often an invalid. One can understand that each woman strived to possess him. An entire generation of women grew up, grew old, and died as eternal fiancées or widows.

And the Stalinist arrests continued after the war as well— with renewed strength. Those who had managed to spend time abroad, especially the partisans who fought with liberating forces in other countries, were sent to the camps; those who had been held prisoner in German camps were sent away; homeless adolescents and orphans, often turning to crime to survive, were also sent to the camps. Sometimes it is said that the entire country spent time in the camps, and this is actually a fair statement. Women—especially the wives of prisoners—were also arrested, but by and large it was men who did time. They returned desperate people; alcoholism was rampant among them; many had become criminals in detention. They would commit crimes and burglary and be sent back again. The intelligentsia was often arrested for political reasons, and the level of education, enlightenment, and just plain civilized behavior was extremely low.

Add to this the constant psychological and physical stress of periods of famine and chronic food, housing, and consumer shortages well beyond the imagination of most Westerners, and it becomes obvious that all these catastrophes were bound to have a devastating effect on the family and relationships between the sexes. Disastrous shifts in the Russian consciousness were bound to occur, developing and strengthening its worst traits. Most foreigners who visit our country deal primarily with the city culture of Moscow and Leningrad. The psychology of rural, provincial, small-town culture is less well known to foreigners—but I am talking mostly about this small-town culture, since the intelligentsia in most countries around the world is quite similar.

A Soviet woman's dream is to not have to work—but work she must, because salaries are very low. It is impossible to live on a husband's salary alone. There can be almost no discussion of a career in the Western sense of a progression upward—a career is tied in with enormous psychological difficulties and adds so insignificantly to one's salary that it isn't even worth trying. A career is more likely to give power than money, but most Soviet women feel they have enough power as is. Why should she want some kind of intangible political power over abstract people who don't want to submit, when right within her grasp is a full-fledged, seductive, constant, palpable power over the members of her family, over every object, chair, bed, broom, curtain, pot or pan, keys, the dog, the schedule, and menu?

Until very recently, a "career" meant relinquishing the personal, private life that provided Soviet people with respite and protection from the claims of the state, in order to participate in the meaningless parades, endless meetings, and lying speeches of the public domain. An honest person tried his or her best not to participate in this "official" life. Those who did get involved in the hellish machine were broken: either it destroyed all traces of individuality and compromised them morally and ethically, or—if a person rebelled—it threw him out of society, sometimes sending him as far as Siberia.

Of course, in our society everyone felt suffocated by public life, by the total absence of freedom. But men suffered from it to a greater degree than women, since women have always had the loophole of "domestic life" to fall back on. Men had no such loophole in our society. At the beginning of the sixties a special law was devised against "parasitism," i.e., the failure to work at a job authorized and recognized by the state. Though this law was used primarily as a tool against political dissidence, it was also directed against men who wished to choose their profession freely and thus be masters of their own fates. The Nobel laureate Joseph Brodsky was convicted under this very law.

Women have rarely been prosecuted under this insane law. In the Soviet Union, women have the de facto right not to work if they don't want to, although the law theoretically applies to both sexes. But it is used against women only in exceptional cases — if the woman's behavior is excessively "antisocial," for instance, if she is a prostitute, a thief, an alcoholic, beats her children, and her neighbors also complain about her. But these are the extreme exceptions. For years, our society regularly punished, persecuted, imprisoned, and humiliated its male population, for men could not withdraw from the role of public citizen as easily as women. One of the ironies of the Revolution is that it did in fact succeed in making men and women equal — by taking away the rights of every member of society.

Although the picture that I have painted here may seem gloomy, my words are dictated not by a wish to judge, but by compassion for our people, who may often seem emotional barbarians to outsiders. And I feel an enormous sympathy for Francine Gray, who was not frightened off and did not turn against the people she met, the Russian men and women whose living portraits fill the pages of her book. There is a Russian proverb: "Learn to love us when we're filthy dirty — anyone can love us when we're clean." That's what she did.

The possibility of misunderstanding and not hearing each other always exists. If a desert dweller and a citizen of a lush tropical island begin to chat about the sun, water, and wind, it's not likely that their opinions will coincide. Knowing Soviet life, I read Francine Gray's book, noting mentally: true . . . that's exactly right . . . American readers — those who don't know our country at all — might think entirely the opposite. "How unlikely," they might think, "how could that possibly be true?"

We are too different; in many respects we are opposites. It's simpler not to listen, not to believe, to shut ourselves off inside the cozy curtains of the usual stereotypes. I end this article with a strange uncertainty that I will be understood correctly, the same feeling that people have on parting with someone they have just met and don't know too well. "It seems I was in top form today and spoke well," thinks one of them. "What a strange nose he has, what a dreadful suit, and what stupid relatives," thinks the other. "Drop in again," they both say. After all — they're neighbors.

1990

The Great Terror
and the Little Terror

Review of *The Great Terror: A Reassessment,* by Robert Conquest (Oxford University Press, 1990)

L AST YEAR Robert Conquest's *The Great Terror* was translated into Russian and published in the USSR in the journal *Neva.* (Unfortunately, only the first edition was published. I hope that the second, revised and enlarged edition will be published as well, if it is not suppressed by the censorship so recently revived in the Soviet Union.) The fate of this book in the USSR is truly remarkable. Many of those who opened *Neva* in 1989–90 exclaimed: "But I know all this stuff already!" How did they know it? From Conquest himself.

The first edition appeared twenty years ago in English, was translated into Russian, and infiltrated what was then a closed country. It quickly became an underground best seller, and there's not a thinking person who isn't acquainted with the book in one form or another: those who knew English read it in the original, while others got hold of the Russian text, made photocopies at night, and passed them on. The book gave birth to much historical (underground and émigré) research, the facts were assimilated, reanalyzed, argued, confirmed, elaborated. In short, the book almost achieved the status of folklore, and many

Soviet people measure their own history "according to Conquest," sometimes without realizing that he actually exists. This is why many readers, especially the younger ones, thought of Conquest's book as a compilation of "commonly known facts" when they read it for the first time. The author should be both offended and flattered.

This is a book about the Stalinist terror, about the Great Terror, which began in the thirties and continued—growing and fading—until the death of the Great Tyrant in 1953.

The very expression "Great Terror" leads to the idea of the "Little Terror," which remains necessarily outside the confines of this book. Of course, no one can write a book about Russia that includes everything, explains everything, weaves together the facts and motifs of history, revealing the root system that every so often puts out shoots and suddenly blossoms into the frightful flower of a Great Terror. I'm reminded of the protagonist of Borges's story "Aleph," who tried to create a poem that described the entire universe—but failed, of course. No one can possibly accomplish such a task.

The Little Terror in Russia has been around from time immemorial. It has lasted for centuries and continues to this very day. So many books have been written about the Little Terror! Virtually all the literature of the nineteenth century, which is so valued in the West, tells the story of the Little Terror, sometimes with indignation, sometimes as something taken for granted, and tries to understand its causes, explain its mechanisms, give detailed portraits of its victims: individual personalities, entire classes, and the country as a whole. What is Russian society and why is it the way it is? What can and must be done in order to free ourselves of this all-permeating terror, of total slavery, of fear of any and everyone? How do we ensure that an individual's fate does not depend on others' whims? Why is it that any revolution, any attempt to rid Russia of terror, leads to an even greater terror?

Russia didn't begin yesterday and won't end tomorrow. The

attempts of many writers and researchers to explain Russian horrors by the Bolshevik rise to power are naive. The sigh of relief that in recent years has been heard more and more often in the West is naive as well: the cold war is over, Gorbachev has come, everything will soon be just fine. (The events of the last few months have shown the West what has been clear to Soviet people for almost two years: nothing good can be expected from Gorbachev.)

Human life is short. For many people, delving into history's depths is boring, frightening, and they have no time for it. Furthermore, in the West the sense of history has weakened or completely vanished: the West does not live in history, it lives in civilization (by which I mean the self-awareness of transnational technological culture as opposed to the subconscious, unquestioned stream of history). But in Russia there is practically no civilization, and history lies in deep, untouched layers over the villages, over the small towns that have reverted to near wilderness, over the large, uncivilized cities, in those places where they try not to let foreigners in, or where foreigners themselves don't go. Even in the middle of Moscow, within a ten-minute walk from the Kremlin, live people with the consciousness of the fifteenth or eleventh century (the eleventh century was better, more comprehensible to us, because at that time culture and civilization were more developed in Russia than in the fifteenth century). When you have any dealings with these people, when you start a conversation, you feel that you've landed in an episode of *The Twilight Zone.* The constraints of a short article don't allow me to adequately describe this terrifying feeling, well known to Europeanized Russians, of coming into contact with what we call the absurd, a concept in which we invest far greater meaning than Western people do. Here one needs literature — Kafka, Ionesco; one needs academic scholars like Levy-Bruhl with his study of prelogical thought.

Archaeological digs have been carried out in the ancient Russian city of Novgorod, once an independent republic that carried on independent trade with the West. The earth reveals deep layers of the city's history. In the early ones, from the eleventh or twelfth century, there are many birch-bark documents and letters written by simple people that testify to the literacy of the population. And there are also remains of good leather footwear. In the fifteenth and the sixteenth centuries, when Novgorod had been conquered by Moscow, letters disappear, and instead of leather boots, *lapti* appear, a kind of slipper-like shoe made from bast.

The sixteenth century, when Ivan the Terrible ruled, was also a time of Great Terror, perhaps even the first government-wide terror in Russia, a terror that is horribly reminiscent of Stalinist times. It is particularly appalling in what would seem to be its inexplicableness, its lack of precedent: after all, there wasn't any Lenin, there were no Bolsheviks or revolutions preceding Ivan the Terrible. It was during his reign that someone said: "We Russians don't need to eat; we eat one another and this satisfies us."

The backward motion of history, the submersion of culture under a thick layer of gilded, decorative "Asiatic savagery," government piracy, guile elevated to principle, unbridled caprice, extraordinary passivity and lack of will all combined with an impulsive cruelty; incompletely suppressed paganism, undeveloped Christianity; a blind, superstitious belief in the spoken, and especially in the written, word; the sense of sin as a secret and repulsive pleasure (what Russians call Dostoyevskyism). How can all this be described, how can one give a sense of the ocean from which the huge wave of a Great Terror periodically rises?

Robert Conquest investigates only the Great Terror, not touching on the Little one. He sees its roots in the Soviet regime that formed before Stalin, in the very principles and organization of the Soviet state. In his own way he is absolutely right; this is true, and every investigation must begin somewhere. I merely wish to remind the reader once again (and Robert Conquest knows this very well) that the Soviet state was not created out of thin air, that its inhabitants were the inhabitants of yesterday's Russian state who awoke one fine morning to find themselves under the so-called Soviet regime. The October revolution and the civil war that soon followed led to the exile and destruction, or decivilizing, of the Europeanized Russian population (by Europeanized I mean people who were literate, educated; who possessed a work ethic, a developed religious consciousness, respect for law and reason; and who were also familiar with Europe and the achievements of world culture). Those who survived and remained in Russia lost the right to speak their mind and were too frightened or weak to influence anything. Russian society, though it wandered in the dark for centuries, had nonetheless by 1917 given birth not only to an educated class but to a large number of people with high moral standards and a conscience, to honest people who were not indifferent to issues of social good. This is the intelligentsia—not really a class but a fellowship of people "with moral law in their breast," as Kant put it. Lenin hated them more than anyone else, and they were the first to be slaughtered. When Maxim Gorky wrote to Lenin in their defense, saying that "the intelligentsia is the brain of the nation," Lenin answered with the famous phrase: "It's not the brain, it's the shit."

The savage, barbaric, "Asiatic" part of the Russian empire was invited to participate in the "construction of a new world" and its members received certain privileges, some people in word alone, others in fact. What this section of the population really represented, what it was capable of and what it aspired to, no one actually knew, particularly the Soviet leaders, whose notions about the "people" derived exclusively from their own theories; the model for the "worker" was taken from the German or English working class, and the peasant was entirely dreamed up. Arrogant, impatient, cruel, barely literate people took advantage of the historical moment (the war dragging on, the military leadership's lack of talent, thievery in the army and the rear guard; a weak tsar; and after the February Revolution, a weak transitional government, widespread disorder and chaos, a dissatisfied people, etc.) to carry out what they called a revolution but what was actually a counterrevolutionary coup.

As is well known, Lenin's initial idea was to hold onto power for no less a period than the French Commune once did. This desire to become a chapter heading in a history text is quite characteristic of bookish, theoretical thinking. Then he intended to suffer a defeat, go underground, and work for a real coup. However, no one ended up taking power away from the Bolsheviks: they were better organized and much more cynical and unscrupulous than any of their opponents. Seizing power turned out not to be too difficult. But governing the Russian empire was almost impossible. (Even today no one knows how.) Terror became useful.

In one of his telegrams, Lenin exclaims indignantly: "We're not shooting enough professors." Isn't this a portent of typical Stalinist methods: destruction by category? Under Stalin, arrest by category became a regular thing: today they're killing miners, tomorrow they're destroying railway engineers, then they'll get around to peasants, then historians of local customs (students of local lore, history, and economy were almost completely destroyed for being "spies"). One of my grandfathers, Mikhail Lozinsky, was a well-known translator of the poetry of Shakespeare, Lope de Vega, and Corneille who spoke six languages fluently. He was frequently interrogated in the early 1920s for participating in the "Poets Guild" literary group; the ignorant investigator kept trying to find out where the "Guild" kept their weapons. This was under Lenin, not Stalin. His wife (my grandmother) was jailed for several months at the same time, perhaps because so many of her friends were members of the Social Revolutionary party. She later recalled that she had never before or since had such a pleasant time, or met so many intelligent and educated people. In 1921, my mother's godfather, the poet Nikolai Gumilev, was shot on a false accusation of involvement in a "monarchist plot." (There were other deaths in our family, but fewer than in some. The hatred many felt toward our family because of this was typical, and was expressed in the following way: "Why is it that they've lost so few family members?") Gumilev's wife, the famous poet Anna Akhmatova, referred to these relatively peaceful times as "vegetarian."

Cannibalistic times didn't emerge out of thin air. The people willing to carry out Bolshevik orders had to ripen for the task. They matured in the murk of Russian villages, in the nightmare of factory work conditions, in the deep countryside, and in the capitals, Moscow and St. Petersburg. They were already there, there were a lot of them, and they could be counted on. "God forbid we should ever witness a Russian revolt, senseless and merciless," our brilliant poet Pushkin remarked as early as the first quarter of the nineteenth century. He knew what he was talking about. Was Lenin counting on the senselessness and mercilessness of Russians, or did he simply fail to take them into account? Whatever the case, by fate's inexorable law he, too, was victimized by his own creation: his mistress, Inessa Armand, was apparently killed; power was torn from his paralyzed hands during his lifetime; it is rumored that Stalin murdered Lenin's wife, Nadezhda Krupskaya, by sending her a poisoned cake. It is merely rumored — no one knows precisely. (The vision of this rather stupid, self-assured old woman — who forbade children's stories because they were "unrealistic" but who was honest in her own way and not malicious — eating a spoonful of cake with icing and poison provokes mixed feelings in me. Mea culpa.)

And how could a Russian revolt be anything but senseless and merciless, when the Russian government had exhibited a senseless lack of mercy toward its own people for centuries? From time immemorial the subjugated Russian classes have been required to inform their sovereign of anyone who for whatever reason seemed suspicious to them. From the mid-seventeenth century on, the law prescribed the death penalty for failure to report a crime committed or intended. Not only the criminal but all of his relatives must be reported. Thus, for example, since unauthorized flight abroad was considered a crime, the escapee's entire family became criminals, and death awaited them all, because it was supposed that they could not have been ignorant of the intended betrayal. Interrogation was carried out under torture, and of course everyone "confessed."

The Stalinist regime didn't have to invent anything three hundred years later, it simply reproduced the political investigation techniques that were already a longstanding tradition in the Russian state. It merely included more of the population, and the pretexts for arrest became more trivial. But perhaps there was no significant difference? After all, neither the seventeenth nor the eighteenth century had their Conquest, someone to describe in scrupulous detail every aspect of what occurred.

The parallels between arrests in the eighteenth century and the twentieth are so close that it's hard to shake the feeling that time has stopped. In an article by the Soviet historian Evgeny Anisimov on the history of denunciation, I read about something that happened in 1732. A man informed on a certain merchant, claiming that the merchant had called him a "traitor." The merchant was arrested (pronouncing "indecent words" was a political crime which brought suffering, torture, Siberia). With great difficulty the merchant was able to prove that the word "traitor" referred not to the other man but to a dog sitting on the porch (the merchant was speaking out loud about the fact that the dog would betray him: it would follow whoever fed it better . . .). A witness was found who confirmed that a dog actually was wandering around the porch during the conversation. This saved the merchant.

Two hundred years later, in the 1930s, a herdsman was arrested and sent to the Stalinist camps for referring to a cow as a "whore" because she made advances to another cow. His crime was formulated as "slandering the communal farm herd."

Of course, those who don't agree with me, who see a fundamental difference between the Russian and Soviet approaches, will say that totalitarian thinking in the Soviet period becomes all-encompassing. Previously, a dog was simply a dog, an animal; but now a cow becomes an integral part of the regime. He who affronts the cow's honor is aiming—in the final analysis— at the well-being and morals of the People. And they are also right. I only want to say that totalitarian thinking was not invented by the Soviet regime but arose in the bleak depths of Russian history, and was subsequently developed and fortified by Lenin, Stalin, and hundreds of their comrades in arms, talented students of past tyrants, sensitive sons of the people. This idea, on which I will insist, is extremely unpopular. In certain Russian circles it is considered simply obscene. Solzhenitsyn has often denounced those who think as I do; others will inevitably try to unearth my Jewish ancestors, and this explanation will pacify them. I'm speaking not only of our nationalists and fascists but about a more subtle category: those liberal Russians who *forbid* one to think that Russians can *forbid thinking*.

In 1953, when Stalin died, I was two years old. In one of my earliest childhood memories it is summer. There's a green lawn, bushes, and trees—and suddenly from the bushes emerge two huge people, many times greater than life size; they are wearing long white overalls, and pillows take the place of their heads; eyes and laughing mouths are drawn on the pillows. Instead of legs, they have stilts. I remember the childlike feeling of happiness and wonder, and something similar to a promise that life would contain many more such wondrous surprises. Many years later, in a chance conversation, I learned that this small group of merrymakers was imprisoned that summer for an unheard-of crime: "vulgarity."

When I read *The Great Terror,* I carefully followed Conquest's detailed descriptions of the lengthy, notorious trials of the 1930s, the investigation of the police apparatus's cumbersome mechanisms, the network of destinies, biographies. This is all assembled into such a complex architectural edifice that I cannot help but admire the author who undertook an investigation so grandiose in scale. The reader comes away feeling that the author knows every event of the Soviet years, that no remotely accessible document has escaped his attention, that he hasn't neglected a single publication in the smallest provincial newspaper if it might throw light on one or another event. Ask him what happened to the wife of comrade X or the son of comrade Y — he knows. The only question he can't answer is: Why?

Conquest does ask this question in regard to Stalin and his regime: he meticulously and wittily examines the possible motives of Stalin's behavior, both rational and irrational; he shows the deleterious effect of Bolshevik ideology on the mass consciousness, how it prepared the way for the Terror. A particularly wonderful quality of this book is also that when questions, ideas, or suppositions arise in you, the reader, the author invariably answers these mental queries a few pages later, develops the thought you've had, and figures things out along with you, bringing in more arguments on both sides than you ever thought possible. I was especially struck by this in the third chapter, "Architect of Terror," which sketches a psychological portrait of Stalin, and in the fifth chapter, "The Problem of Confession," where Conquest explores the motivations and behavior of Stalin's victims.

This book is not a storeroom of facts but a profoundly analytical investigation. Instead of getting tangled up in the abundance of information, you untangle the knots of the Soviet nightmare under the author's patient direction. Having finished this book, no one can ever again say: "I didn't know." Now we all know.

But the question "Why?" remains unanswered. Perhaps the only answer is "Because." Period.

My first English teacher, the daughter of Russian-Ukrainian immigrants, was once married to an American. They lived several years in America, and in the mid-1930s, like many other naive Western people who believed in socialism, they came to the USSR. They were immediately arrested and sent to prison. Her husband didn't return, but she survived. "But I'm not guilty of anything!" she screamed at the investigator. "No one here is guilty of anything," answered the exhausted investigator. "But why, then?" "Just because" was the answer.

What lies behind this "Just because"? Why were two merry-makers arrested for "vulgarity"? After all, someone took the trouble to inform, someone else to listen and apprise the authorities, a third person took the trouble to be on guard, a fourth to think about it, a fifth to send an armed group to arrest them, a sixth . . . and so on. Why, in a small, sleepy provincial town in the 1930s, did the head of the police, sitting on his windowsill in an unbelted shirt, waving away the flies, amuse himself by beckoning passers-by and arresting those who approached (they disappeared forever)? Why, in 1918, as the writer Ivan Bunin wrote, did peasants plundering an estate pluck the feathers off the peacocks and let them die to the accompaniment of approving laughter? Why, in 1988, in Los Angeles (I witnessed this), did a Soviet writer, in America for the first time, take in at a glance the pink, luxurious mass of a Beverly Hills hotel and daydream out loud: "Ah, they should drop a good-size bomb here"? Why, in Moscow, in our time, did a woman, upon seeing a two-year-old child sit down on the floor of a shop and refuse to get up, start yelling: "Those kinds of kids should be sent to jail! They're all bandits!"? And why did a group of women, including the saleswomen and cashiers, gather around her and join in: "To jail, to jail!" they shouted. Why do Russians immediately start stamping their feet and waving their hands, hissing "Damned beast," if a cat or dog runs by?

This question "Why?" has been asked by all of Russian literature, and, of course, a historian cannot answer it. He almost doesn't have the right—facts are his domain. Only some sort of blind bard, muttering poet, or absurdist playwright can answer this question.

In Russia, in contrast to the West, reason has traditionally been seen as a source of destruction, emotion (the soul) as one of creation. How many scornful pages have great Russian writers dedicated to Western pragmatism, materialism, rationalism! They mocked the English with their machines, the Germans with their order and precision, the French with their logic, and finally the Americans with their love of money. As a result, in Russia we have neither machines, nor order, nor logic, nor money. "We eat one another and this satisfies us." Rejecting reason, the Russian universe turns in an emotional whirlwind and can't manage to get on an even footing. Looking into the depths of Russian history, one is horrified: it's impossible to figure out when this senseless mess started. What is the source of these interminable Russian woes? The dogmatism of the Russian Orthodox Church? The Mongol invasions? The formation of the empire? Genetics? Everything together? There is no answer, or there are too many answers. You feel there's an abyss under your feet.

The enslavement of the peasants, which continued for three hundred years, provoked such a feeling of guilt in the free, educated classes of Russian society that nothing disparaging could be said about the peasants. If they have certain obvious negative characteristics, then we ourselves are to blame—that is the leitmotif of the nineteenth century. All manner of extraordinary qualities—spirituality, goodness, justice, sensitivity, and charity—are ascribed to the Russian peasant and to the simple people as a whole—everything that a person longing for a normal life among normal people might hope to find. Some voices of alarm break through Russian literature, the voices of people trying to speak about the dark side of the Russian people, but they are isolated, unpopular, misinterpreted. Everyone deceives everyone else and themselves in the bargain. The revolution comes, then another, and a third—and a wave of darkness engulfs the country. The cultured classes are destroyed, the raw elements burst forth.

Cultural taboos forbid us to judge "simple people"—and this is typical not only of Russia. This taboo demands that a guilty party be sought "high up." It's possible that such a search is partly justified, but, alas, it doesn't lead to anything. Once an enemy is found "up above," the natural movement is to destroy him, which is what happens during a revolution. So he's destroyed, but what has changed? Life is just as bad as ever. And people begin ever new quests for enemies, detecting them in non-Russians, in people of a different faith, and in their neighbors. But they forget to look at themselves.

During Stalin's time, as I see it, Russian society, brutalized by centuries of violence, intoxicated by the feeling that everything was allowed, destroyed everything "alien": "the enemy," "minorities" — any and everything the least bit different from the "average." At first this was simple and exhilarating: the aristocracy, foreigners, ladies in hats, gentlemen in ties, everyone who wore eyeglasses, everyone who read books, everyone who spoke a literary language and showed some signs of education; then it became more and more difficult, the material for destruction began to run out, and society turned inward and began to destroy itself. Without popular support Stalin and his cannibals wouldn't have lasted for long. The executioner's genius expressed itself in his ability to feel and direct the evil forces slumbering in the people; he deftly manipulated the choice of courses, knew who should be the hors d'oeuvres, who the main course, and who should be left for dessert; he knew what honorific toasts to pronounce and what inebriating ideological cocktails to offer (now's the time to serve subtle wines to this group; later that one will get strong liquor).

It is this hellish cuisine that Robert Conquest examines. And the leading character of this fundamental work, whether the author intends it or not, is not just the butcher, but all the sheep that collaborated with him, slicing and seasoning their own meat for a monstrous shish kebab.

1991

Misha Gorbachev's Small World

Review of *The Man Who Changed the World: The Lives of Mikhail S. Gorbachev*, by Gail Sheehy (HarperCollins, 1990)

YOU HAVE TO BE quite fearless, an adventurer, extraordinarily self-assured, to offer American readers a book about a country that you yourself do not understand. Gail Sheehy possesses all these qualities in abundance. As she correctly indicates, "A mystery is what no one knows. The Soviet Union used to be a nest of secrets. Now it's all mystery — even to its own leadership." A secret that's become a mystery is pretty hard to handle. Sheehy has written a book on the enigmatic president of a country that she has not studied, explaining the incomprehensible in terms of the unknown, and vice versa.

It is hardly surprising, therefore, that she got tangled in contradictions at the outset, was tied up in knots by the middle, was hopelessly stranded by the end, and scrambled out after 400 pages into the index (which is nearly useless, because it seethes with mistakes), without having convincingly answered any of the questions that she herself posed. Sheehy modestly refers to her book as "an X-ray of history," but it is not nearly so probing. If a medical metaphor is wanted, I would sooner compare what she has produced to a dermatologist's examination. It's skin deep.

The reader will learn a lot of surprising things from this book. For instance, that "diabetes is definitely a familial disease and would therefore be widespread in a closed ethnic society such as Russia, where people marry and reproduce, for the most part, with other Russians." Sheehy seems not to know that there really is no such thing as a Russian, genetically or racially; a more diverse people would be hard to find. (Besides, there are about 150 million of them.) The reader also learns from Sheehy that the "Peredvizhniki" (more commonly known in the West as the "Wanderers") were "a group of seventeenth-century Russian classicists," when in fact they were critical realist painters of the late nineteenth century who broke with the Academy. (In seventeenth-century Russia there was not yet, nor could there have been, any such groups, nor any classicists.) The reader will also take away that Potemkin, one of Catherine the Great's favorites, was an architect, when his contribution to architecture, as is known, consisted of ordering the construction of decorative facades to hide the poverty and destitution of Russian villages from the empress when she rode about the country to survey her lands.

The reader is also asked to believe that Russians hate Tatars, which supposedly explains the population's friendly dislike of Raisa Gorbacheva: "Because of her wide cheek span, she is believed to have Mongol ancestors, an unappealing feature in a society that bears undisguised hatred for the Tatar-Mongols stemming from Russia's long subjugation by both." This "both" is especially endearing, since really only one people is under discussion, not two. If, in her headlong plunge into Russian affairs, Sheehy had relied less often on the help of the KGB, the Central Committee staff, Party bureaucrats, and would-be mistresses of Gorbachev (what a pity that no real mistresses could be found!), then she might have observed a completely different picture. Russians love to talk about their Tatar heritage. Educated Russians will inevitably quote Napoléon, who is supposed to have said, "If you scratch a Russian, you'll find a Tatar." Cursing the historical, almost mythological Tatars, Russians will look for the mythological Tatar in themselves.

Russians take particular pleasure in self-disparagement. They like to rub salt in old, historical wounds. (The writer Bunin called this phenomenon being "moved by your own perdition.") Sometimes it seems that if it weren't for the Tatar-Mongol yoke (which lasted not 500 years, as Sheehy thinks, but about 300), the Russians would have nothing to talk about. Fusing self-abasement and pride is a Russian characteristic, well described by Dostoyevsky. Raisa Maksimovna's wide cheekbones are not her personal features, they are a trait typical of many Russian faces, which Sheehy could have noticed herself, and which Russians know perfectly well.

The number of illiterate mistakes in this book is beyond counting. I will enumerate a few of them, mixing the silly and the serious. There is no journal called "Banner and Strength" (*Znamia i sila*), but there is one called "Knowledge Is Strength" (*Znanie—sila*). "Imenikirovna Sanitorium" is a chimera; it is the "Sanatorii imeni Kirova," or the Kirov Sanatorium, or the Sanatorium named after Kirov. *The Catcher in the Rye* was not "just published" in the Soviet Union; it was translated into Russian and published in the 1960s, has been frequently reissued since, and is one of the most popular American novels in Russia (which says much about the Russian mentality). And there is this surprising sentence, which serves as an excellent test of Sheehy's competence in matters Russian: "For a thousand years—500 under the yoke of the Mongol-Tatars, and 500 more from Ivan the Terrible to Lenin—the Russian people had no experience of liberal democracy or economic competition."

Everything has been swept into this remarkable sentence, as if into a black hole: the pre-Mongol period; the first republic, Novgorod; the unification of the Russian principalities; the rapid growth of the country from the small kingdom of Muscovy to the giant that included the unembraceable expanses of

Siberia (where there was no serfdom and economic competition abounded); the reforms of Peter the Great; the Decembrist uprising; the reforms of Alexander II; the emancipation of the serfs; Russian capitalism of the nineteenth century; and many, many more important things. Not to mention that the Tatar-Mongol yoke ended not with Ivan the Terrible but 100 or 200 years earlier, depending on how you count. All in all, Sheehy seems to have trouble with math. She assures us that she was the owner of a 260-megabyte computer, which was worth only $350. As far as I know, computers of that capacity are used only in things like Star Wars. And she gave hers to her stool pigeon–chauffeur. Generous.

Almost all the proper names in the book are garbled. A single individual's name is sometimes spelled different ways in the body of the text, and in the index it becomes entirely unrecognizable. (Brezhnev's son-in-law suffers terribly: one time he appears correctly as the daughter's husband Churbanov and another time as her lover Cherbonov.) Scolding Russian society for its patriarchy and its oppression of women, Sheehy nonetheless doesn't bother to do Russian women the honor of spelling their names correctly, to say nothing of often changing their surnames into the masculine form, removing the feminine grammatical endings. I, too, have the misfortune to be mentioned in Sheehy's book, and my surname is also misspelled. Worse, a conversation is ascribed to me that actually happened in a different place, at a different time, and under different circumstances than Sheehy describes. She may not care how she presents me, but I do: my story about how I interceded with the editors of a journal on behalf of certain young poets who were rejected as insufficiently traditional is transformed into a story about how I supposedly begged to be admitted to the Writers' Union. In the Soviet Union we have always believed that Americans are legendary for their work ethic, their honesty, their sense of responsibility. Now I wonder.

Sheehy would seem to be closer to the mark when she writes

that "for seven decades under their Marxist masters, [Soviets] have been isolated from the civilized world, forbidden to travel to the West, and insulated from the great currents of social, political, economic, and spiritual thought." Well—almost. Those seventy years that everyone talks about now—everyone who wants to simplify things, to straighten out history and dump everything on the Bolsheviks as everything was previously dumped on the Tatars—were a complex and heterogeneous period. It was possible, though it was difficult, to travel to the West until about 1928, so ten years can be dropped right away. And limited travel (for a particular kind of person, at particular times, and at the price of fantastic humiliation) became possible again after 1956. So there's another thirty years to be dropped, or at least qualified. It adds up to quite a difference. And it should not be forgotten that in the 1920s and 1930s some Western influence did exist. In those years the most influential Western politicians, writers, and philosophers visited the Soviet Union. They arrived in a country swathed in barbed wire, surveyed the Kremlin tables heavy with caviar and cognac, and heartily extolled the wonders of communism. They preferred not to hear the half-stifled moans of the victims.

This book, in short, is not to be trusted. It doesn't even hold together as a book, though Sheehy's pretensions to having created something monumental are clear from her title, *The Man Who Changed the World*. We are given the World, and the Man (Gorbachev), and the author, who has broken through the KGB's cordons and made it to the hero's hometown, so as to see the hero's mother, his neighbors, his chickens, and his classmates, all with her own eyes. Breathlessly, she broke through. Breathlessly, she looked. And with what did she return? Nothing much. Was it worth all that investigative zeal just to discover that Misha had two grandfathers, and that one of them spent time in prison and the other sent people to do time in prison— a typical Soviet biography that sheds no light at all on our hero's personality and achievements?

It is true that Sheehy displayed a certain persistence and cunning in getting to a village to which others don't have access; but her feats and her accomplishments occupy a central place in the first half of her narrative. The reader is offered long and allegedly exciting stories about how Gail thought that Sergei might inform on her, but it turned out to be Oleg who informed. What a surprise! I can assure Sheehy that she was informed on by Oleg *and* Sergei, and by Arkady and Pyotr and Ivan (if she met anyone by these names), and by another couple of dozen people who smiled and helped her; and by Sergei Ivanko (an old, renowned villain whom Vladimir Voinovich made the subject of a great satire), to whom she expresses her gratitude in the introduction. Her chauffeurs informed on her, as did her maids, her translators, her neighbors, and certainly Gorbachev's villagers; and they informed not out of any evil intent but mechanically, indifferently, as a matter of course. And those who were not actually required to inform couldn't help it anyway: their apartments, their telephones, and their automobiles were bugged, the Moscow apartment that Sheehy inhabited was bugged, and so was the apartment of her kindly neighbors, from whom the naive and tactless Sheehy tried to borrow an egg (which, under current Russian conditions, is something like borrowing change from a beggar's cap because you're too lazy to go to the bank).

Please do not ask me for proof of this mass informing. I may assert that the sun rises in the morning and sets in the evening without appealing to astronomical theories. This is the way things are. And everyone knows this: every single step, every look, every breath of an American reporter who's trying to unearth the details of the personal life and the murky past of the number-one man in the Soviet Empire is observed, recorded, and filed in a dossier. To expect that Soviet people will tell the truth to such an American reporter is ridiculous. Some will and some will not; and you'll never know who is telling the truth, because without knowledge, experience, and informed intuition in a society like Soviet society, you can't learn anything.

Still, Sheehy has a theory, of which she is very proud. Her theory, as is well known, is that people pass through several "lives" within their lifetimes. Or, in a word, they undergo "passages." Sheehy has no compunction about transporting this dubious flight of American pop psychology to the Soviet Union. Thus Gorbachev is supposed to have undergone a transformation into a reformer, or a revolutionary, or something. (For some reason Sheehy fails to apply her theory to Raisa Gorbacheva.) Did Gorbachev change the world or did the world change Gorbachev? Sheehy calls this a "philosophical riddle," and boldly takes the second hypothesis as her point of departure (thereby refuting the title of her book). Never mind that at least 2,000 years ago the Romans noted that the times change and we change with them. But let us even grant that a "philosophy" underlies the "riddle." The important question is whether, as a result of Sheehy's "philosophy," we will be enlightened about these changing times, about the processes that have taken place in Soviet society during the seventy years of its existence.

Now, our country possesses certain peculiarities that verge on the fantastic, and its inner geometry is decidedly non-Euclidean. Our roads are Mobius strips; our parallel lines cross as many times as you like; the sum of the angles of our triangles is infinite. You knock a hole through the wall of the fortress and you find yourself inside a swamp; the wall didn't actually enclose anything. Russia is an accursed but bewitching place. It has its own logic, which the most intelligent Russian people have been unable to explain. All they could do was describe it, weep over it, and pray for it.

Sheehy appears in Russia, however, brimming with confidence, a self-proclaimed philosopher and a self-satisfied sociologist. Like Cuvier, who recovered the image of prehistoric animals from a single bone, she tries to reconstruct Russian society from random shreds of evidence. But she doesn't know how to distinguish a bone from a boulder, and instead of full-blooded and frightening dinosaurs, she produces an impossible bestiary of talking hens and fish with eyeglasses. After visiting one market, for example, she asserts that Soviet markets are "open-air stalls . . . operated by migrant sellers from the Central Asian republics." In fact, most Moscow markets are covered pavilions where people from all over the country sell their wares—from the Ukraine and the Caucasus, but mostly from the Moscow area. For that matter, things are often sold through surrogates, or fake "communal farmers"; the goods are frequently stolen from state stores, since they can be sold at the markets for ten times the price. And to keep everything under wraps, bribes are paid to the police, the Party secretaries at all levels, and so on, upward and upward until the money reaches—guess who?

Sheehy tells us that she decided to live in the Soviet Union just the way that Soviet people supposedly do. To this end, she pockets the salt and pepper given out with breakfast in the airplane, though I wonder how many days she planned to get by on this quantity of spices. It's a nice detail—except that Soviet people, when they steal, steal by the wagonload. If a train full of goods stalls in a provincial station, whole brigades of thieves will appear, open the sealed doors with experienced hands, and carry off every last item. Sometimes the guards and the station manager help, too. They take hundreds of thousands of rubles' worth at a go, sometimes millions, depending on what the loot is. If you want to live like us, my dear, you better get used to our scale of operations!

Interpreting the behavior of Russian people, Sheehy ascribes motivations to them that are based on her own hastily conceived errors and homegrown theories. In this, of course, she is not alone. It has become fashionable, for example, to rebuke Russians for their indignation at Raisa Gorbacheva's behavior: male chauvinists, that's what they are. It doesn't occur to Sheehy that, unlike the American president, who is elected freely by at least half the voting population, our president, or general secretary of the Communist Party, is elected by nobody. He lands on our heads all by himself, with all his stupidity, his tactlessness, his dishonesty, his shady past and unpredictable decrees. If *he* is unavoidable, however, like rain in autumn, or like old age, or like fate, *she* is not. If he has won the right to torment us (and Russians don't doubt that the authorities exist solely in order to torment) as the result of a long, dirty struggle with other, weaker tormentors, she has not.

Raisa jabs at us—robbed, humiliated, and half-imprisoned people that we are—with her well-manicured fingers decorated with diamonds bought with our money. She screeches at us with a mouth that has tasted countless delicacies, while our children are half-starving. This woman can elicit nothing but intense scorn. She didn't struggle for power with anyone, she received it as the result of luck, happy circumstance, and now she sets out loudly and shamelessly to make use of what she has not earned. Instructing whole peoples and republics on how they should behave, she reproaches children in the Baltics for speaking their native language instead of Russian, and she tells the Ukrainians that their capital, Kiev, is a Russian city, because "that's what's written in the textbooks." If the president had, say, a brother who traveled everywhere with him, screamed, gave orders, made scenes in museums and instructed the professional staff on what they should and should not do, took over state culture as though it were his own property, got himself a gold credit card and bought diamonds with the taxpayer's money, the reaction to that man would be precisely the same as the reaction to this woman.

As befits the product of a tabloid mentality, Sheehy's book is lousy with "big names." Andropov's son and Brezhnev's grandson touchingly discourse on the problems of the Soviet mafia as if it were something to which they had no relationship. The excited American correspondent comes to the conclusion that "'organized crime' is indeed an oxymoron in the Soviet context. Crime is no more organized than agriculture." A big mistake: criminal activity is extremely well organized in our country. It's organized on the lowest level, from the pickpockets and the train thieves, to the highest level, where, in essence, the whole government is stolen, all rights and all freedoms are embezzled and handed out to people piecemeal, in the form of privileges.

"When did Gorbachev find out that socialism doesn't work?" Sheehy asks anxiously. The answer is simple: he knew that nothing works while still in his mother's womb. That's why he embarked on a Party career. Such a career was the only way that he could find for himself a warm place within a dysfunctional system—a dangerous place, perhaps, but a privileged one. "Who suggested the idea of glasnost to him? Who first began talking about perestroika?" Another anxious question. Sheehy sets out to guess, naming first Gorbachev's boss and patron Fyodor Kulakov, then Raisa. It never occurs to her that not only the ideas of glasnost and perestroika, but the very terms themselves, have a history more than 150 years old.

In the correspondence between the Russian revolutionaries and emigrants Herzen and Ogarev, in the middle of the last century, we read about hopes for "glasnost" and "perestroika." Russian writers, revolutionaries, and dissidents of all parties and all periods have ceaselessly talked about the necessity of reform and of freedom of expression—with variable results. Herzen and Lenin and perhaps Saltykov-Shchedrin (the nineteenth-century satirist who described the vices of Russian society and Russian psychology so exactly that his works could have been written only this morning) would have been required reading for the Gorbachevs at university.

In fact, Sheehy patronizes Gorbachev, painting the picture of a witless provincial whose "older comrades" or wife taught him everything. She patronizes him by thrilling over his ability to quote Pushkin or Lermontov, not knowing that each and every Soviet schoolchild is forced to learn poems by heart (and prose as well!) over the course of ten years of schooling. It's a bit like exalting Gorbachev for knowing his multiplication tables. And she patronizes him by calling him a "master strategist" merely because as a young flatterer he was able to carry off the most banal sort of manipulation: he ordered his assistant to lose at billiards to a high-placed official and thus gained the official's good graces.

There is no need to marvel over the enigma of Gorbachev's soul just because he tells the Soviet people that "I am a convinced Communist" and then tells Margaret Thatcher that he is no longer a Communist. No theory is required for an explanation. It's quite simple: he says whatever will go over better with the listener. (If he had said the opposite, now *that* would be truly inexplicable.) Similarly, it would be curious to consider why the general secretary of the Communist Party was ashamed of his title and decided to call himself president, after the Western fashion. After all, there are grander appellations that would have been closer to the truth. The answer, again, is simple. The term "president" soothes the Western ear and creates a subconscious image of democracy, a foggy vision of legitimacy. It brings free elections to mind. A president may receive loan credits more easily than a general secretary. It's no wonder that President Bush keeps repeating that President Gorbachev is resolved "to continue to move along the path of reform and perestroika," despite the obvious meaninglessness of such claims.

In order to arrive at "the truth," Sheehy has used all possible sources: honest and dishonest, clean and unclean. She has questioned intelligent people and idiots, the experienced and the inexperienced, without, it seems, being able to distinguish one from the other. There is not a trace of a critical attitude toward her material. Instead there is her trite theory of "passages." There are moments of intelligence scattered about the book, and occasionally we are given the observations of people who understand the situation well, but they are lost in a sea of ignorance and preconception.

And yet there remains the really important question: Why did what happened in the USSR in the mid-1980s happen? Or better still, what *did* happen? Of all the theories current in the So-

viet Union to explain the events of the last six years, I have a favorite. It is that the Kremlin got hungry.

If every morning, at the moment you awake, food appears
before your open, waiting mouth, then you won't change a
thing. You will think: *All is well. Glory to labor.* You will eat your
fill and turn over on your other side and go back to sleep. If one
fine day, however, nothing appears before your open mouth,
you will wake up. Surprised and annoyed, you will swing your
legs over onto the cold floor, and you will look for the reasons
for this catastrophe. And when you see that the fridge is empty,
and that there are only crumbs left on the table, and that the
canned goods are gone, besides which the toilet is broken and
the garbage disposal stinks, you will begin to wonder what's
going on. Where did that food come from in the first place anyway? What can be done to make it come back?

Sometime around 1985, the general level of collapse in the
Soviet Union had reached such staggering proportions that reform could be expected at any moment. The Soviet historian
Andrei Amalrik, who immigrated to the West (and soon after
died in a car crash), wrote a book called *Will the Soviet Union
Survive until 1984?* Many of his prophecies have come true, not
least his timetable. The country survived until 1984, but it could
no longer exist as it was. Everything contributed to this: the un-
believable corruption, the complete moral disintegration of the
government and the people, the hopeless economy, the defeat in
the Afghan war.

The dissident movement, which had begun in the 1950s
merely as an expression of dissatisfaction with the regime, grew
in size and in strength throughout the 1960s and the 1970s, taking different forms—from religious groups to armed plots,
from samizdat to social escapism. By the mid-eighties, the dissidents—those who were engaged in the struggle for human
rights and in the distribution of forbidden political tracts and
prohibited literature—were reduced to very few, since nearly
everyone who was the least bit active was either in prison or had

emigrated. But there was almost no need for the dissident movement anymore; everyone else had already been enlightened.
(The authorities, too, were enlightened: dissident literature was
much more accessible to them than it was to regular people.
KGB agents sold dissident works, made money on them, and
then informed on the buyers.)

The official economy kept on collapsing, and nobody knew
what to do about it. Entire branches of industry, especially in
the southern and Asian republics, were transferred (secretly) to
private hands; a lively and effective capitalist economy, the so-
called black market, emerged through the official but non-func-
tioning structures. Remember that business in our country was
criminally prosecutable. Prison or the death penalty awaited
a major businessman, who therefore required the services of a
Party bureaucrat to cover him, to "legalize" his underground activity. If the business failed, or if the deal fell through, it was the
businessman who suffered, and the bureaucrat simply moved
on. This system of unsinkable Party bureaucrats, this caste of
people with immunity, is called the nomenklatura.

What happened in Brezhnev's time was that the number of
bureaucrat-ideologists shrank and the number of bureaucrat-
businessmen (that is, of corrupt people) grew. And that was just
fine. The ideological Communist is a danger to humanity. Certain that he is right, and confident that he can remake the
world, he is an ascetic who demands asceticism from those surrounding him. He is proudly devoid of human weaknesses, such
as the love of eating, buying, falling in love, relaxing, and just
doing nothing. Nor does he permit others to have them. He
wants to subordinate all of humanity to himself, since all people
are brothers; and he will stop at nothing.

The corrupt Communist, by contrast, knows that he is a
petty thief, and he recognizes that other people also want to
steal. He loves comfort, and he recognizes that others love it,
too. He will not start a nuclear war with the West because it
would destroy all those warehouses with all those goods. And

the best thing about the corrupt Communist is that he doesn't give a damn about others. He's too busy with his own affairs. He will pay attention to you only if you get in his way. The ideological Communist, however, thinks about you constantly: you are his nourishment, you are the clay from which he will sculpt the human being of the future.

The corrupt Communist knows that he is a nobody, but he really, really wants to live well. In a situation of free competition, he would most likely lose out to the businessman, the farmer, and the intellectual. Therefore he works out a system of privileges so that access to all the blessings of the world belong only to the chosen. Occasionally he will reward the obedient slave, perhaps with a trip abroad (that is, to the magical kingdom of consumer goods). According to the rules of the game, however, the slave must pay for this upon returning: he must tell those who are not allowed out that everything is quite awful abroad, that people everywhere are out of work, are scavenging in garbage heaps and killing each other on the streets, where they also sleep. (This is rather like the medieval Arab traders, who, afraid of competition, spread rumors that a "sea of gloom" lay west of Gibraltar.) These people are naturally bound to each other by a round robin of bribes and base actions. There is a file on each of them, and they all know it.

It is obvious that Gorbachev belongs to the corrupted segment of the Partocracy. He is supposed, however, to be a "true Communist," with socialism in his heart and his blood, who cannot allow the introduction of capitalism (though he can take advantage of its fruits on his trips abroad). A faithful student of Lenin, he cannot allow private ownership of land (though he can live for free in luxurious villas at our expense). As if we didn't know that the main Leninist trait is the lack of scruple. As if we didn't know that Lenin became disillusioned with socialism and introduced the New Economic Policy, that is, he returned to capitalist principles.

Gorbachev introduces elements of a free society, then forbids what he himself has made possible, depending on who leans on him the hardest. It is pretty clear by now that he doesn't have an opinion of his own about most matters. By habit, he defended a one-party system; and when society pressured him and demanded multiple parties—please, be my guest, it's up to you. And last fall he began "liking" the Communist Party and its affairs once again. This lack of principle has even given birth to the myth that Gorbachev deliberately says the opposite of what he means, that he is secretly in sympathy with the liberals but is afraid to say so openly, and so he hints, winks, gesticulates, speaks in riddles. Only recently has it become apparent that Gorbachev doesn't care about the intelligentsia, as he doesn't care about any other class of society.

It is wrong, I think, to suppose that Gorbachev thought up the reforms and was only waiting for the opportunity to begin remaking a totally unsuspecting society. The necessity for change in the Soviet Union was felt by everyone. The universal impossibility of continuing to live half-starved under the cover of the old dogmas was putting pressure on the authorities. But the old guard was still alive and strong. In 1982, Brezhnev died. Then the other dinosaurs started dying. After Stalin's death, people shed genuine tears; after the deaths of Brezhnev and Andropov, people laughed; after Chernenko's death, they guffawed. And how could they not? A man comes to power, declares himself a genius, and kicks the bucket.

When Gorbachev fought his way to the throne, however, or when he was placed upon it by his colleagues, he changed tactics. He began to play the simple, earnest, democratic fellow. He removed all the posters from the streets and—this amazed everyone—removed all the meaningless announcements about the greatness of the Soviet people, all the pompous idiocies like "The Party Is Our Helmsman," "You Are Walking the True Path, Comrades," "Glory to the CPSU," "The Party Is the Mind, Honor, and Conscience of the People," and so on. Gorbachev didn't hang his own portrait (and thus the portraits of the lower-echelon bosses automatically disappeared). He started traveling around the country and "meeting with the simple people." The simple people weren't used to such honors; they had been spat upon or punished for decades.

It doesn't take much to warm the soul of a tortured human being. I remember a radio broadcast of Gorbachev's "meeting with the people" in Siberia. "Maybe you need some help with something, comrades, what do you say?" he asked in a domestic, caring, "fatherly" voice. And in reply there came this soul-splitting cry from a woman in the crowd: "Felt boots for my child! Size 22 felt boots!" To which Gorbachev retorted, "We'll work, and life will straighten itself out, comrades," as he has preached many times since. Gorbachev would also visit the apartments of ordinary people, supposedly without warning, though they say that the day before the unexpected visit detachments of un-known people would run in and quickly renovate the premises and equip the amazed hosts with good dishes, a gilded samovar, and rolls that had long since disappeared from the shops. (After Harun al Rashid's departure, however, the samovar and the cups were taken away.) And he visited schools, which were also reno-vated overnight, and plants and factories, which had been cleared of drunk workers and suddenly decorated with flowers.

The art of erecting Potemkin villages has not died in our country. Good traditions die hard. When Richard Nixon came, all the houses on his way to the Kremlin were freshly painted, and one building, a particularly old-looking one, was torn down and a little square was made in its place. At night truckloads of grassy, daisy-covered turf were laid down to cover the empty space. Since then the popular name for this plaza has been Nixon Square. And Ronald Reagan has no idea how personally grateful I am to him for coming to meet Gorbachev in Moscow. They painted my building (only the facade; the backside was left as it was) and renovated the church that stands in our court-yard (the one that Sheehy, incorrectly once again, describes as "newly working," when in fact the church still contains a warehouse, an archive, and a typesetting plant) and carted off the garbage that had been there for three years (the hulls of rusted cars and two old sofas).

The rumors that Gorbachev had descended from the clouds and was wandering among us mortal folk gave us hope. Previously they just yelled at us: "You can't!" "Don't you dare!" "Don't go there!" "Stop it!" "You're under arrest!" Suddenly there appeared an affectionate, smiling, understanding man with words of greeting: "Yes, my dears, I know how hard it is for you. But be patient and you'll get your felt boots." And he came in spring.

April, May, June, dreams, hopes! The refuse heaps blossomed with yellow flowers. Lonely old women stirred in the crypts of communal apartments. ("Only one toilet for forty-eight rooms," as Vladimir Vysotsky sang.) One-armed war veterans crawled out into the sun to sell old galoshes and copper door handles stolen at night from the entryways of old buildings. Drunks also moved out of their apartments and into the gardens to drink their half-liter bottles in a threesome amid the lilac and the tulips. (Do you know how to divide a bottle evenly in three parts when you only have one glass? You don't know anything! In each half-liter bottle there are twenty-one "glugs," and there are seven "glugs" in a glass. That's how it's always been, and that's how it will always be. What do we care about wars, revolutions, Reformations, Renaissances, elections, oil crises, sexual revolutions, stock exchange crashes? Gulp down the seven glugs in a glass among the lilac bushes and fall asleep to the song of the sparrows, for a thousand years. And if there's nothing to nibble on, to wash down the drink, then we sniff our sleeve, which is why—just in case—we never wash our jackets.) At the markets and flea markets, around the few churches that still function, holy fools, prophets, and enchanters seduced the crowd with a new myth: Mikhail the Marked One had come, on his forehead there was a sign, his appearance was foretold in the Bible. God had given him seven years, and then he would fall, and once again there would be gloom and war and desolation.

The people sang, drank, and composed myths, while the intelligentsia sat at their televisions and their jaws dropped to their knees: the new ruler was getting rid of the old government. Almost every day another minister went, almost every week another Party secretary. Nobody knew why he was doing this, and each class or group chose to understand it in its own way. The intelligentsia decided that its voice had been heard at last and that the Party system was being dismantled. The Partocracy was confused and petrified with fear. The people decided that you didn't have to do anything or be afraid of anyone.

This was a very important moment for Gorbachev: he had to decide who was reliable. He chose the intelligentsia, consciously or intuitively. It was a brilliant move. First, no tsar in Russian history had ever done this. Second, satisfying the demands of the educated classes, demands that they had formulated long ago and had been insisting on for years, was quite simple. And they weren't really asking for much: freedom of expression, freedom of conscience, freedom of movement, the freedom of elections, respect for human rights. That was all. No goods had to be produced. It was clear, moreover, that all these freedoms would serve to reinforce Gorbachev's role. How could he refuse to yield such trifles? And how he was loved for these concessions!

He played a different game, however, with the Partocracy. Accustomed to fawning before higher-ups and to pressuring their subordinates, accustomed to doing nothing concrete, to producing a lot of empty talk, they were shaken from their usual rut by the very mystery of what was happening. They were so baffled that it was easy to sweep them from their posts. When someone has fainted, you can quickly throw them out the door.

There remained the question of the people, an unknown quantity. Who are they, and what do they want? For the last thousand years, nobody has been able to answer this question. Gorbachev's advisers informed him that the people were drinking in the lilac bushes and were completely covered in sparrow droppings. Who would feed the Party? Not the intelligentsia! Who really needed the intelligentsia, anyway? And here Gorbachev made his first, and perhaps his most serious, mistake. He forbade the people to drink.

The intelligentsia forgave him this (they were "moved by their own perdition"). The Partocracy was happy. Here was a concrete task, and a familiar one: to fight, to root out, to fire people from their jobs. They set to tearing out grape vines, paving over rare vineyards in the Crimea, uprooting muscat so fine and so expensive that "the people" couldn't get near it. They only counted the monstrous losses when the campaign was over. During the campaign, however, the people cursed Gorbachev, bought up all the sugar, perfected their knowledge of moonshine manufacture, and most important of all, grasped that they could do everything their own way and not get caught or punished. An epidemic of hoarding began. Sugar, soap, matches, and lightbulbs disappeared, and then sheets and pillows, and then clothes, shoes, eggs, and finally bread.

Gorbachev couldn't do anything about any of this. He kept meaning to straighten everything out, but he was busy creating the image of a peacemaker in the West. I don't waste too much time over the question of why Gorbachev (or his advisers at the time) made peace with the United States and let go of Eastern Europe. I see these things practically: if they let it go, it means they couldn't hold on to it any longer. Eastern Europe was what we call a "suitcase with no handle": hard to carry, but a shame to leave behind. It must have become too heavy to carry. It was also hard to hold together the essentially collapsing Soviet Union, hard to repeat again the empty slogan "The Party is our Helmsman" when nobody was listening.

People die because they grow old. They grow old because they have lived a long time. Communism died because it had lived a long time, degenerated, and grown weak; not because Gorbachev had a willful grandmother, or because Raisa whispered "Free the people, darling" into her husband's ear, as Sheehy would like to imagine. There is much less of Gorbachev's will involved in everything that has happened in our country than is usually thought. Having chosen a Party career from the start, he aspired to rise as high as he could (although he probably didn't count on reaching the position of general secretary; but then each soldier carries a marshal's rod in his backpack, as a French proverb says). And having ended up on top, he tried to hold on to the position he had gained.

We do not yet know who proposed Gorbachev for the top and who supported him (our analysts now think that it was the military-industrial complex), but his initial behavior, when you look back on what happened, bears the mixed traits of boldness and indecision, ignorance and a fine knowledge of human nature (in its Party version), recklessness and cold calculation. Having grown up under conditions of Brezhnev's stagnation, Gorbachev knew his small world and the people in it extremely well, and supposed that he knew how to change it. But he did not know the larger world and its problems; and when he destroyed the habitual structures with his own hands, he ceased to understand his immediate surroundings and took one false step after another.

He is, really, a fit object for pity: a provincial individual who received a bad education at a bad time, was later the all-powerful boss of a mineral waters resort, and servant and nanny to the Moscow bosses; a man who knew more about the sick, gurgling intestines of the authorities who came to cure their innards with the sparkling waters than he did about the actual life of his tormented country. He didn't handle well — how could he have handled well? — the chaos that he created when he let the genie out of the bottle. He couldn't handle the stubborn, cunning, patient people, who were used to deceiving far more difficult customers than the paunchy chatterboxes that descended for a minute from the gilded heights to advise the people to "work better" and then disappeared again into the palace beyond the clouds, surrounded by a triple wall with armed guards.

After his first mistake came his second, and then his third. He betrayed the intelligentsia. Having received every imaginable (and unimaginable) support from it, having become the first ruler ever supported by the intelligentsia, which historically has opposed every regime, Gorbachev decided that he was strong enough, and grew deaf and blind to the demands for freedom and respect for human rights that the intelligentsia never tired of presenting to him. And he betrayed the businessmen, major and minor, a live force capable of leading the country out of its economic dead end. He appealed to people who knew how to work, who had initiative and wanted to better their lives with their own hands. He let them believe in justice, and published laws and promised that these laws were genuine; and then six months later he annulled them and burdened businessmen with absurd, punitive taxes. Most important, he poisoned the public against the businessmen, pointing to them as the reason for the country's ruin. His actions in regard to "cooperatives," questions of privatization, and "monetary reform" (the recent confiscation of the people's money) were a mockery.

He set the army against himself, antagonized the generals and then gave in to them, when they were already annoyed. He antagonized the officers and didn't give these disenfranchised, dependent people anything in return. He turned all the republics against him by speaking ambivalently about independence and then using tanks to suppress all attempts to acquire this independence. He angered the West, his only real support, with all of the above. But the most important thing is that he turned the simple people against him, those who are now hysterically supporting Boris Yeltsin, those whose stubborn, cunning psychology, whose changeable, superstitious, and unpredictable personality he thought he could disregard.

The simple man, daydreaming for centuries in the lilac bushes, opened his eyes and reached for his bottle, only to find that his bottle had been taken away. He looked around and saw that he was surrounded by the same old dirt, horror, and ruin, that the lilac was covered with the thick soot of industrial waste, that the sparrows were radioactive, that babes in arms had become thieves and adolescents had become murderers, that whole trainloads of girls were setting off to the cities to become hard-currency prostitutes.

And then, from behind the Kremlin's battlements, the simple man heard a drawn-out cry: "Hey, people! Don't drink, work! Work, 'cause we're getting awfully hungry in here!" They want to eat in the Kremlin. But they want the people to provide the food for nothing. For a long time "their" policy was growling and barking. Since 1985, they've changed tactics: smiles, charm, laughter. Previously no one ever saw "their" wives (it was embarrassing to show those morose behemoths in brocaded bags to enlightened humanity). Now an elegant lady in Parisian outfits can even help the cause, assist in the procurement of credits, most-favored-nation status, food parcels.

The trusting and well-wishing West seized the bait, and as yet it doesn't want to let go. In a letter sent to a Soviet newspaper, an enthralled American wrote to suggest that the beleaguered Gorbachev abandon the Soviet Union, receive American citizenship, and run for president of the United States. "We'll all vote for you," he promised. Well, president is perhaps a bit much. The role of governor, however, might suit him — governor, let's say, of the state of Idaho. The handsome, warm, smiling, well-dressed, well-spoken Misha would look marvelous. But Americans might never see potatoes again.

1991

Yeltsin Routs Gorbachev

EVERYBODY KNOWS how to pull off a coup d'état. You must identify and destroy your principal enemy, so that the crowd has no one to support; you must cut off all communications that might assist your enemy in making contact with the outside world; you must dispatch troops into the centers of potential resistance (troops that differ in nationality and religion from the people you wish to suppress); and you must mollify and reassure the people by immediately distributing food, drink, and goods.

But nothing of the kind was done in Moscow. It was clear from the reports that everyone was disappointed by the performance. Even the defenders of the Russian White House were wondering: Why didn't they cut off our telephones? And why didn't they sever our satellite connections with the Americans? And who was the asshole who dispatched the Taman division, that Potemkin village of the Soviet army, composed mostly of Moscow boys who are the lucky sons of high-ranking officials, a division that exists solely to show foreigners that our soldiers are handsome and well fed?

Ted Koppel asked this same question of the very wise Aleksandr Yakovlev. And Aleksandr Nikolayevich answered correctly: "Fools." And repeated several times, with laughing eyes, "Fools. Fools." Asked why Gorbachev got involved with these fools, Yakovlev answered that it is a personal mystery and one should ask Gorbachev himself for the answer. Of course, everybody *does* ask Gorbachev, but he says only: "This was my mistake. I trusted them, especially Kryuchkov and Yazov."

We have heard this answer endless times. Indeed, we have been hearing many things for a long time. But did we grasp the clear and unambiguous signs, the voices that were warning us? It seems to me that we had the answers long ago to the questions that we are asking now.

If we had not been so afraid on the night when those thousands of people stood around the White House in the Moscow rain and nobody knew what to expect, and if the capacity for clear and calm thinking somehow had not failed us, it would have been obvious the moment that we saw the faces of the plotters and the trembling hands of Gennady Yanayev, and heard the incoherent, stammering speeches of these creeps, and especially when we heard the laughs of the journalists who covered their pronouncements, that the coup had collapsed. Fools generally do not realize that they are fools, that one can read their faces like an open book, that it is impossible to conceal your own nothingness.

Still, what about Gorbachev? How to explain that he chose each of these scoundrels the way one chooses melons at the market, studying them carefully to determine their ripeness, sniffing them, and finally taking them along? Or that he didn't listen to dozens of his close advisers, to hundreds of well-meaning citizens in the parliamentary institutions, to tens of thousands of common people who tried to shout the truth loudly for him, using all possible means, radio, newspapers, TV? He had even been careful to select his own man, the disgusting Leonid Kravchenko, as head of Soviet television, a man who gagged the mouths of all free-thinking TV journalists, destroyed excellent political and cultural programs, fired lots of good people, and retorted to those who protested: "I came to carry out the will of the president." And lastly, how to explain that Gorbachev took no action against Valentin Pavlov, Boris Pugo, Vladimir Kryuchkov, and Dmitri Yazov, when they tried to depose him openly in June? "We have no differences with Comrade Pavlov," Gorbachev said on that occasion.

So what *is* the matter with him? The answer is that Gorbachev is simply of a piece, from head to toe, with those who made the coup. He was always a participant in the plot: not the plot that was carried out on August 19, but the plot that has always existed, which is the plot of the Communist Party against the people, of parasites against their own serfs, of dictators against democracy. One judges a man by his actions, and all of Gorbachev's actions showed that he desperately tried to stop the reforms in which he did not wish to participate any longer. The logic of democratic development, after all, required that he, too, be swept from his post and stripped of his position, his perquisites, his glory.

Perestroika was started largely in order to provide a better life for the Party authorities, but things got out of hand. Instead of feeding the Party more fully, perestroika saw the people moving — awkwardly, looking nervously over their shoulders, fighting bitterly with one another — toward democracy. (Gorbachev liked to speak not of democracy but of democratization, which prompted the joke that the difference between democracy and democratization is like the difference between a canal and canalization — i.e., a sewer system.) When the dangerous question of party privileges inevitably arose, Gorbachev tried to avoid it in every way. True, he had to sacrifice a few especially extravagant swindlers; but it is an old Russian tradition to appease the angry crowd by throwing a few boyars from the terrace of the palace onto the pitchforks below.

Meanwhile, in those early years of perestroika, Boris Yeltsin, who was still not widely known in Moscow but was quickly gaining popularity, happened to be one of those odd people who are indifferent to privileges, who really do like to work and really do believe in the work ethic. Yeltsin destroyed the cozy nest of the high-ranking Party officials who were his colleagues in the Moscow branch of the Party; he fired the thieves and insisted that those who remained get to work. Word soon got out that this man was honest, straightforward, genuinely interested in doing something for the people. His popularity soared.

It was then that the famous personal clash between Gorbachev and Yeltsin occurred, the details of which are still unknown. Word has it that Yeltsin spoke of Raisa in a way that her husband did not like, and attacked the privileged position of the general secretary himself and his reluctance to renounce the old style of life. Yeltsin was ousted from all his positions, suffered a heart attack, and became a hero. Indeed, he achieved the status of folklore: he was a Stenka Razin (a Robin Hood), a fool at court who dared to speak the truth to the king and paid the price. The enthusiasm for Yeltsin was extraordinary. Nearly everybody voted for him in the first elections for the Soviet Parliament. He was so popular in Sverdlovsk, where he used to live, that the citizens bought up all the tickets to all the trains to Moscow, and traveled there in great numbers to cast their votes, to increase his plurality in the capital.

It was not long before there were two "parties" in the Soviet Union. There was the party of Yeltsin, consisting of all the democratic forces, plus the crowd, plus a part of the intelligentsia, plus assorted common people who wanted a change; and there was the party of Gorbachev, the party of central government, of empire, of the traditional institutions of Communist rule. All the forces in the party of Gorbachev, or "the center," were bent on the destruction of Yeltsin. The battlefield was all of the Soviet Union, every precinct of Soviet society, because the party of Yeltsin seemed to have representatives everywhere. So Gorbachev and his people began to take coup-like actions: to slander or, better, to kill Yeltsin (there were a number of attempts on his life), to cut off his communications (they attempted to ban him from television and later delivered Soviet television entirely into the hands of hard-liners), and so on. The most successful operation was to turn the nationalities against one another in the Baltics, in Nagorno-Karabakh, in Ossetia, and elsewhere.

The "center" watched with pleasure as the feeling of helplessness grew in the camp of its enemy, whose arsenal consisted mainly of good intentions. Whenever democrats accomplished something constructive, a presidential decree banning all similar initiatives followed. The "center" attempted to prosecute businesspeople, to take away their money, to choke them with taxes, to search their offices and apartments, to arrest them. They banned demonstrations in Moscow, stationed troops in the city, invented unconstitutional measures to deprive democrats of the few freedoms that remained. The Communist Party and the KGB collaborated almost openly.

Last December, as his closest economic and political advisers have testified, Gorbachev stopped replying to letters, to telephone calls, to other direct appeals. Eduard Shevardnadze quit. Magazines could not be printed because the price of paper increased tenfold. (The Party press, of course, was not affected.) Why didn't the "center" close the country's borders? It did not fear the brain drain. Conservatives don't need brains. Anyway, the brain drain was actually a drain of democrats, and this suited the powers perfectly. They knew that it would be easier to deal with those who stayed behind.

In the aftermath of the great event, I must recount an intriguing story that I heard last summer in Moscow. It was told to me, secondhand, by one of the most respected democratic leaders in the country, who is a People's Deputy and a member of the Supreme Soviet. I had asked for his opinion of the strange incident in which Yeltsin fell into the river, which was reported all around the world. According to the reports from Moscow, a drunken Yeltsin, carrying flowers, was on his way to see a certain lady, who worked as a maid in a village in which only high-ranking Party officials lived. At the door of her house—again, according to the reports—Yeltsin was met by his rivals for her affections. Yeltsin tried to get rid of them, shouting: "Do you know who I am?" To which they replied, "Now you will know who we are." Whereupon they beat him up, threw him in the mud, and chased him away. It was said that Yeltsin went to the river to wash off the mud, and fell in. Then he began a quarrel with some policemen nearby, and managed to draw the head of Moscow police into the incident, and in no time at all there was an international scandal. Yeltsin never offered a comprehensible explanation of the episode, though there was a bizarre exchange about the incident between him and Gorbachev, as if it were a matter of significance. Gorbachev's delight at Yeltsin's trouble was plain.

My friend told me that what we had all heard was bullshit. He had established the truth from a reliable source, which was this. It was Prime Minister Nikolai Ryzhkov's birthday, and Yeltsin, who used to work with Ryzhkov in Sverdlovsk, decided to throw convention to the winds and use the occasion to make peace, to restore his relations with his political rivals. He bought flowers for Ryzhkov and his wife, and set out for Ryzhkov's dacha, which was protected by cordons of police. At each cordon he was stopped and interrogated, and slowly he approached the dacha. When he appeared at the house, Ryzhkov's guards announced that Yeltsin was there and wished to see him. The appearance of their enemy at the door, uninvited and in flagrant violation of protocol, outraged the company within. And that company, according to my friend's source, included Gorbachev.

Gorbachev barked an order: "Give that piece of shit a good bath!" Yeltsin was seized, dragged into the house, and it was not long before he found himself drenched. Then his wife and daughter were summoned to retrieve him, and in the time it took them to reach the dacha and the wet and humiliated Yeltsin, the KGB trashed their apartment. When they returned home, they found their place turned upside down and a note threatening Yeltsin with retaliation against his wife and his daughter if he reported the incident. Thus it was that Yeltsin found himself at the center of a scandal that he could not, or would not, explain.

That same evening, said my friend, "I went to bed without knowing what had happened, and as usual I unplugged my telephone, which otherwise never stops ringing. Early in the morning, however, I was awakened by the phone. It was Kryuchkov. 'Good morning, my dear,' said the chief of the KGB, as if we were old friends. 'Did you hear what Boris did yesterday? What a tough guy! Imagine, at his age, he still has a mistress!'" And Kryuchkov proceeded to tell my sleepy friend the version of the scandal that became known around the world the following day.

When Kryuchkov hung up, my bewildered friend sat up and realized that his unplugged phone had rung anyway. In the early hours of the morning, the chief of the KGB had called and merrily told a ribald story about Yeltsin that should be of no interest to him. The only possible explanation was that a provocation had been staged, however clumsily, into which they wished to draw him. My friend, you see, is a man known for his honesty, and the KGB thought that his honesty would be useful: the version of the incident that *he* circulated would be believed. How they managed to make his phone work remains a mystery. My friend suspects that they entered his apartment while he slept and reconnected it. When he told me this story, he was at my apartment. He told me that he was being watched by the KGB, and showed me the car outside my window. We went into the courtyard of my building, where a church stands. A painter was sketching the church. When my friend left, the painter left, too. So did the car.

I have heard many firsthand accounts of Gorbachev's rudeness, which do not surprise me, since rudeness is a characteristic trait of high Party officials. And I have often thought that there is a limit to the humiliation that you can inflict upon someone else. If you push your victim over the line, you may break him forever, which is the objective of Communist regimes, or you may make him stronger, and impossible to break. Under intense pressure, coal turns into diamonds.

Maybe something of that kind happened to Yeltsin, who has been humiliated by many, many people, including his former colleagues in Moscow, the mass media of the United States (who made him into a buffoon), and the American government. These were all people without a sense of history, with a misplaced sense of propriety, and a tendency not to see beyond appearances. There has been much snickering about the fact that Yeltsin drinks, that he arrives late at breakfasts with rich and influential people, that he demands an audience with the American president. Only a week before the coup, *Newsweek* reported that Yeltsin eats caviar and butter with his fingers.

This need to present Yeltsin as a wild, disheveled, Rasputin-like figure, to mock him publicly, could be forgiven (why not have some fun at a politician's expense?) if the stakes were less important than the disposition of power in the world's other superpower, which owns a spectacular nuclear arsenal and works hand in hand with the terrorists of the world. I may be exaggerating, I know, but still I believe that if the Russian public were as prudish, and as easily offended, as the American public, if Russians were to play along with Kryuchkov's plan and agree that a colorful private life discredits a political leader, and therefore turn their backs on Boris, then the coup of August 19 would have succeeded, Gorbachev would be dead, the cold war would be revived, Eastern Europe would be stained with blood, and Russian tanks would be in Berlin. (Recall the uncertain fate of the nuclear codes during the days of the coup.) Fortunately for Russia, scandals of the Gary Hart–like variety leave us indifferent.

It appears that everybody underestimated what has taken place in Russia during the past two years. In the United States, more attention was paid to Mrs. Bush's dog than to Boris Yeltsin. But the dog, who is extremely cute, never put her paw to a nuclear button. Gorbachev's command did. And step by step Gorbachev let the coup happen. What provoked the plotters, in fact, was not that he was moving with them but that he was not moving as fast as they wished to move, and so they decided to get rid of him. *That* is what Gorbachev meant by "treachery." After all, they had a deal: he wanted only to be No. 1, and they had agreed.

The fact that he himself had betrayed the country did not occur to him. For the truth is that lately Gorbachev more and more openly stood at the head of the resistance to reform. And this was more and more openly discussed in the Soviet media. In the West, however, nobody wanted to listen. He is so nice, he has such a winning smile, he has such a tasteful wife. President Bush repeated and repeated that Gorbachev confirmed his commitment to the path of democratic reform and we must help him in every way possible and blah blah blah. The fact that conservatives in the Soviet Union were loudly demanding Gorbachev's resignation contributed to the mass deception in the West.

A Russian who reads American newspapers and watches American television cannot recognize his or her country from these reports. I am acquainted with many Western journalists. They speak pretty good Russian. They are intelligent. They understand what is happening. But what do we read in their reports? Typically, we read this:

MOSCOW, JUNE 14—Soviet people are experiencing hard times. "We are experiencing hard times," says Ludmilla, thirty-six, a fat woman with a tired face, and the mother of two children.

Ludmilla does not know what she will feed her children if famine comes. She does not know what will happen tomorrow. She does not know what will happen in a year. "I don't know," she says, shaking her head.

"I don't know either," says Yuri, twenty-five, a young businessman with closely cropped hair, in blue jeans and a Pepsi T-shirt. What does Yuri think of America? "Oh, you are happy people, you Americans," says Yuri. "You can drink Pepsi every day."

Soviet people want democracy. They want to drink Pepsi and wear jeans. They don't know whether they will be able to wear jeans in a year.

Meanwhile, Soviet newspapers and magazines during the past year have been bursting with real information and fine analysis. Of course they, too, have been stupid, vulgar, ridiculous, and uncertain. But together the strengths and the weaknesses of Soviet journalism have amounted to all the material that a thoughtful person requires for an understanding of the Soviet Union today. The affiliation of various papers with various organizations; their mastheads and their tables of contents, and the changes in their staffs; the numbers of copies printed and the manner of their distribution (by the newsstands or by hawkers in the streets, in Moscow or all over the country); the presses at which the papers are printed; the prices of the papers (the democratic papers cost more); the typical whereabouts of the various editors (Vitaly Korotich of *Ogonyok* is in New York, Yegor Yakovlev of *Moscow News* is in Moscow); the scandals among the editors and writers (thirteen editors of *Ogonyok* recently left and founded the new magazine *Russian Visa;* Vitaly Tretyakov recently left *Moscow News* and founded the *Independent Gazette;* the war led by Anatoly Lukyanov for *Izvestia,* in which hard-liners tried to take control of the paper) — all this was breathtaking, and together formed a battleground of Tolstoyan proportions.

The showdown between the party of Gorbachev and the party of Yeltsin, in short, has been clearly visible. So was the birth, and the quick growth, of what Russians call the "third force," or fascism, which found a great deal of nourishment in the atmosphere created by Gorbachev. In the last elections for the Russian presidency, 7 percent of the voting population gave their votes to Vladimir Zhirinovsky, the leader of the so-called Liberal Democratic Party who is generally believed to represent the KGB. He pretended to speak for the political center, and with amazing ease he obtained an audience with Gorbachev, who is inaccessible to the democrats. Our conservatives played glasnost for all it was worth, and enjoyed to the ugliest their right of free speech. And Gorbachev, who is certainly not a fascist, was well-disposed toward these people. Why, then, need we speculate about his political orientation?

Human ingratitude is a marvel. Yeltsin surrounds himself with democratic forces and people tired of communism. Gorbachev promotes the scoundrels to the highest posts in the land. Yeltsin issues decrees to loosen the deadly grip of the party. Gorbachev issues undemocratic decrees that are simply unconstitutional. The smartest people take Yeltsin's side. Gorbachev's command consists of fools and knaves. Gorbachev falls victim to his own intrigues, casts the country into danger, and nearly perishes himself. Yeltsin, in unequal battle, with no weapons, wins the day, and saves the life of Gorbachev and his family. It becomes plain to everybody in the country that the Communist Party and the KGB lack all legitimacy and deserve to be dismantled, and Gorbachev solemnly proclaims his faith in the ideals of communism. After two days of post-coup pressure, Gorbachev reluctantly concedes and quits the Party, in defiance of the very ideals to which he swore fealty only a few days before. And what is the result, at least in the days immediately following the crisis? The Western media still awards laurels to Gorbachev. His departure from the Party is discussed reverently, as if it were his doing, not Yeltsin's.

Human blindness is also a marvel. I doubt that the historian and commentator Stephen F. Cohen would like to live under communism. But when Yeltsin destroys the Communist Party, a criminal organization if ever there was one, which cast its shadow over half of the world and almost an entire century, and was responsible for the death of scores of millions of people, the only thing that Cohen worries about, at least on television, is that Yeltsin is not playing according to democratic rules, that in his bold and peremptory blow against the Party he does not follow the rules of the democratic textbook—as if democracy in the Soviet Union could be born in any other way, as if democracy is a Platonic thing that is indifferent to the circumstances in which it finds itself, and must follow clear and ideal formulas.

A man who watches a wolf devouring his child does not begin a discussion of animal rights. And if he does, he is doing the wolf's work. I can understand, in a way, the hypocrisy of a man like A. Shalnyev, a correspondent for *Izvestia* who deplores the undemocratic closing of *Pravda,* who says that he would prefer that *Pravda* compete with the democratic press in a free market, which is a bit like proposing that a beggar compete with Donald Trump in a free market. Shalnyev was a faithful servant of communism even before perestroika. I expect nothing else from him. But the homemade leftism of those who were lucky enough to be born in a free society is another matter. It is not less foul because it is so familiar.

I am grateful to Stephen F. Cohen for reminding us of the danger of what he called the "mob." I share these anxieties. I insist, however, that the historian's erudition is glib and misapplied, that the people who surrounded the White House in Moscow and brought the first stirrings of real democracy to Russia do not deserve to be called a mob. This time the crowd was not the mob. This time the crowd was the people. It was one of those rare moments when the crowd is transformed, by truth and by danger, into something higher, not something lower. Every one of the men and women who assembled outside the Russian Parliament building left his or her home alone, and headed in the rainy night toward the danger without any certainty that they were joining anything larger or safer than themselves.

It is amazing, this sweet and shared sensation of the road to freedom, this sudden smashing of the prison doors, this deep intake of oxygen after decades of foul vapors. My phone rings endlessly. American Russians are calling, Russian Russians are calling. They call to congratulate all of us, and to laugh with joy. Never in my life did I expect to hear so much Russian laughter.

1991

The Future According to
Alexander Solzhenitsyn

Review of *Rebuilding Russia: Reflections and Tentative Proposals,* by
Aleksandr Solzhenitsyn, translated and annotated by Alexis Klimoff
(Farrar, Straus & Giroux, 1991)

A S IS WELL KNOWN, Alexander Solzhenitsyn supposes
that there is a single truth, that the truth is one. The
combined evidence of his work, especially his polemical
articles, suggests also that he believes it is known to him alone.
This sense of high exclusiveness became clear in 1974, immediately after his expulsion from the Soviet Union, when Russian
émigrés, who would have gladly embraced this émigré by com-
pulsion, ran into a hastily erected fence. It turned out that, in
the mind of the involuntary émigré, they were all bad, since
they had left Russia of their own will. (The horrible circumstances that forced them to flee, to save their lives and the lives
of their families, were not taken into account.) But he, Solzhenitsyn, was good, since he had been expelled against his will.

Russian writers should not leave the motherland, they
should stay home. Why? Because. Russian writers should not
think about money. Russian writers should not criticize Russia
(though they are obligated to curse the Soviet regime). Russian
writers should not have their own opinions about other Rus-

sian writers (how dare Siniavsky love Pushkin so uncanonically, not the way the Leader and Teacher commands that he should?). It turned out, in short, that everyone should or should not do one thing or another, and that only Solzhenitsyn knew what precisely that thing was. Submit—or be condemned and excommunicated.

Russians learned a good lesson. For the umpteenth time they had raised up an idol, and for the umpteenth time, having barely settled on his pedestal, the idol began to kick, bite, and spit in their faces, and to demand the most terrible sacrifice: that they relinquish their free will, their liberty to reason and to feel, that they forsake, in other words, everything that constitutes individuality. The confusion and the dismay that this exposure of Solzhenitsyn caused among Russian émigrés actually benefited Russian thought and letters. The spat-upon matured from the experience; they left the Buddha behind to meditate on the far side of his fence, and they busied themselves with more productive matters than burning incense and offering flowers and honey to the little god.

Now, about the fence. As we know, on the mainland (as émigrés often refer to Russia) Solzhenitsyn's works were categorically forbidden. The émigrés that he shunned in their common exile were also forbidden. Thus, information about what was really going on between them in distant, inaccessible, legendary America didn't get through to Russia, or it arrived in distorted form. It was for this reason, and not only because of his extraordinary personal courage, that Solzhenitsyn gradually acquired the attributes of a quasi-mythological figure. Indeed, he was transformed into an archetype from Russian folklore, into one of those immortal, omnipotent, and often ornery old people who lives in a distant, inaccessible place, on an island or a glass mountain or an impenetrable forest, once-upon-a-time-in-a-far-off-kingdom. The famous writer came to be imagined rather like the ancient characters Koshchei the Immortal or Grandfather Knowall or Baba Yaga, a powerful old crone who lives in the forest behind a pike fence decorated with human skulls.

The "immortality" of this man who had suffered from cancer, was miraculously cured, and was then transported by a supernatural power (by the KGB, and through the air) to the final point beyond the ocean, beyond the river of forgetfulness into a fairy-tale world, facilitated the formation of the myth. In Russia it was claimed that the fence around the Solzhenitsyn estate in the woods of Vermont was high and impenetrable, topped with barbed-wire snares, like a labor camp. It was whispered that the gates were guarded by vicious German shepherds that didn't understand Russian or English, but only Old Slavonic (the sacred language of the Church); in mythological terms, that is, the dogs responded only to certain magical formulas.

The legend about the fence has persisted, with different variations, for fifteen years. I remember when it was born, and I have seen it take root and grow thick with outlandish details. Just recently Solzhenitsyn was visited by the director Stanislav Govorukhin, one of the few who have been allowed into the inner sanctum. And what was the very first thing that the visitor reported back to his listeners, who hunger for bedtime tales? That the fence was not what we had thought, that it was only an ordinary wire fence guarding the grounds from deer, that it was neither very tall nor very strong. (Now who asked him to go and destroy a myth?)

The immortal and irascible old wise men of Russian folklore rarely have direct dealings with anyone. The role of press spokesman or messenger is usually played by a quasi-magical woman, who is close to the old man but is kind and favorably disposed toward the people. It might be Vasilisa the Beautiful, captured by Koshchei to be his wife and housekeeper, and to scratch his head at night; or the lass Chernavka, who serves Baba Yaga and scratches her heels before bedtime; or one of those nameless girls who warn mortal guests about the host's bad mood. Solzhenitsyn's wife plays this role: she delivers his manuscripts to the outside world and conveys his refusal (or, rarely, his agreement) to be interviewed. It is she who sometimes responds to Russian writers who have dared to request an audience, "Alexander Isayevich approves of your story, but you needn't come. He won't see visitors." Which brings to mind the skulls on Baba Yaga's fence. They were all that remained of the unfortunate travelers who tried to break into the enchanted enclave without the requisite passwords and skills, and without availing themselves of the messenger's friendly assistance. They got what they deserved.

The consummation of the Solzhenitsyn myth is the half-joking conviction of Russian émigrés that the Solzhenitsyn in Vermont is not the "real" one, that there has been a switch, that the KGB sent a double and the "real" Solzhenitsyn rotted somewhere in the Gulag. In the eighteenth century, Russians spoke much the same way about Peter the Great, who traveled to the West and returned infected with Western ideas: Russians should wear German clothes, shave their beards, and smoke tobacco; Russian women should wear décolleté dresses and dance with men. It was whispered that Peter had been switched, and that the figure who returned to Russia was the Antichrist. In the Russian popular imagination, the West, where the sun goes down, is a bewitched location that denotes night, cold, death, the corridor to another world (which is why all those magical elders live in the West). The unseen line that divides "East" from "West" is a magic site where people are transformed. A transfiguration takes place, a turning inside out, a metamorphosis; werewolvery, werefolkery.

The mythopoeic model of the "wise old man behind the fence," of the "magical grandfather," has existed since preliterate and dark times. Anyone who conforms to this archetype, deliberately or not, is doomed to immortality. Thus the tyrant Ivan the Terrible, whose reign spread fear across the land, is remembered with a respect that has not diminished over the last four hundred years, while softhearted Boris Godunov, who tried to reform and to enlighten, is regarded with contempt and pity. Ivan the Terrible killed countless people, but he is honored; Boris Godunov may or may not have killed one sickly boy, the tsarevich Dmitri, but the populace will not forgive him. Similarly, Stalin is much more popular than Lenin among our conservatives, who boast of their closeness to the people, their nationalism, their roots. (They are right, the proximity is obvious.) Stalin's fence was higher, his guard was more fearsome, and he himself was far more enigmatic than the "open" Lenin. He also killed many more people, so clearly his sorcery was more powerful than Lenin's. Of course, both Lenin and Stalin dwelt behind the Kremlin's fence, possessed superhuman (more correctly, inhuman) wisdom and the ability to foresee the future (a perennial characteristic of our folklore about leaders); and both are immortal. (Neither of them was buried when they died, and Lenin remains unburied today.) One official slogan declared, "Lenin Lived, Lenin Lives, Lenin Will Live," and another one, "Stalin Is Lenin Today."

Every culture and every nation has its own powerful sources of mythological radiation. As long as these sources are alive, the nation recognizes itself. Certainly mythological models are very strong among Russians. As long as myths are alive, "Russia" is alive. "What is Russia?" Solzhenitsyn has asked, as have millions of others. The land? The language? The traditions? Well, it could be claimed that Russia exists when and where Russian mythological models are reproduced. If they operate in Moscow or Siberia, in New York or Vermont, then Russia is there, too. In this sense, Solzhenitsyn is a profoundly Russian character — and a profoundly pagan Russian character, though he considers himself a Russian Orthodox Christian.

In this sense, the struggle of "Russia" with the "West" is a battle with foreign sources of mythic radiation. And the underestimation of this "Russian voodoo" leads to mistakes and misunderstandings. Take the case of Western aid, for example. The Russian attitude toward it has been described in the press more or less accurately. The Russians want this help (everyone wants to eat!), but they are ashamed of it (such a big, rich country, and we are forced to take leftovers from the Germans, whom we defeated in the war); they are grateful for it (how can you not thank the giver for his kindness?), but they are suspicious of it (they'll feed us, lull us into letting down our guard, and then demand half our country!).

But another element is left out of the picture. No one talks about it, you are not supposed to mention it. It is that Russians secretly feel that the West is *obligated* to feed them, that this is only just and fair, the result of some special sorcery at work, or of the magic word or smile or threat or spell that sets the aid of enchanted powers in motion. In this way, for example, did lazy Emel, the hero of a Russian fairy tale, catch a pike in the river. The fish begged to be released, and Emel agreed, on the condition that the fish promise to help him on a regular basis. The pike would do all of Emel's work for him, provide him with food and drink, rescue him from any peril. And at the end of the tale Emel naturally married the tsarevna and received half a kingdom as her dowry.

The fairy tale doesn't allow for any doubt that the pike will keep its word. Magical creatures may not deceive. Humans, however, may deceive; and so, in relation to foreigners, Russians feel that we will always trick them, but they will not trick us. The foreigners—well, they're not really quite human, they only appear to be like us, but they really don't have souls, they're empty inside, they're mechanical (as Dostoyevsky wrote), they are werefolk, they came from the West, the land of dangerous wonders and sumptuous treasures. They know how to cast magic spells, how to make money, gold, riches, and so let them serve us. (After the revolution in 1917, bankers were jailed and interrogated about how they made money: What do you need to do it, what is the secret? The frightened, astonished bankers muttered something about labor and the laws of economics, but the peasant-born secret policemen only laughed: Come now, you can't fool us! Tell us your secrets!)

◆ ◆ ◆

The little book by Solzhenitsyn that has recently appeared in English was published in Russian in two Soviet newspapers in September 1990. It appeared in the United States, in other words, after the revolution of August 1991, when the Soviet Union almost ceased to exist, when all the cracks and schisms, previously hidden under a deceptively smooth surface, suddenly emerged, tearing apart a huge power in all imaginable and unimaginable directions. The previous reality no longer exists, the old facts are obsolete, the logic of history, once unknown to all of us, now manifests itself before our very eyes, frightening peaceful citizens and awakening emotions that people never even suspected they possessed.

In this sense Solzhenitsyn's book is completely outdated, though not by any fault of his own. Still, in another sense, in another dimension, in the mythological space in which the writer and his faithful audience dwell, this text is not in the least dated. Indeed, in essence it can never become dated, for it is the stuff of myth. In this myth, in this ideal world, a Great and Kind-hearted Russia, populated by a Wise and Just People, endures. Evil Forces (communism, Soviet power) cast a temporary spell on the People and turn them from the path to the One and Only Truth, but these powers will be defeated by the Wisdom of the People.

Since this space is mythic, moreover, its size is not all that important. Thus, according to Solzhenitsyn in his book, a smaller Russia is better: in a smaller Russia, there will be fewer aliens. Time also is a secondary consideration, and therefore the writer speaks of prerevolutionary Russia as if it continues to exist, petrified and immobile, in some dreamtime. Having established these fairy-tale parameters, it is only natural to furnish them with a fairy-tale Russian people; and this, in turn, requires the mythmaker personally to determine the criteria for belonging, the criteria of true Russianness, and hence to approve, to thunder, to command.

What is to be done with the former Soviet Union, which occupies one sixth of our planet's landmass? Two hundred and eighty million people. More than 130 nationalities. Myriad religions, faiths, superstitions, sects. A babel of languages. The broadest spectrum of political views and passions. And everyone is wretched, everyone sees an enemy in his neighbor, everyone is running from someone or chasing others. The Soviet Union has collapsed, and yet it has not collapsed. The process continues. How much iniquity, blood, and injustice will we have to witness? The terrifying example of Yugoslavia stands before us. What is to be done?

I don't know. I am in no position to give any advice. I can only observe and ask more questions. Solzhenitsyn, by contrast, has the answers. "Should," "should," "should," "should," he hammers from the pages of his essay. Solzhenitsyn proposes his own formula for the collapse of the country, based not on real (and perhaps unsolvable) problems but on a mythological paradigm in which Russia, surrounded by aliens, occupies the center. Solzhenitsyn is not stupid or ignorant; he cannot fail to understand that the conflicts of kindred peoples (Russians and Ukrainians, for example) are often more acrimonious than those of very different peoples. But reality doesn't have much place in his picture of the world. For him, Ukrainians are brothers, while Armenians, say, are not. His rigid and immutable design can only frighten and offend those who have other sympathies and other ties.

The English title of Solzhenitsyn's essay is *Rebuilding Russia*. It is not entirely precise. A more literal translation of the original would read: "How We [Should] Arrange Russia." The translator, Alexis Klimoff, has dropped that important "We," thereby dampening the author's clearly expressed desire to emphasize his membership in an exclusively Russian fellowship, and his intention to participate in the plans for rebuilding. In the original Russian, that "should" is implied rather than stated, but it is heard by every Russian ear. And "rebuilding" is also, really, an incorrect translation. Though the word "rebuilding" in fact conveys the idea of Solzhenitsyn's essay, Solzhenitsyn's own word craftily evades and flirts with the dictionary. For the word *obustroit* describes, more precisely, the process of turning a dwelling into a comfortable place: I'll put the wardrobe here, the bed there, the table over in the corner. I do not mean to be overly harsh toward the translator, for the task is titanic. One must translate Solzhenitsyn first into Russian, and then from Russian into English.

The Italian writer Tommaso Landolfi has a story about a man who learns Persian. Inspired by the divine harmonies of the language, he writes a marvelous poem. He is convinced that it is a work of genius, and seeks out the reaction of specialists. But it turns out that no one (other than his joker-teacher, who disappears) knows this "Persian" language. Such a Persian simply does not exist. The nasty prank torments the poet, since he cannot share the treasure that he possesses. He tries to translate his masterpiece into accessible Italian: no good, it's not right, it's merely a pale copy with little meaning and less poetry. The great beauty that has been revealed to him must remain unknown to others.

Solzhenitsyn is in a similar situation. Unlike the unfortunate poet, however, he himself invented this "Persian" language, which swaddles his speech and his mind in a thick shroud. In this particular text I counted more than 100 words that are not used in the Russian language, and my tally, I am certain, is not complete. It's not that these words are entirely incomprehensible: recognizable Russian linguistic roots show through each of them, the prefixes and the suffixes are more or less Russian, the nouns stand where nouns should, the verbs indicate action. A number of words, however, are transformed beyond recognition, so that as you read you have to stop and think, is this a verb? Imagine that your cat suddenly grew a cow's head. You might not object, but you would certainly pause to wonder if it will drink milk or produce it.

Solzhenitsyn may have invented some of these words. Others he clearly found in his favorite book, Vladimir Dahl's *Reasoned Dictionary of the Living Great-Russian Language* (1863–66). That lexicon is a marvelous collection of words that were and still are used in Russian, but as befits a dictionary, it is a storehouse, a treasury. It unites words in that imaginary, intellectual, theoretical space called language. No real individual speaks this language. Real individuals know only a part of it—otherwise we wouldn't need such collections of words.

Solzhenitsyn got his hands on Dahl relatively late—in 1946, when the future writer was about thirty. It's obvious that he was bowled over by this Aladdin's treasure trove of language, and he grabbed more gems than he was able to carry. I remember an interview Solzhenitsyn gave quite some time ago, in which he talked about how, with the help of his children, he was revising Dahl's dictionary with a view to determining which words Russians needed and which they did not. There is also a work that he recently compiled and published on the basis of that effort, the *Russian Dictionary of Linguistic Expansion,* a recommended list of words that are now little used or obsolete.

Again, these are wonderful words for a dictionary, but they are unthinkable as recommendations for the actual speech of real people; a joy for the historian, but incomprehensible to the contemporary ear; appropriate in rare contexts (a quotation of direct speech, a quarrel, a historical novel), but absolutely impossible in today's language, written or spoken. If medical instructions were to be written in the language of *Beowulf,* or judicial opinions in the language of Joyce, or road signs in cuneiform writing, if CNN's anchors appeared on the air in bathing suits and the president read a speech wrapped in a yashmak, then you might scream with frustration, even though you probably don't have anything against either *Beowulf* or bathing suits.

In Solzhenitsyn's little book, at least two lexical layers are clearly delineated. First, there is his "Persian," which includes verbs, adverbs, and nouns meaning "crazy," "doom," "to rob," "neglect," "blindness," "to spoil," "unfortunate," "bad," "very bad," and "horrible," and also "befriend" and "together." The meaning of a good half of these words can be reconstructed only by spotting their roots. This "Persian" vocabulary is rich, inexhaustible, very expressive and, given the context, incredibly tasteless. And it is incorporated into a syntax that is equally unintelligible — not Russian literary syntax but that of "popular" or "peasant" speech. This, of course, is no accident. Even if you ignore the meaning of what is said, and consider the style alone, it becomes quite clear that the writer is speaking to the "people," the "muzhik," the "peasant" — an imagined and generic peasant, to be sure. Addressing these archetypes in this archaic and obsolete language, Solzhenitsyn rails and curses. Others — notably foreigners, city-dwellers, and contemporaries — are not his intended interlocutors. Through his mythological fence Solzhenitsyn conjures a mythological Russia-dweller and summons the spirit of the Russian land with spells and incantations. All are supposed to respond, mere mortals as well as the entire pantheon of our folklore: the talking steeds, wise ravens, all-powerful pikes, mice, hobgoblins, mermaids, and domestic spirits.

The second layer of Solzhenitsyn's language consists largely of political terminology: "Parliament," "party," "democracy," "bureaucracy," "economy," "majority" and "minority," "monopoly," "voting," "procedure," "lawyer," "legislation," "proportional system," "information," "statistics," "national," and many other such words. The syntax in the section where these words dominate is normative, clear, easily mastered. This, too, is no coincidence. When you switch from magic to reality, you have to speak comprehensibly. There are no mermaids in parliament.

Solzhenitsyn's article is divided into two almost equal parts, which consist, in turn, of fourteen short "chapters" each. In the first half of his book, the author speaks of the past and the present, and in the second half he gives his ideas regarding the future. I counted the frequency of "strange" words and locutions in both parts. In the first part there are 127 such expressions; in the second, 21. They are distributed among the fourteen chapters of each part in the following manner: in part one—12, 16, 11, 11, 6, 8, 12, 6, 7, 3, 8, 12, 11, 4. In part two—1, 1, 1, 1, 2, 2, 0, 5, 1, 5, 0, 0, 1, 1. This is surprising only at first glance. After all, it is in the first half of his text that Solzhenitsyn denounces, appeals, curses, and prophesies—and the apocalyptic mode, as is well known, requires inarticulateness, fervor, and hysteria. If a prophet runs about barefoot, his beard flailing in the wind and his trembling hands lifted heavenward, you listen to him. If the prophet is calm, polite, clean-shaven, and properly dressed, you won't give him the time of day.

It is impossible to expound a proposal for governmental organization in the tone of someone who has just been stung by a scorpion. Not that Solzhenitsyn is mad. Quite the contrary, he knows perfectly well where he is and what he is doing. Here's what he does. He identifies and juxtaposes two principles: "the people" and "the individual." According to Solzhenitsyn, the interests of the people are good, but the interests of the individual are bad. The people want to live a quiet, worthy, well-fed life; the individual wants to grab, to seize, to appropriate, to enjoy. Who are these greedy, disgusting creatures? Young people, the people of television and radio, speculators from the "shadow economy," bureaucrats, all political parties (by definition), the city of Moscow, the nomenklatura, 75 percent of "glasnost's troubadours," teachers, athletes, the military, the Communists, the KGB, the intelligentsia. The government is on the take, industry is "mindless and rapacious," the peasant estate has died out.

Taken individually, in short, everyone is no good. Perhaps this is true, but then how did all these scoundrels manage to constitute a good people? The answer is that "the people" is not "constituted of." According to Solzhenitsyn, "the people" is a living organism, not a "mere mechanical conglomeration of disparate individuals." This, of course, is the old, inevitable trick of totalitarian thinking: "the people" is posited as unified and whole in its multiplicity. It is a sphere, a swarm, an anthill, a beehive, a body. And a body should strive for perfection; everything in it should be smooth, sleek, and harmonious. Every organ should have its place and its function: the heart and brain are more important than the nails and the hair, and so on. If your eye tempts you, then tear it out and throw it away; cut off sickly members, curb those limbs that will not obey, and fortify your spirit with abstinence and prayer.

Having described quite colorfully the horrors and the consequences of communism, and sketched a broad (and in many respects accurate) picture of the country's desolation, Solzhenitsyn commands twelve (or eleven and a half) republics to separate "unequivocally and irreversibly" from Russia proper, in the name of the people. He would leave only the Ukraine, Belorussia, and the Russian part of Kazakhstan in a "Russian Union." He similarly allows more than one hundred minority nationalities and ethnic groups to remain part of Russia. "Should they wish to be with us, more the credit to them." And what should be done if one of the twelve "big" republics doesn't want to separate? "With the same resolve we—that is, those remaining—will then need to proclaim our separation from them." "We"—the three Slavic peoples—merge into a single whole and keep one hundred smaller ethnic groups for ourselves, while banishing the twelve larger peoples utterly without regard to their desires. (There are chapters called "A Word to the Great Russians," "A Word to the Ukrainians and Belorussians," and "A Word to the Smaller Nationalities and Ethnic Groups," but the rest are not found worthy of the patriarch's "words.")

Solzhenitsyn knows perfectly well the horrors of such forced separation—what it means to cut across the lives of nations, cultures, families, and lands that are closely intertwined—but with biblical cruelty he divides people into "ours" and "not ours." To the Ukrainians, he cries: "Brothers! We have no need of this cruel partition. The very idea comes from the darkening of minds brought on by the Communist years. Together we have borne the suffering of the Soviet period, together we have tumbled into this pit, and together, too, we shall find our way out." But he is short with "aliens": "Panels of experts representing all concerned parties must begin deliberations" to figure out a separation plan. "This sorting process might well take several years."

On the one hand, brothers. On the other hand, commissions of experts. Who are these experts? What is the nature of their expertise? Where did they gain the experience that confers upon them such authority? Will this be something like the medieval councils of doctors, professors of phlegm and black bile, in velvet berets with quill pens and saws near at hand for the necessary and justified amputations? Or will the commissions consist only of "brothers"? But can "brothers" really be relied upon if, as Solzhenitsyn himself quite rightly says, we "have been hurled back to a state of semibarbarity," and "there is no guarantee whatever that the new leaders now coming to the fore will immediately prove to be farsighted and sober-minded," and "of all the possible freedoms, the one that will inevitably come to the fore will be the freedom to be unscrupulous," and our souls have been "destroyed," and glasnost is defended by "tainted voices," and three of every four defenders of glasnost are unrepentant "toadies of Brezhnevism," and tens of thousands of intellectuals ("smatterers") have "festering moral sores," and our merchants are "sharks bred in the murky waters of the Soviet underground," and "our glasnost is bedecked, festooned with the same old plump and heavy clusters of lies," and so on?

Consider the chapter "Family and School," which is structured like the rest of them. First, the lamentations: woe is me, woe is us, alack and alas, all is lost! Then the advice on how to correct the situation: begin with children. But since the children have to be taught, begin with the teachers. But since the teachers also have to be taught, begin with the teachers of the teachers. Throw out all the textbooks. Rework everything. Change the university curriculum. But who, again, should do all this? The festering intelligentsia? The mendacious authorities? The wealthy sharks? And if, sharing Solzhenitsyn's horror of this vicious cycle of woe, I should attempt to do something by myself, without waiting for the proper help, well, what awaits me is the lash of control:

> In the near future we can probably also expect to see the appearance of tuition-charging private schools which will surpass the standards of the school system in particular subjects or in some other specific educational aspects. But such schools must not institute irresponsibly arbitrary curricula; they should be under the supervision and control of local educational authorities.

We have come full circle. We have arrived not at freedom but at control. The unfortunate children, with whom the writer started, are abandoned and forgotten. They were only there for decoration, for rhetorical purposes, to attract attention.

Voting and elections, according to Solzhenitsyn's plan, are not necessary, since "the majority" cannot know what is better for the government and what is worse. In the Russian Union our lives are to be managed by a Sobornaya Duma, or Collective Council, which consists of representatives of the estates. (The writer clarifies that the estates are not the same thing as the trade unions: the unions fight for material welfare, "higher wages and other benefits," while the estates are based on a "common creative impulse," or, as the Russian has it literally, "spiritual co-creativity.") Moreover, these representatives — "the most worthy" — are to be appointed (without voting) by the method of "polling the wise men" (the model here is "the mountain people of the Caucasus") or some other equally enigmatic procedure. (But who will conduct the poll, one wonders? Who will determine the degree of wisdom? Of what does this wisdom consist? How will the disagreement of protesters, stupid people, and those armed to the teeth be resolved? Can the wise man be bought with money? Does he know human passions, weaknesses, fears?) Then, having received the highest authority, the Sobornaya Duma "will have the power to interdict any law or any action by a government institution or agency, and to mandate changes or corrections," for "moral principles must take priority over legal ones," and "any secret organization . . . will be subject to criminal prosecution for conspiracy against society."

If, at this point, the reader cannot dispel the feeling of déjà vu, he is right. The social organization that Solzhenitsyn proposes has already been attempted by a man named Lenin. The similarities between Lenin and Solzhenitsyn are striking, and they make the differences seem inconsequential. Lenin had "soviets," Solzhenitsyn has "zemstvos," and both are forms of local "self-determination." According to Lenin, socialism is a matter of inventory and control; according to Solzhenitsyn, the future of Russia is a matter of inventory and control. For Lenin, there is the wisdom of the party. For Solzhenitsyn, there is the wisdom of the elders. For Lenin, the intelligentsia is "shit." For Solzhenitsyn, it is filth, pus, hypocrisy. (His polemical essay "Our Pluralists" is entirely directed against the intelligentsia, which he accuses of a diversity of opinion.)

Solzhenitsyn believes that "party rivalry distorts the national will." Lenin thought much the same and destroyed all parties save his own. Both, naturally, cite the will of the people, but neither will allow this people to vote and elect representatives. Lenin detested Russian Orthodoxy and made atheism the government religion. Solzhenitsyn does the opposite, with the same fervor: atheism should be forbidden. Both hate the rule of law. Lenin called the rule of law "bourgeois," which for him was a synonym for "Western, democratic," and enough has been said of Solzhenitsyn's attitude toward the West. The fact that both of them say that "some things may be taken" from the West does not really change the situation. Both, in fact, took personal advantage of the most important things that the West has to offer: its freedoms of speech, the press, action, and movement. Both, living in the security of the West, worked out projects to deprive Russia's inhabitants of freedom, projects that prefer "opinions" to laws, that promote the "moral feeling" of the minority as the ruling power, that call for "democracy" without elections. The apogee of arbitrariness is Solzhenitsyn's statement that "power is a call to service and it cannot be the subject of interparty competition."

Russian readers, who are better acquainted with Lenin's works than they care to be (Lenin was required reading in school and university), immediately notice that even the title of Solzhenitsyn's work, "How We Should Arrange Russia," recalls the title of Lenin's "How We Should Reorganize Rabkrin" (the *rabkrin* were committees of inspection run by workers and peasants). Russia, in sum, has already been "arranged" once according to Solzhenitsyn's plan. And the wise men whose opinion was higher than the law found a cozy place for the writer: a freezing bunk in the Gulag.

Human beings are awful, there's no denying it. My neighbor is especially awful. He behaves badly, looks strange, likes things that repulse me, and wants things I've already got my eye on; and worst of all, he dares to think the very same of me. History knows two opposite ways of handling such vile creatures. The first is to forbid everything. Fire (Sodom and Gomorrah), water (the Flood), wholesale deaths, inquisition, wars, witch hunts, the Gulag—it's all been tried, but without much apparent success. Tell a human being "No!" and you can bet that the moment you turn your back he'll be up to his old tricks.

The second way is to allow everything, to let people themselves work out laws, and to let those laws regulate the incessant flares and sparks of human caprice and need. Laws (like money, which reformers of humanity also hate) were not invented by wily scoundrels, as Solzhenitsyn and Lenin think. Laws are the result of the natural, collective efforts of humanity to establish a single measure on the path to some sort of justice in an imperfect world. For all their flawed approximateness, they have somehow saved humanity from arbitrariness, tyranny, and madness. It is perfectly true that everyone's moral sense differs, that everyone is piqued by different things, but that is precisely why any attempt to substitute "moral feelings" for law inevitably leads to the kind of situation in which, instead of getting a ticket for illegal parking, you and your entire city would be engulfed in fire and brimstone.

Invectives against human insatiability and calls for voluntary self-limitation, when they are not accompanied by specific indications of "how many seeds you must have before you can call them a bunch," may provoke alarm in the sensitive Russian. Can Solzhenitsyn himself have overstepped the mark? Might he, too, have become a shark? Worried, the simple soul scans the pages of Solzhenitsyn's books, of articles on him, of Michael Scammell's biography, in search of models to emulate. And one finds: fifty acres of land . . . two houses on the lot . . . twelve volumes of collected works . . . a second wife . . . three children . . . a son at Harvard when he could have studied at a little Vermont college . . . a son playing piano and giving concert tours when he could have stayed home and beat humbly on a toy drum. Money? The author's income is not publicized, but as early as 1974 there is mention of $2 million to $3 million dollars. What a relief! The threshold of self-limitation established by the prophet of Vermont is clearly unattainable in actual Russian life. Russians may sleep soundly.

If someone in Russia were to take Solzhenitsyn's recommendations seriously and set about fulfilling them point by point, the country would collapse within a month. If Solzhenitsyn took over the real Russia with its real population, it's likely that uprisings, pogroms, and conflagrations would commence within a week. Russian people, of course, are no gift. Obedient but not acquiescent, submissive but willful, lazy but pliant—everyone wants to have a go at governing them, at deciding for them. Referring to the "Will of the People" (with capital letters, of course), Solzhenitsyn's pen frequently slips and accidentally declares that no one knows what this will is or how it may be determined. On those occasions when he does detect traces of that will's free manifestation, however, he can find no kind words for it. Here's what the people have chosen to embrace from the West: the "continuous seepage of liquid manure—the self-indulgent and squalid 'popular mass culture,' the utterly vulgar fashions, and the byproducts of immoderate publicity." But "popular," "mass," "vulgar," and "public" are all words that describe the people, and these, after all, are *its* music, *its* fashion, *its* byproducts, however revolting they might be or seem. The people in theory always diverge dramatically from the people in reality; and the horror of this truth is sooner or later discovered by everyone who pretends to the people's spiritual leadership, by everyone who knows how things should and should not be done.

Having settled in the most atypical state in the United States, built himself a fence, refused to allow mere mortals to enter (except for the few who agree to scratch his heels), Solzhenitsyn unconsciously and instinctively submerged himself in myth. But, as often happens with Russians, he overdid it. His drama, as I see it, lies precisely in his Russianness: in the fact that he so completely and without any doubt identifies himself with Russia, being flesh of its flesh and blood of its blood. And this proves that, although there is absolutely nothing Western about him, not the tiniest wrinkle, he is nonetheless only a part of Russia, and not Russia itself. For Russia is broader and more diverse, stranger and more contradictory, than any idea of it. It resists all theories about what makes it tick, confounds all the paths to its possible transformation. One can describe and explain Russia in a thousand ways, but as soon as the theorist and the dreamer lays down his pen, satisfied at last with his description, diabolical laughter will sound from the emptiness behind him, and the undried ink will evaporate, leaving not a trace on the white page.

1992

Pushkin's Children

CERTAIN TRICKY QUESTIONS arise from time to time in literary circles. No one knows who first asked them, and they often seem a pointless game. For instance: Would you, as a writer, continue to write if you ended up on an uninhabited island and it seemed that no one would ever read your work? Many writers answer: Yes, of course I would, I don't need a reader, I'm my own reader, I'm incapable of *not* writing, I am my own source of inspiration, no one should come between me and God, and so forth. It's impossible to judge the sincerity of such feelings. After all, there aren't any uninhabited islands left, are there?

In fact, more and more Russian writers seem to have found themselves on just such islands.

To understand how they arrived there, we might consider a few well-known points. Throughout the entire history of Russian literature, the Russian writer has never been seen by the reading public as "simply" a poet, journalist, philosopher, or scribbler—that is, as a person freely expressing his or her own thoughts and feelings or merely entertaining the reader. The Russian writer has always been seen as a prophet or preacher, a dangerous free-thinker, or a revolutionary. The very ability to manipulate words and to articulate one's thoughts placed the individual in a suspect position. The word was seen as a weapon far more fearsome than poison or daggers. A murderer might be sentenced "only" to long-term hard labor, but a person could receive the death penalty for reading forbidden poems. Even one's unproven presence in a place where a song insulting to the government had allegedly been sung could lead to exile. This is precisely what happened at the beginning of the nineteenth century to the writer and dissident Alexander Herzen, who was forced to emigrate and spend the rest of his life in exile. Such has always been the situation in Russia, but it acquired a particularly threatening aspect with the birth of a genuine, full-blooded literature in the early nineteenth century. And this threat has persisted right up to this day.

This is a wonderful point of view. It proclaims the primacy of literature over life, of dreams over reality, of imagination over facts. It says: Life is nothing—a fog, a mirage, fata morgana. But the word, whether spoken or printed, represents a power greater than that of the atom. This is an entirely Russian view of literature, without parallel in the West. And everyone in Russia, it seems, shares it: the tsars and their slaves, censors and dissidents, writers and critics, liberals and conservatives. He who has articulated a Word has accomplished a Deed. He has taken all the power and responsibility on himself. He is dangerous. He is free. He is destructive. He is God's rival. And for this reason, all of these daring, bold, outspoken, powerful magicians, from Alexander Radishchev in the late eighteenth century to Andrei Sinyavsky in the twentieth century, have been playing with life and death.

Naturally, when such power is attributed to the Word, the writer begins to feel a particular responsibility. Not surprisingly, most great Russian writers and poets have not only accepted this responsibility but have used the power of their words to address the most important social and political problems of their day: freedom (or, more accurately in Russia, the lack of it), the individual, human rights, and so on. A line from the nineteenth-century poet Nikolai Nekrasov is often quoted: "You're not required to be a poet, but a citizen you're obliged to be." This formulation harked back to the executed Decembrist Ryleev, who said: "I am not a poet, I am a citizen." But, in essence, it was part of Nekrasov's polemic with Alexander Pushkin, the father of all our contemporary literature.

Pushkin was a poet who is remarkable for, among other things, the fact that from the outset he stood above this flat, pragmatic point of view, which is so seductive in Russia. Pushkin's point of departure was that the writer should teach no one and make no appeals but be free to sing as best he could, whatever came his way, and to listen to his inner voice—in short, to create on an uninhabited island. Pushkin himself lived on a sort of uninhabited island, but his manuscripts, sealed in the bottle of time, floated on the waves into the future and are still out there. His small circle of admirers and contemporary readers didn't appreciate him as he deserved. People read much into his works but did not see everything that was there. They didn't see the most important thing—his inner freedom. (In order to understand this idea fully, one must, it seems, possess one's own inner freedom, and that is one of the most difficult things on earth to acquire.) Pushkin's contemporary readers appreciated the harmonious beauty of the poet's verse and the dry precision of his transparent prose, they understood his hatred of slavery and his defense of simple, oppressed people, and they saw his profound comprehension of Russian history, his delight in female beauty, his encyclopedic knowledge and astonishing ability to describe Russian life. They praised his humor, his alternately lighthearted and melancholy frame of mind, the tragic nature of his worldview—and quite rightly, for all this was in his verse. But the motif of inner freedom remained in the shadows, as if obscured behind opaque glass.

After Pushkin's death, this motif became downright unpopular. What inner freedom could there be when despots ruled, when there were no laws and human beings were traded like cattle, when whole peoples and classes were doomed to a brutal life? The only freedom that could be discussed was social — and a number of writers took it upon themselves to call for revolutionary changes or peaceful reforms (in accordance with their individual temperaments and political views), while others turned their attention to the moral reeducation of man, seeing salvation in the process of self-perfection, in religion, in the search for national roots, or in a special mission for Russia and the Russian people. These were marvelous writers, great writers, writers of international renown: Nikolai Gogol, Fyodor Dostoyevsky, Lev Tolstoy . . . But not one of them possessed that inner freedom, and none was able, or dared, to allow himself that inner freedom. Instead they voluntarily donned the fetters of moral duty: service to the tsar, to God, or to the People. Pushkin alone, who described himself humorously as "that homely descendant of Negroes" (one of his ancestors was from the royal family of Ethiopia, kidnapped as a child and brought as an exotic sideshow to Russia, where he subsequently was made a nobleman), was able to formulate the only ordinance that an artist can accept — inner freedom. Pushkin alone, whom his contemporaries thought an empty, worldly, frivolous man, a philanderer and naughty child, dared to ask the question: "Whether it depends on the tsar or depends on the People — isn't it all the same to you?" The irony is that after his death admiration for Pushkin grew and grew until he himself became, for many Russians, God, tsar, and the People, an idol, an icon, holy writ. Mindlessly repeating Pushkin's idea about freedom as a magic formula, an incantation, no one bothered to delve into its essence. Not one of Pushkin's admirers would allow you to be free of Pushkin himself.

This, by the way, was what happened in our own time with one of the few genuinely free Russian writers, Andrei Sinyavsky. Desiring to be dependent neither on the tsar nor the People, Sinyavsky, a descendant of the Russian nobility, hid under a Jewish pen name, Abram Tertz, and sent his manuscripts out of

Russia to the West, until his identity was uncovered and he was sent to the camps by an enraged government. To many people, this made him a hero, the mouthpiece of freedom. But in the camp, Sinyavsky decided to write a book about Pushkin, which he also published in the West after he emigrated. And suddenly the defenders of freedom ostracized Sinyavsky, simply because he had dared to address Pushkin as a mere mortal. (The most amusing mistake was made, as always, by Solzhenitsyn, who unleashed the full weight of his *malleus maleficarum* on his fellow prisoner but landed right on the icon. He accused Sinyavsky of printing an "obscene street poem" about Pushkin, not suspecting that the mildly ribald little ditty was composed by Pushkin, who was writing ironically about himself in the third person.) And so it is: God is free, but that's his own business, and all of you, who love God, are obliged to be his slaves.

Submitting to a moral but not to a creative imperative, Russian writers condemned themselves to all manner of suffering and torment. It was not only that the authorities and society cruelly punished the love of freedom — that goes without saying. The problem was also that the struggle of the poet and the citizen within any given writer usually resulted in the death of the poet. The brilliant Gogol, seeing his vocation as pointing people toward the true path to moral salvation, wrote the second volume of *Dead Souls,* in which, apparently, he tried to create a morally uplifting image of the positive hero. We aren't certain what he wrote, since, unhappy with the results, Gogol burned the manuscript and then went mad, falling into a state of religious gloom. But the sparkle of Gogol's early works dims and dies out toward the end of his life. In the last years of his life, Lev Tolstoy also ceased to be a brilliant artist, having driven himself into the narrow, cramped cage of forced morality. He didn't stop being a brilliant personality, but his preaching, the primitive pieces for children, and the moralizing tracts for peasants are no more than a curiosity against the background of his great novels. Fortunately, Dostoyevsky avoided such an inglorious end—perhaps he was saved by the indomitable passions that raged in his soul. Nevertheless, the ideological slant of all his works is obvious. Writers of a lesser stature surrendered more quickly. And the very few who did not wish to sacrifice art on the altar of service to the Fatherland, Truth, or the People were subjected to such ferocious criticism by the "progressive thinking" sectors of society that they were literally terrorized, as though they had committed the most heinous of crimes against humanity. Dostoyevsky's indignation at Afanasy Fet's innocent lyrics, "Whispers, timid breath, the nightingales trilled," is well known. This is simply disgraceful, wrote Dostoyevsky indignantly, and he speculated what an insulting impression such empty verses would have made if they'd been given to someone to read during the Lisbon earthquake!

Some people protested: Yes, of course, Dostoyevsky is right, but we aren't having an earthquake, and we aren't in Lisbon, and, after all, are we not allowed to love, to listen to nightingales, to admire the beauty of a beloved woman? But Dostoyevsky's argument held sway for a long time. It did so because of the way Russians perceive Russian life: as a constant, unending Lisbon earthquake.

And then these civic passions started to wane, and there began to appear here and there poets and artists for whom freedom and beauty had more meaning than truth and morality. The break began at the end of the nineteenth century, just when the great literature of ideas seemed to have degenerated into banal journalism and liberalistic concoctions on politically correct themes—the women's question, the improvement of mores, popular education, health care, etc. Suddenly all this began to dim. In the Chekhovian, unpoetic fin de siècle, when, as many thought, the giants had all died and only the dwarfs were left, the shoots of a new, unfamiliar art, which at first irritated many people, began to sprout. Despite the pressing "needs of the people," modernism was born in Russia, and it was all the more striking for its utter lack of practical application.

Many people considered it a form of madness and delinquency. Lev Tolstoy himself, who at the time sought his moral peace by covering the roofs of neighboring peasant huts with straw thatch and plowing the peasants' poor land, tore himself away from his unproductive voluntary labor to condemn the "decadents" with what he thought were venomous reproaches. And, of course, the "new art" was at first ridiculed by the entire previous generation of liberally inclined professors, teachers, political figures, lawyers, and other respectable people. This was a generation that read literature only to find "artistic" confirmation of what it already knew: that the peasants feed us and we must therefore love them; that women are also human beings; that poverty is bad; that we must help the poor and somehow reorganize society. But there were also readers bewitched by the unusual qualities in the new writing. The Russian Europeans, who believed in the formula "Light comes from the West," could not help but eventually respond to the new appeals and new voices. And just as eighteenth-century Russians experienced the influence of the French Enlightenment and nineteenth-century Russians were affected by the French Revolution, so early twentieth-century Russians imbibed and transformed the new French art — impressionism in painting, symbolism in poetry. (Isn't this why writers and artists flocked to Paris after the catastrophe of 1917 — to the promised land of art and freedom — only to discover that no one needed them there?)

During the years before the revolution, the arts flourished in an extraordinary manner, and Pushkin's weighty words suddenly sounded with renewed force and acquired fresh significance. The "new art" discovered that the word is magical in and of itself and not only because people are willing to kill for it. This art discovered, or rediscovered, that man is not only a member of society but a strange animal with five senses, with a variety of often untamed sexual needs, a capricious, whimsical being with unruly moods, hysterics, and perversions; that the world is large and unfathomable; and that there is such a thing as the delight of exotic, unseen countries and islands—Africa, Egypt, Ceylon, India, Japan—which are interesting not only for their statistical profiles, their undeveloped industries, and oppressed working people but for their religion, history, philosophy, mysticism, aromas, fiery sunsets over the water, snakes, lotuses, kimonos, tea ceremonies, hashish, and the unusual beauty of their women and men.

The new art fell in love with camellias and tuberoses, the colors lilac and green, seashells, bracelets, sails, the smoke of bonfires and the dust of the road, dreams and ravings, mystical illuminations and divination by cards and palmistry; it fell in love with the carnival, the theater, ancient Greece, and the ascetics; it was enchanted by languor, anguish, and tears, and it cried not because it had no money to buy a cow or to pay the moneylender but because the Ideal was unattainable, because dream and reality were divided by an insurmountable wall, and because the soul strives to reach something somewhere out there, far away, in the clouds: it strives for death, the past and the future, and loquacious numbers and weighty objects have already foretold the approaching destruction of the world, foretold plague, death and affliction, revolution and apocalypse.

Now when we look back with a feeling of sorrow and loss at that legendary time, which seems separated from us by a transparent but impassable barrier, when we hear the dim, underwater voices of those people—their debates and quarrels, their amorous admissions, their unrealized and realized prophecies—we have a vision of the *Titanic* floating in the night and gloom on its way to destruction, a vision of a huge ship brightly illuminated, full of music, wine, and elegant people, a bit afraid of the long ocean voyage, of course, but hoping that the journey will end well. After all, the ship is so large, strong, and reliable!

Russia perished just as quickly as the *Titanic*. And likewise, only a handful of people survived.

Alexander Blok, a brilliant poet who possessed truly prophetic gifts, whom Anna Akhmatova called "the tragic tenor of the era," had a premonition of the fall of the former Russia. He foresaw the revolutionary squall ("the unheard-of changes, unseen storms") and even predicted the coming destruction and catastrophe ("O, if you knew, children, / The cold and gloom of the coming days!"), but he didn't know and could not imagine that instead of the cleansing though perhaps deadly wind for which he was prepared, a thick, malodorous mist would descend over the land. Blok says he wrote poetry by listening to an inner music, which he would then transform into verse. When the revolution came, Blok at first listened greedily to the new sounds: "Listen to the revolution with your whole heart!" He wrote a poem in which, he thought, this new music sounded, and then suddenly he went "deaf." According to his contemporaries, he complained of this "deafness" as a physical rather than metaphysical calamity: "I've gone deaf, I've gone deaf, I don't hear anything any more!" he told his friends and his diary. He —a productive, marvelous poet—wrote no poetry in the last three, postrevolutionary, years of his life. To be more exact, he did write one poem. In it he said farewell to the world as he departed "into the darkness of night," as he called it. And it was none other than Pushkin whom he remembered and mentioned precisely in connection with that inner freedom, which, it seems, was his own "music" and which had left him during those fearful months.

> Pushkin! We sang the *secret* freedom
> Following in your footsteps.
> Give us your hand in foul weather,
> Help us in the mute struggle!

After this came silence. Blok, who was by and large a mystical poet, died mysteriously in 1921: He had an unknown illness that resembles AIDS. He began to dry up, to go deaf; he became emaciated and weak, and, once dead, he lay unrecognizable in his coffin, frightening those who had known him. But not all of

Russian literature had been killed. The government was distracted by more important forms of destruction, and Russian artists managed to shine for a short, frightful moment before going down in the abyss of the Soviet night.

Russian literature of the early Soviet period (as well as Russian émigré literature, which is thematically distinct from Soviet but stylistically close) continued to dramatize the theme of the Poet and the Citizen. Those who decisively chose the Citizen drowned in oblivion, and those who chose the path of the Poet surfaced alive. Of course, this theme, which is latent throughout the entire history of Russian literature, has never manifested itself in pure form. Feelings of civic duty were not alien to the great Russian poets of the frightful Soviet period; likewise, stylistic beauty and creative discovery were not entirely unknown to the writers who sold out to the regime and tried to be model Soviet citizens.

One such writer, Andrei Platonov, who passionately believed in communism, wrote a series of novels that he thought glorified the new era and new ideas. But his creativity, his unusual train of thought, and his unprecedented style constituted a devastating attack against the regime. There is no more anticommunist literature than Platonov's: paradoxically his rejection of communism is achieved not by way of open accusations but through his linguistic visions.

But most of them — the young and the old, the smart and the stupid, those who tried to fit in and didn't know how, those who tried to protest, not knowing that it was useless — were sent to different prisons and camps, or shot, or frightened nearly to death, or exiled from the country, or brought to suicide, or forced to exalt their tormentors. Their manuscripts were confiscated and burned, their libraries were destroyed, their archives were taken away and lost, and for a quarter century the country was submerged in communist gloom.

The end of the 1950s — Khrushchev's "Thaw" — brought a new wave of "civic" literature. Writers, especially poets, "spoke the truth," and hundreds of thousands gathered to hear that truth. It was then that the poets Andrei Voznesensky and Yevgeny Yevtushenko became well known. The latter, paraphrasing Nekrasov, coined the famous saying "In Russia the Poet is more than a poet." Cynics, noting how swiftly civic passions in the literary arena were replaced by mercantile passions, repeated these words, adding: "That's why the poet needs more money and privileges." This short-lived dawn of civic literature was replaced, as ever, by a new twilight; the hopes for social reform were extinguished, and from the mid-1960s to the mid-1980s we lived through the period that it is now fashionable to call "the era of stagnation," a period that one must condemn at all costs.

Oh, yes, things were very bad for the citizen during these years. But artists, poets, and writers — miracle of miracles! — flourished in this stifling era, and never has so much been written or read as during these dismal, static, prevaricating years. Literature was valued above everything. Books became a common form of currency. In order to acquire certain rare books, people would spend huge sums or laboriously retype the books themselves on old typewriters. Soviet censorship — the most refined in the world — placed the stamp of interdiction not only on meaning but on style as well, and state presses, instead of cashing in on the huge demand for books and journals, artificially limited the print runs. People stole journals from their neighbors' mailboxes. Thieves broke into apartments in order to carry away books. It was a surprising, paradoxical time — and who could have foreseen that it would be this way? Who would have thought, after the lobotomy Russian culture underwent in the 1930s to 1950s, that living, functioning cells still existed? The external pressure grew stronger, and, as before, words could land you in jail, hard labor, or the madhouse: they could even cause your death. But the writers and readers became more and more cultivated and enlightened; they protected their treasure — the word — from the outside world with ever greater agility and in-

could take a piece of paper, write a lewd ditty in large letters, curse or insult the regime, and go out on the square to all-around approval, holding the poster high above his head.

The regime itself was desacralized. The veil of secrecy was torn from the Kremlin's inhabitants; their saints, their idols, and their beliefs were ridiculed and scorned. And, as is always the case, it turned out that the emperor had no clothes, the temple was empty, and it wasn't even a temple but a third-rate brothel.

The poet no longer had to be a citizen. Citizens took this responsibility upon themselves. The poet could quietly return to poetry. And lo and behold, it turned out that there was no place for writers to return to: all their fuel reserves had already been placed on the Altar of the Fatherland, and there was nothing with which to light one's own fireplace. Those who still had a bit of kindling found themselves on an uninhabited island alone, bewildered, and flustered.

When literature develops naturally, even sudden changes in the age—such as those that took place when modernism arose within the depths of a tired and oversatiated "realistic" literature—are not damaging. Memory and continuity are retained, and even if the new art completely breaks with the old, it still sees and remembers what it broke with, what exactly it was negating. But when everything that had once been is destroyed and trampled, amnesia sets in. Literature directs its senile gaze toward the mirror in the morning and doesn't recognize itself; it tries to understand who it is, where it came from, and whether yesterday existed or was only a dream. It starts everything anew, gets muddled and repeats itself in viscous, uncompliant words: it invents what was already invented long ago, stares at linguistic designs in amazement, not understanding their origin or meaning. Such a literature moves in circles, tries to remember last night's dreams, doesn't understand its neighbor's language, grows irate, and, in its torment, accuses its ancestors. This scenario is now being played out on the ruins of Russian art.

One idea that is currently quite popular is that literature is to

ventiveness. They placed ever greater hopes on this bright, fragile, frightened, self-willed butterfly. Both writers and readers dreamed of external freedom, for, it seemed to them, they had had their fill of Pushkin's and Blok's secret freedom. They could not guess that external freedom might prove disastrous and their inner freedom imaginary.

The wide world which had once been open to the Russian had long since contracted to the dimensions of his apartment. Distant and not very distant lands—Paris and China, London and Ceylon, the seas, islands, nighttime streets of far-off capitals, bright with lights and cars—seemed to be pretty, fabricated fairy tales, in whose existence it was difficult to believe. The Russian tendency to indulge in dreams and fantasy mingled the foreign and unreal in a whimsical cocktail in which it was difficult to distinguish what had already been, what was invented, and what had happened (but not to us). At this time, the literature of the fantastic thrived, as did "village" literature, which was more and more inclined to idealize the lost world of the Russian village, attributing to "the soul of the people" rare virtues that had never existed in reality.

The painful rupture in culture—the artificial, forced darkness that divided the literature of the nineteenth-century Golden Age and the early twentieth-century Silver Age from our barbaric iron period—was traumatic for literature and all the other arts. The *Titanic* seemed to have sunk along with its baggage, and if from time to time corpses floated up to the surface, their facial features were distorted and unrecognizable.

> When an epoch is buried
> No psalms sound at graveside.
> It will have to be garnished
> With nettle and thistle.
> And only the gravediggers labor
> Nimbly. For this cannot wait!
> It's so very, very still, Lord,

You can hear time passing.
And later the epoch will surface
Like a corpse in a spring-swollen river.
But by then the son won't know his own mother,
And the grandson will turn back in sorrow.

This is what Anna Akhmatova wrote about occupied Paris in 1940, but it was not truly Paris that she had in mind.

The books of the Silver Age of Russian literature—the books of Russian émigré writers and the Soviet literature that never reached its readers—all of this would have been lost if not for the love and enthusiasm of Western publishers, who stubbornly and meticulously gathered and published Russian writers, without hope of any great commercial success. They were subjected in the press to the insults and condemnations of the Soviet government and official Soviet literature specialists. These books made their way into the Soviet Union in the suitcases of diplomats, courageous foreigners, and KGB agents who made money on reprints and the resale of books. It was dangerous to read these books in a public place—in the park or on the bus or subway—because the extremely white paper and dark, well-printed letters that distinguished Western books from the yellow-gray Soviet books could be seen from afar, tempting the alert passerby to raise a fuss and denounce the reader. Many incautious people paid with their freedom—or at least with their jobs.

The Russian books of Nabokov, published by the small press Ardis, infiltrated Russian literature in this way. Nabokov was the most mysterious and beloved writer of our day, and the publishers of Ardis—Carl and Ellendea Proffer—acquired the status of quasi-mythical omnipotent beings. Whether we were able to enjoy this divine prose or were condemned to shiver in the dark of ignorance was up to them. Besides Nabokov, the Proffers published many other authors, as did numerous other Western publishers—but Nabokov had the most magical effect of all on

Russian readers of the 1970s. And no word sounded so [...] ing to the Russian ear as the mysterious source of book [...]

Then came the time we all know about, when Go [...] and his like-minded colleagues were obliged by intens [...] pressure to allow "glasnost." And the word flooded the [...]

The circulation of literary journals jumped to a [...] Then to two million. Then four million. Instead of c [...] doses and cautious judgments, all manner of opinion [...] denly available, from the intelligent to the bizarre; all [...] viewpoints appeared in print, from the most democrat [...] most fascistic and misanthropic; all kinds of prose, fro [...] traditional realism to the extreme avant-garde; all kind [...] etry, and religious tracts, astrological charts and calculat [...] prophecies of Nostradamus, the mystical texts of Da [...] dreyev, pornography, the platforms of dozens of politica [...] cooking recipes, rules of good taste from the 1880s, [...] memoirs, autobiographies—all of it overwhelmed th [...] who was accustomed to hiding, looking cautiously arou [...] ing the curtains closed, whispering or pretending to [...] mad, or devoted to the cause of communism (which am [...] the same thing). The word, which had seemed unique [...] was published in editions of millions and lost its magic [...] ties. The reader, elated at first, was eventually overwhel [...] then disappointed. A collector of rare coins might feel [...] thing if he suddenly realized that the pride of his colle [...] no more than the most ordinary coin to be found in an[...] ment store. Everything was lost, everything was desacr [...] one fell swoop. Writers—formerly a caste of priests, [...] seurs of clandestine rituals—were no longer any differ [...] anyone else. If previously a poet could take pride in the [...] of an Aesopian language employed in order to hint at [...] views or to express secret civic protest against the au [...] and if the reader could take pleasure in his own acuity i[...] ing these poetic cryptograms, now people started to [...] What was the point of all this? Now anyone who w[...]

blame for all the woes of Russian society. The accusations vary but for the most part can be divided into two groups. The first holds that Russian letters was involved in shady deals: it taught people how to light fires, throw bombs, called Russia to take up the ax, confused the peasants, and accused the ruling class of parasitism, of sucking the people's blood and gnawing on the people's bones. It gave the revolutionaries a shove—and they lunged. And then you get the Gulag. And then you get 60 million people tortured.

The second version, by contrast, accuses Russian letters of inaction. Instead of looking for the bright side of reality, pointing out the positive and shoring up the healthy elements of society, it listened to the trill of the nightingales, wept in a drunken ecstasy over gypsy songs, drank itself away in bars, allowed itself to be carried off to sunset distances, promised that everything would perish, grow deaf, grow thick with duckweed, and plunged into a deep melancholy, pessimism, and fatalism. And there is some truth to this. Who, after all, are the heroes of Russian literature? Idiots, epileptics, consumptives, thieves, murderers, drunkards, fallen women, idlers, dreamers, fools, nihilists, three sisters whining away for two hours straight on a stage. They loll about on the sofa in stained robes, cut up frogs, lose millions at cards, corrupt minors. They go off with axes to kill old ladies. They slit people's throats once, and then they do it again. Their heads are shaved and they're sent to distant farms. Their heads are shaved and they're sent to the army. They set dogs on children. They hang themselves. They drown themselves. They shoot themselves. Yes, an impressive panopticon! And then you get the Gulag. And then you get 60 million casualties.

The accusations take opposing tacks but come to the same conclusion. But the most remarkable thing about these bitter nihilistic accusations—sounding from the right and the left, from nationalistically inclined government officials as well as from democrats appealing for the equality of all thinking minorities and the recognition of the sovereignty of virtually every village, if each so desires — is that it represents the very same antiquated but nonetheless indestructible belief in the power of the word, in the primacy of the word over life, of the dream over reality, and of imagination over facts. Here is the old belief in the idea that if you can just compose it correctly, then life will be correct, it will be healthy, wealthy, and wise.

Of course, this is naive — to imagine that Russia's pragmatic merchants cut down their poetic cherry orchards because that's what Chekhov wrote: when the orchard meets the merchant it is the orchard, alas, that perishes. Yet now in Russia some of the most intelligent, educated, and talented people — whose cultural ambivalence readers of Dostoyevsky and Tolstoy will recognize — claim that literature should not exist at all, since it goes against God; that the writer is sinful by nature for he competes with the Absolute; that we dare not know, risk, and desire, but should only make our peace, pray, and read Holy Scriptures. These people are frightening because they know precisely what God needs: he needs control over the Word.

The "People," in whose name these new critics of Russian literature speak, do not, of course, listen to these accusations and are not overly interested in philosophical debates. The "tsar" has lost control over current events and has no time for literature. "Isn't it all the same to you — whether to depend on the tsar or on the People?" The words of the poet come to mind ever more often. And it seems that he's laughing, that he knew all this in advance.

What should we write about? What should we speak about? To whom should we appeal? To whom call out? Whom should we amuse and frighten, and to whom should we complain? And how to find one's own voice? And what should we do? Destroy? But everything has already been destroyed. Build? What kind of dwelling and for whom, if the wind is so strong that it will demolish any structure? And when the wind dies down, who is to

ventiveness. They placed ever greater hopes on this bright, fragile, frightened, self-willed butterfly. Both writers and readers dreamed of external freedom, for, it seemed to them, they had had their fill of Pushkin's and Blok's secret freedom. They could not guess that external freedom might prove disastrous and their inner freedom imaginary.

The wide world which had once been open to the Russian had long since contracted to the dimensions of his apartment. Distant and not very distant lands — Paris and China, London and Ceylon, the seas, islands, nighttime streets of far-off capitals, bright with lights and cars — seemed to be pretty, fabricated fairy tales, in whose existence it was difficult to believe. The Russian tendency to indulge in dreams and fantasy mingled the foreign and unreal in a whimsical cocktail in which it was difficult to distinguish what had already been, what was invented, and what had happened (but not to us). At this time, the literature of the fantastic thrived, as did "village" literature, which was more and more inclined to idealize the lost world of the Russian village, attributing to "the soul of the people" rare virtues that had never existed in reality.

The painful rupture in culture — the artificial, forced darkness that divided the literature of the nineteenth-century Golden Age and the early twentieth-century Silver Age from our barbaric iron period — was traumatic for literature and all the other arts. The *Titanic* seemed to have sunk along with its baggage, and if from time to time corpses floated up to the surface, their facial features were distorted and unrecognizable.

> When an epoch is buried
> No psalms sound at graveside.
> It will have to be garnished
> With nettle and thistle.
> And only the gravediggers labor
> Nimbly. For this cannot wait!
> It's so very, very still, Lord,

You can hear time passing.
And later the epoch will surface
Like a corpse in a spring-swollen river.
But by then the son won't know his own mother,
And the grandson will turn back in sorrow.

This is what Anna Akhmatova wrote about occupied Paris in 1940, but it was not truly Paris that she had in mind.

The books of the Silver Age of Russian literature—the books of Russian émigré writers and the Soviet literature that never reached its readers—all of this would have been lost if not for the love and enthusiasm of Western publishers, who stubbornly and meticulously gathered and published Russian writers, without hope of any great commercial success. They were subjected in the press to the insults and condemnations of the Soviet government and official Soviet literature specialists. These books made their way into the Soviet Union in the suitcases of diplomats, courageous foreigners, and KGB agents who made money on reprints and the resale of books. It was dangerous to read these books in a public place—in the park or on the bus or subway—because the extremely white paper and dark, well-printed letters that distinguished Western books from the yellow-gray Soviet books could be seen from afar, tempting the alert passerby to raise a fuss and denounce the reader. Many incautious people paid with their freedom—or at least with their jobs.

The Russian books of Nabokov, published by the small press Ardis, infiltrated Russian literature in this way. Nabokov was the most mysterious and beloved writer of our day, and the publishers of Ardis—Carl and Ellendea Proffer—acquired the status of quasi-mythical omnipotent beings. Whether we were able to enjoy this divine prose or were condemned to shiver in the dark of ignorance was up to them. Besides Nabokov, the Proffers published many other authors, as did numerous other Western publishers—but Nabokov had the most magical effect of all on

Russian readers of the 1970s. And no word sounded so enchant-
ing to the Russian ear as the mysterious source of books, Ardis.

Then came the time we all know about, when Gorbachev
and his like-minded colleagues were obliged by intense public
pressure to allow "glasnost." And the word flooded the land.

The circulation of literary journals jumped to a million.
Then to two million. Then four million. Instead of controlled
doses and cautious judgments, all manner of opinion was suddenly available, from the intelligent to the bizarre; all possible
viewpoints appeared in print, from the most democratic to the
most fascistic and misanthropic; all kinds of prose, from heavy,
traditional realism to the extreme avant-garde; all kinds of poetry, and religious tracts, astrological charts and calculations, the
prophecies of Nostradamus, the mystical texts of Daniil Andreyev, pornography, the platforms of dozens of political parties,
cooking recipes, rules of good taste from the 1880s, exposés,
memoirs, autobiographies—all of it overwhelmed the reader,
who was accustomed to hiding, looking cautiously around, pull-
ing the curtains closed, whispering or pretending to be blind,
mad, or devoted to the cause of communism (which amounts to
the same thing). The word, which had seemed unique and rare,
was published in editions of millions and lost its magical qualities. The reader, elated at first, was eventually overwhelmed and
then disappointed. A collector of rare coins might feel the same
thing if he suddenly realized that the pride of his collection was
no more than the most ordinary coin to be found in any depart-
ment store. Everything was lost, everything was desacralized in
one fell swoop. Writers—formerly a caste of priests, connois-
seurs of clandestine rituals—were no longer any different from
anyone else. If previously a poet could take pride in the deft use
of an Aesopian language employed in order to hint at political
views or to express secret civic protest against the authorities,
and if the reader could take pleasure in his own acuity in decod-
ing these poetic cryptograms, now people started to wonder:
What was the point of all this? Now anyone who wanted to

could take a piece of paper, write a lewd ditty in large letters, curse or insult the regime, and go out on the square to all-around approval, holding the poster high above his head.

The regime itself was desacralized. The veil of secrecy was torn from the Kremlin's inhabitants; their saints, their idols, and their beliefs were ridiculed and scorned. And, as is always the case, it turned out that the emperor had no clothes, the temple was empty, and it wasn't even a temple but a third-rate brothel.

The poet no longer had to be a citizen. Citizens took this responsibility upon themselves. The poet could quietly return to poetry. And lo and behold, it turned out that there was no place for writers to return to: all their fuel reserves had already been placed on the Altar of the Fatherland, and there was nothing with which to light one's own fireplace. Those who still had a bit of kindling found themselves on an uninhabited island alone, bewildered, and flustered.

When literature develops naturally, even sudden changes in the age—such as those that took place when modernism arose within the depths of a tired and oversatiated "realistic" literature—are not damaging. Memory and continuity are retained, and even if the new art completely breaks with the old, it still sees and remembers what it broke with, what exactly it was negating. But when everything that had once been is destroyed and trampled, amnesia sets in. Literature directs its senile gaze toward the mirror in the morning and doesn't recognize itself; it tries to understand who it is, where it came from, and whether yesterday existed or was only a dream. It starts everything anew, gets muddled and repeats itself in viscous, uncompliant words: it invents what was already invented long ago, stares at linguistic designs in amazement, not understanding their origin or meaning. Such a literature moves in circles, tries to remember last night's dreams, doesn't understand its neighbor's language, grows irate, and, in its torment, accuses its ancestors. This scenario is now being played out on the ruins of Russian art.

One idea that is currently quite popular is that literature is to blame for all the woes of Russian society. The accusations vary but for the most part can be divided into two groups. The first holds that Russian letters was involved in shady deals: it taught people how to light fires, throw bombs, called Russia to take up the ax, confused the peasants, and accused the ruling class of parasitism, of sucking the people's blood and gnawing on the people's bones. It gave the revolutionaries a shove—and they lunged. And then you get the Gulag. And then you get 60 million people tortured.

The second version, by contrast, accuses Russian letters of inaction. Instead of looking for the bright side of reality, pointing out the positive and shoring up the healthy elements of society, it listened to the trill of the nightingales, wept in a drunken ecstasy over gypsy songs, drank itself away in bars, allowed itself to be carried off to sunset distances, promised that everything would perish, grow deaf, grow thick with duckweed, and plunged into a deep melancholy, pessimism, and fatalism. And there is some truth to this. Who, after all, are the heroes of Russian literature? Idiots, epileptics, consumptives, thieves, murderers, drunkards, fallen women, idlers, dreamers, fools, nihilists, three sisters whining away for two hours straight on a stage. They loll about on the sofa in stained robes, cut up frogs, lose millions at cards, corrupt minors. They go off with axes to kill old ladies. They slit people's throats once, and then they do it again. Their heads are shaved and they're sent to distant farms. Their heads are shaved and they're sent to the army. They set dogs on children. They hang themselves. They drown themselves. They shoot themselves. Yes, an impressive panopticon! And then you get the Gulag. And then you get 60 million casualties.

The accusations take opposing tacks but come to the same conclusion. But the most remarkable thing about these bitter nihilistic accusations—sounding from the right and the left, from nationalistically inclined government officials as well as from democrats appealing for the equality of all thinking minorities and the recognition of the sovereignty of virtually every village, if each so desires — is that it represents the very same antiquated but nonetheless indestructible belief in the power of the word, in the primacy of the word over life, of the dream over reality, and of imagination over facts. Here is the old belief in the idea that if you can just compose it correctly, then life will be correct, it will be healthy, wealthy, and wise.

Of course, this is naive — to imagine that Russia's pragmatic merchants cut down their poetic cherry orchards because that's what Chekhov wrote: when the orchard meets the merchant it is the orchard, alas, that perishes. Yet now in Russia some of the most intelligent, educated, and talented people — whose cultural ambivalence readers of Dostoyevsky and Tolstoy will recognize — claim that literature should not exist at all, since it goes against God; that the writer is sinful by nature for he competes with the Absolute; that we dare not know, risk, and desire, but should only make our peace, pray, and read Holy Scriptures. These people are frightening because they know precisely what God needs: he needs control over the Word.

The "People," in whose name these new critics of Russian literature speak, do not, of course, listen to these accusations and are not overly interested in philosophical debates. The "tsar" has lost control over current events and has no time for literature. "Isn't it all the same to you — whether to depend on the tsar or on the People?" The words of the poet come to mind ever more often. And it seems that he's laughing, that he knew all this in advance.

What should we write about? What should we speak about? To whom should we appeal? To whom call out? Whom should we amuse and frighten, and to whom should we complain? And how to find one's own voice? And what should we do? Destroy? But everything has already been destroyed. Build? What kind of dwelling and for whom, if the wind is so strong that it will demolish any structure? And when the wind dies down, who is to say what it will leave in its place: snowdrifts, desert sands, forest, swamp, or open seas? The Russian writer at the end of 1991 feels like a senile old man on an uninhabited island in the company of indifferent goats and mindlessly cawing parrots. He doesn't know what to do. Make paper boats and fashion hooks from ballpoint pens? Look for a ship to show up over the horizon with people from the other world? Wait until he's carried away by a wave? Or simply sit still until, perhaps because of an earthquake, bare new islands arise, worthy of his imagination.

1992

The Death of the Tsar

Review of *The Last Tsar: The Life and Death of Nicholas II*, by Edvard Radzinsky, translated by Marian Schwartz (Doubleday, 1992), and *Nicholas and Alexandra: The Family Albums*, by Prince Michael of Greece, translated from the French by Catherine O'Keeffe (Tauris Parke Books, 1992)

A T A DINNER after an art exhibition opening in the mid-1970s, I was seated next to an elderly woman, and was told in a whisper that she was ninety but had all her wits about her. We started talking, and the conversation turned to Nicholas II. The old woman, as it turned out, had once been something like a lady-in-waiting at the court. She sighed: "Everyone always says he was such a tyrant. But why, really? They always served such fresh cream at table."

This sort of slightly mad logic is increasingly popular in the Russia of 1992. Every day the myth gains ground: before the revolution, life was marvelous (for everyone); after 1917, no one ever saw fresh cream except for members of the Politburo—who were all as old as Methuselah by the time they had crawled to the collective throne, and were no longer able to digest anything but mineral water. One woman I know swore to me that at the beginning of the century her grandfather, a simple worker, a typesetter, drank up most of his weekly pay in the inns, and with the leftover change was still able to buy gold rings with emeralds to appease his wife. The peasants were swimming in grain. The proletariat breakfasted on caviar. Gendarmes were polite, traders were honest, priests were pious. Why was all this so? Because we had the tsar. Cream, emeralds, church chimes, Fabergé Easter eggs, honest and enlightened merchants, upright women, clear streams filled with sturgeon . . .

Cloudy images of a Russian paradise, a Golden Age, torment our present daydreamers, provoking acute attacks of nostalgia for what probably never existed: revolutions don't happen in paradise. But reality is offensive: the green glades of silky grasses that beckon seductively from afar turn out to be littered with tin cans and cigarette butts on closer inspection. Better to reject reality and love your dream, to concoct a fairy tale about a kind, concerned tsar, his well-fed, grateful people, and their mutual affection. It seems that Nicholas II belonged to this type of dreamer; he convinced himself that the simple people were good and adored the tsar, and that the crowd was being stirred up by troublemakers who should be caught and punished. Driven by this delusion, he managed to destroy himself, his family, the country, the empire, the people, and the cream of the nation for several generations into the bargain.

When I was a child there was a popular joke about Nicholas II being posthumously awarded the Order of the October Revolution, "for creating a revolutionary situation in the country." Was he professionally incompetent? Or was the autocracy doomed? Or was the doom of the autocracy destined to be embodied in the incompetence of this man, who neither wanted nor knew how to rule, but only loved to stroll, chop wood, and take photographs? These three views, the human, historical, and mystical, respectively, each have their supporters, and their arguments have never been and never will be resolved. Nonetheless, everything about Nicholas II's life continues to excite the imagination of writers and readers around the world: the strange, Oblomov-like passivity of this quiet, blue-eyed family man, his submissiveness to fate combined with a suicidal obstinacy and egotism, the fateful family and historical circumstances (an imperious, hysterical spouse, a sickly heir; war with Japan, war with Germany), and, of course, the terrible end in the cellar of a house in the Urals. The more fairy-tale motifs and mythological clichés that can be detected in the story of the last Russian tsar, the more enthusiastically writers set pen to paper and the more avidly readers grab their books from the shelves.

Edvard Radzinsky's *The Last Tsar,* a book about the life and death of Nicholas II, has become a bestseller in the United States. In the 1970s, Radzinsky studied at the Historical Archives Institute in Moscow, and he went on to become a successful playwright. The playwright in Radzinsky clearly defeated and trampled the professional historian. In this sense the entire book is a battlefield for the author's two careers: if the playwright erects a triumphal arch, the historian raises only a few paltry molehills. Not only does the book have no footnotes, but the bibliography seems merely an ornamental twist, a modernist caryatid that doesn't trouble itself with holding up weight but is simply there to gladden the passerby.

Doubleday, the publisher, followed the author's lead: the book opens with a map that is no more useful than a decorative arabesque. St. Petersburg (renamed Petrograd in 1914 and Leningrad in 1924) peacefully coexists with Kuibyshev (which was Samara until 1935), and in place of the Arctic Ocean we find the Atlantic. On this map the Amur River flows in a circle, and another river, unknown to geographers, boldly joins the Black Sea with the Caspian; Russia and Siberia are divided by a border, Sweden and Finland are not, and so on. (Russia is, of course, a fantastical country, but not to that extent.)

From the first pages of this book Radzinsky declares his distrust of all witnesses: "Participants are, after all, biased," he writes, and even supports this view with a proverbial saying, "He lies like an eyewitness." He therefore dismisses all—all!—

the statements of eyewitnesses on the circumstances surrounding the tsar's death. He discards the work done by others and wants to do everything himself, to find voluntary rather than forced testimony by the participants in the execution. This isn't easy: wherever you go, everyone lies. I sympathize with the author's difficulties. But lying, perhaps humankind's primary weakness, is precisely what historians must overcome through their meticulous work, which is not unlike that of the criminal investigator.

Of course, it's probably harder to discover the truth in Russia than anywhere else. In what other country will the conservators of archives look you straight in the eye, assure you that the documents you need do not exist at all, and then—how capricious is human nature!—secretly break all the rules and risk their jobs to bring you the "nonexistent" documents around by the back stairs, as happened to Radzinsky himself. Having satisfied your curiosity, they automatically induct you into the circle of the initiated, the liars. From now on you will be bound by the round robin of a double standard. You, too, will lie to newcomers, uninitiated seekers of the truth; if you let something slip, you betray the people who entrusted the secret to you. The lie becomes the guarantee of your good behavior. Such is Russia: it's hardly surprising that our playwrights are much better than our historians.

Bound by vows of silence, moving through a world of whispers and stolen documents, Radzinsky was unable to carry on his research openly for many years, and when he could (parts of his book were published in the Moscow weekly *Ogonyok* in 1989), it turned out that almost everything had already been done by others. As a result of his research on the circumstances surrounding the tsar's death, Radzinsky turned up what was already known—that is, that we don't know anything for certain. It seems that a group of eleven or twelve men, led by the Bolshevik Yakov Yurovsky, shot eleven people in a cellar: the tsar's family, three servants, and a doctor. Some of the victims simply refused to die immediately—the bullets bounced off their bodies and flew around the room—so they were finished off with bayonets. Then the corpses were taken into the forest, undressed, and robbed. It turned out that the women's corsets were stuffed with diamonds, which is why the bullets rebounded. The bodies were buried, then reburied in another place the next day, and for some reason two of them were burned. When the White Army seized Yekaterinburg a week later, an investigation was conducted, but the grave was not found. A grave thought to be that of the royal family was discovered in recent years and was opened twice: in 1979 and again in 1991 (remains from this grave are now being examined by scientists in England). At least two bodies were missing. What does this mean? Were they the ones burned? Or did some survive?

From a dramatic point of view, Radzinsky's book is marvelously constructed. We all know the end of the story, but those who would like to relive it from the beginning can now have it served up under a delectable sauce of bad omens and sinister portents. The action unfolds to the rustle of the tsar's diaries, known for their vacuity and a triviality that seems almost indecent in an autocrat. Nicholas strolled, drank tea . . . strolled, drank tea . . . Faced with the danger of sudden death, his perplexed cry echoes loudly in this context. "What, what?" was all he had to say when, during his trip to Japan, in 1891, a mad policeman suddenly attacked him and struck him on the head with a saber. "What, what?" he asked in bewilderment on hearing the death sentence, just moments before the bullet pierced him in the cellar of the Ipatiev house in 1918. ("That's what!" his murderer, Yurovsky, cried out in irritation and then fired. Indeed, how else could one respond? From 1896, when he ascended the throne, or perhaps even earlier, in 1881, when his grandfather, Alexander III, was killed by terrorists, Nicholas repeatedly received unambiguous signals: look reality in the face, something must be changed, otherwise things will end badly. But he never understood.)

Objects also resound in Radzinsky's book, with an echo that, far from diminishing, inevitably rises to a crescendo. When, still a bachelor, the young Nicholas receives the long-awaited acceptance of his beautiful intended and gives her a diamond brooch as a token of his love, Radzinsky's experienced hand stops the frame on that distant, sparkling April day and, tearing through the curtain of the future, shows us the burned remnants of this very brooch, retrieved from the filthy campfire where the clothes of the dead empress were burned.

The mystical motif of the tsar's unlucky number seventeen is likewise struck in melancholy chords. On January 17, 1895, Nicholas gives his first important speech as a monarch; his voice breaks and he suddenly shouts, frightening an old noble, who drops the traditional gift of bread and salt—a bad omen. On October 17, 1905—seventeen years to the day after the crash of the tsar's train in Borki when the entire family almost died—he is forced to sign a manifesto granting Russia a constitution, a very unpleasant moment for the tsar's pride; Rasputin was murdered on December 17, 1916 (he had promised Nicholas that with his death both the tsar and the country would perish, which did in fact happen). The year 1917 brought the February and October revolutions; and finally, on July 17, 1918, the tsar was executed. The mysticism of numbers and omens is historically meaningless but pleasing to the philistine—for example, the ceremonial cannon shot fired during the 1905 Epiphany celebrations, just days before Bloody Sunday, turned out to contain live ammunition and miraculously wounded not the tsar but a namesake, the gendarme Romanov. All these gothic trappings facilitate the creation of tension in the book. One need not dwell on the well-known story of Rasputin—only a very lazy writer would fail to make use of that. The narrative is adorned with other delightful details as well: the empress, mistress of one sixth of the world's surface, used to sell her old, unfashionable clothes to second-hand clothes buyers but would remove the mother-of-pearl buttons, replacing them with bone or glass.

Toward the finale, the tension rises and it is impossible to put the book down. The author skillfully slows the action, prolonging the denouement and tormenting the reader with a blow-by-blow account of the royal family's last journey: the bloody truck makes its way at night through forest and swamp, laden with corpses . . . or did it carry half-living people? (Yes or no? Yes or no?) Radzinsky deftly breaks the story at the right place in order to project the reader years ahead and show a tantalizingly indistinct picture: an elderly denizen of the Gulag, a patient in a psychiatric hospital, who assures everyone that he is the tsarevich Alexis, that he had managed to escape. He looks like portraits of Nicholas II, is a hemophiliac, and suffers from cryptorchidism, as did the royal heir. He answers all questions about the tsar's family correctly and without hesitation. The doctors are stumped. Cured, he again dissolves into the abyss of the Gulag, carrying his secret with him.

Then there's the servant girl Demidova, the one who reportedly covered her head with a pillow and squealed when she was shot, who was then stuck with a bayonet, whose corpse was burned on the edge of the mine. According to a story Radzinsky tells, Demidova, it seems, lived until World War II (but how, one asks?), never left the apartment where she was hidden by her brother, and was said to scream at night . . .

Could any of them really have escaped execution? I don't know, I don't know, Radzinsky seems to say, while dropping more and more hints that anything might have happened, that the KGB knows far more than it's willing to tell, that the murderers Pyotr Yermakov and Yakov Yurovsky may have been bound by a terrible secret. They came up two corpses short and, afraid of being held responsible, could have staged anything at all: for instance, the burning of two corpses (an action that does in fact seem pointless). Hence the lies and confusion in their stories: they burned all of them—no, just Alexis and the empress—no, Alexis and Demidova—no, no, Alexis and another woman . . . perhaps Anastasia?

The main preserver, bearer, and revealer of secrets in the

book turns out to be a man Radzinsky calls his "mysterious guest," an old Cheka agent whose work gave him access to archives and information unavailable to others, and who at one time personally knew one of the murderers and has long been interested in the royal family's fate. The reader is asked to take Radzinsky's word for it that this old man really exists. In keeping with the rules of the detective story genre, he appears at the book's end; nameless and tittering, he offers his version of events. His version is neatly set forth and quite plausible—but no more so than other versions.

Despite the literariness of this character, we are prepared to believe in both the old man and his theory. According to him, during the bloody truck's last journey, following the execution, one of the guards discovered that two of the victims were still alive, and saved them, hiding the poor unfortunates. As if in indirect evidence of such a possibility, the old man refers to vague information that the wife of the truck's driver, herself a Bolshevik, left her husband and, a few years later, when dying, sent to tell him that she forgave him. From this murky "fact" the conclusion is drawn that the driver could have confessed to his revolutionarily inclined wife that he had saved or helped to save two of the victims—and that this galled her. We are also supposed to be overwhelmed by the fact that the driver's young son was named Alexis, as was the tsarevich.

Anything could have happened, so why not this version? In the West, beginning in the 1920s, various men and women turned up claiming to be the tsar's children. The most famous and unfortunate figure among them was Anna Anderson, whom many recognized as Anastasia (and others categorically denounced as an impostor). The investigation dragged on for years. Two trials in Germany were not able to give an official answer—positive or negative—to the enigma. However, expert handwriting analysis (independently conducted on two occasions) and study of evidence on the shape of her ear (a procedure that some criminologists consider as reliable as fingerprints but that is less well known to the public), among other things, led specialists to conclude that Anna Anderson was indeed Anastasia. For those interested, I can recommend Peter Kurth's *Anastasia: The Riddle of Anna Anderson* (Little, Brown, 1983), a conscientiously documented, clear, and entertaining book.

Radzinsky includes Kurth's book in his bibliography and appears to paraphrase a couple of pages from it. But his account is so cloudy that my suspicions were aroused. This turned out to be useful: I read Kurth's book. My conclusion: the proverb "He lies like an eyewitness" must be applied to Radzinsky himself. Either he never actually read Kurth's book (and thus deceives the reader when he dismisses the serious documents that Kurth cites), or he read it and didn't know what to do about the existence of this evidence. Skepticism regarding Anna Anderson or even the possibility of the princess's escape is more than understandable; but it would seem that the testimony of German experts during the trials is too serious a matter to be simply disregarded, especially since Radzinsky goes on to childishly tickle the reader's imagination with the story of the errant wife of the truck driver (who died without saying anything at all to anyone). The impression arises that Radzinsky, experienced playwright that he is, knows that "unsolved mysteries," mystical numbers, and bad omens — the inventory of a mythmaker — are more exciting than sober analysis and scientific expertise, that "an elevated deceit is dearer to us than a host of lowly truths," as Pushkin said. An ominous, anonymous old man, a secret police agent, pulled out of a hat at the right moment, makes a better story than German specialists with their boring facts.

But any complaints regarding Radzinsky pale against what can be said about the luxurious photograph album with commentary by Prince Michael of Greece, a distant relative of the tsar. The very genre of Radzinsky's work allows for a certain indulgence in fantasy and emotional coloring, but in his own way he is as honest and conscientious as an Impressionist who depicts a cathedral in fog as many tiny colored points. Prince Michael opts for the tactics of a mad Dadaist: he draws a horse and captions it a chicken. The material that he ravages is priceless: photographs from the family albums of the tsar and excerpts from the family's diaries located in former Soviet archives. Most of the photos were taken by the family members themselves: the tsar and his children were all amateur photographers, and we often see the tsarevnas with cameras in hand.

Some of the photographs are magnificent, others so-so, and this makes them even more touching. The family members eat, drink, laugh, read, jump, lie in bed ill, play with the dog, ride horses, embrace dirty village children, flirt, study, make faces, and play tennis. They wade in streams, rolling up their pants and lifting their skirts. They lounge on the beach. Swing on swings. And when you know that this cheerful pretty girl will be run through by a dull bayonet, that this coquettish young woman will be doused with acid and thrown into an icy mine, that this shy child will be heckled in her last days by drunken guards who will make her leave the door to the toilet open and comment on her actions with taunting jeers — you begin to feel the tragedy of this unique family, which allowed itself to be carefree, as if it were like any other family.

What, you ask, is more precise than a photograph? What could be simpler than to quote a document? Why, human fantasy, a passion for mythification, a love of fairy tales and stereotypes! The peculiarities of this book begin before the book does. The caption to the photograph on the frontispiece reads: "During a voyage on the Imperial yacht, Standart, Alexis, wearing a cap belonging to one of the sailors, plays in the water with an old teapot." It is indeed Alexis whom we see in the photograph, but the four-year-old is clearly wearing his own specially made sailor's cap, and he's not holding a teapot but a child's watering can. For all the tsar's personal "modesty" — on which Prince Michael insists to the point of absurdity — I feel sure that the

Russian emperor could have afforded to have a hat made for his sick son and didn't have to borrow a cap from one of his subjects. (A myth comes into play: the unpretentiousness of the royal family.)

On the first page of his preface, Prince Michael assures us that he was one of the first to be shown these photographs by the Russian archivists. But Radzinsky had examined them twenty years earlier and notes that surprisingly, like Nicholas and Alexandra's diaries, they had not been classified. (Another myth: the KGB is supposedly all powerful and omnipresent.) Prince Michael ends his preface with a conceit that is perhaps pretty but inaccurate: he says that the tsar's last diary entry was made just hours before the execution, and it read, "God save Russia." In fact, however, as we know from a reproduction of the last page of this diary in Radzinsky's book, the tsar's diary stops three days before his death, and the last entry says: "Weather is warm and pleasant. We have no news from the outside." (The myth: the sensitive tsar had a subtle intimation of his death but was more concerned for the country than for himself.)

Having warmed up, the prince abandons himself to fantasy: as he has it, the Crimea is part of the Mediterranean, and Alexis was named in honor of the first Romanov tsar, although the first Romanov tsar was Mikhail (Michael) and not Alexis. If the name of the mountain Ai-Petri does indeed mean Saint Peter, it might befit the prince of Greece to know that it is in Greek and not Tatar. If the prince sees flowers on a hat, he writes that it is a feather hat; if the family is sitting on a mattress, the prince sees grass and moss. He calls leafy bushes pine; flowering branches are poplar. He turns measles, a rather dangerous illness, into the mumps, and Peter II, who died as a fifteen-year-old boy, into the husband of Catherine the Great. He dislikes Anna Vyrubova, the empress's close friend, implying that her friendship with the empress had ulterior motives, and picks on her whenever possible. With plebeian snobbism, he contrasts the empress's "elegant outfit" with the "disgraceful furbelows" of her subject, though the greatest contrast is between the figures of the two women: the empress was slim while Vyrubova was overweight. Whenever he sees a photograph of the royal family wading in the water, he inevitably informs us that the water is "bitter cold," "frozen," or "freezing" (and in so doing emphasizes the myth of the Russian emperor's spartan character).

I have to say that this talk about freezing water drove me over the brink. The obstinate stereotype that in Russia it is never anything but cold is one that I come across almost every day. It might be forgivable in inhabitants of equatorial climes, but it isn't in Europeans, and certainly not in the authors of luxury albums who boast of kinship ties with the Russian imperial family. I've studied the origins of this myth as far as possible. It seems to have begun with Ambrogio Contarini, who visited Moscow in 1476–77. Contarini writes that "this country is remarkable for its incredible cold, such that for nine months of the year people stay in their homes." Sigismund Herberstein, who was in Muscovy in 1526, echoes him. "The cold is sometimes so extreme there that the earth cracks, and at such times water poured into the air and spittle from the mouth freeze before reaching the ground."

I, too, love fairy tales, but I would like to remind the taletellers that we are now living in the twentieth century and that the global climate has changed. In Holland, for instance, it's no longer possible to skate on the canals, despite all the pictures we've seen. Moscow is not Siberia and has had a normal, moderate mid-European climate for centuries. The Gulf of Finland, where my home town of St. Petersburg is located, gets quite warm, even hot, in the summer. Since the gulf is something like a shallow, sheltered puddle, in which even two-year-olds bathe, the Russian emperor was not obliged to "train" in order to wade in this lukewarm soup.

Beginning with inaccuracy and myth, the book ends with inaccuracy and myth: the last photograph shows Alexis with a dog that purportedly shared the boy's terrible fate. In fact, though, this is only a dog, and though the Bolsheviks were monsters, they didn't murder this particular dog. The dog in the photograph was rather large, while it is known that the dog that was shot was small enough to be held in a sleeve. The lap dog's corpse was found — along with a woman's finger, pearl earring, and other things — by the White Army investigators in 1919.

Prince Michael of Greece was asked to do a simple job: write a few words to accompany clear, straightforward photographs. The task was facilitated by the fact that in a number of cases the diary entries and letters explained the meaning of the photographs. The tsarevich writes, for example: "Papa was still asleep. I went to his bed with a pillow." In the picture we see the tsarevich with this very pillow on his head. He's showing off for the camera. The prince pointlessly asks, "Why is he wearing this strange fabric as a kind of turban?"

These useless captions might seem hysterically funny. But I'm not laughing. I find it endlessly, nauseatingly sad and offensive that a peasant child named Bolyus who is shown in one photograph is listed in the index as a "pet," that the place names, landscape, climate, history, and geography of my country are carelessly treated, as if it were some distant, unseen Herodotean land inhabited by dogheaded beings. It irks me that the workers of Russian archives and Western publishing companies imagine that a distant royal relative is, by right of birth, a more suitable author than a prosaic but common-sense historian, and thus that his shamelessly crude job doesn't need checking.* The increasingly popular myth of the autocracy's mystique inevitably turns into ordinary social racism. Although this is an-

---

* In contrast, see *Before the Revolution: St. Petersburg in Photographs, 1890–1914* (Abrams, 1992), a fascinating collection of photodocuments on the life of prerevolutionary St. Petersburg, which has an absorbing preface and foreword by, respectively, historians James Billington and Dmitri Likhachov, and is accompanied by interesting, informative, and accurate historical commentary. The royal family is unlucky, however: the only mistake I found in this otherwise marvelous album is a caption misidentifying all the tsar's daughters.

other story altogether, the Russian Orthodox Church, adding the royal family to the roster of saints, preferred, as if mocking Christian teaching, not to pay any attention to the modest, truly loyal, and worthy people who worked for the family: Doctor Botkin, the cook Kharitonov, the servants Trupp and Demidova, who were shot because they didn't flee and didn't betray their masters but remained faithful to them to the end.

At present in Russia it is fashionable to hold that our misfortunes of the last seventy years are retribution for the murder of the tsar, who served such fresh cream. Repentance can, of course, be a useful thing, but only if we don't forget that all these years the tsar's bones have lain in a pit mixed in with those of the people who got the cream, warmed it, served it, and then cleared the monarch's leftovers from the table: the bones of those who, unlike their "modest and charming" lord and "always elegant" lady, decided to carry out their professional duty as they understood it.

Whether or not the tsar is to blame for the people's fate, or the other way around, in death they were finally united in a communal grave, and they deserve at the very least that the truth be told. And if you can't manage that—then, according to Russian custom, you should take off your hat and be silent.

1992

Kitchen Conversations

Review of *Classic Russian Cooking: Elena Molokhovets's "A Gift to Young Housewives,"* translated and introduced by Joyce Toomre (Indiana University Press, 1992)

A LL RUSSIANS are familiar with Lenin's famous saying: "Every cook should know how to run the government." One wonders what Lenin, who never boiled an egg for himself, could possibly have known about cooks? There was, however, one cook in Russia whose ability to govern her own diminutive empire Lenin himself might have envied.

In 1861, a young provincial Russian housewife, Elena Molokhovets, who knew how to prepare tasty meals, published a collection of 1,500 recipes. Hardly an event of any note, you might think. First of all, it was far from being the first and of course was not the last cookbook in Russia. Furthermore, 1861 was the year in which the peasants were freed from more than three hundred years of serfdom, an era of stormy transformations in Russian society, of liberal reforms and hopes. The movement for the emancipation of women from traditional domestic dependence was gaining strength, and thousands of young women yearned to escape their patriarchal homes to freedom; they dreamed of the university bench and not of cooking.

Nonetheless, this very book, appearing at what might have

seemed the most inopportune moment, was fated to acquire instant, unprecedented popularity and to live for decades. Growing in size and complexity, Elena Molokhovets's *Gift to Young Housewives* went through dozens of editions and lived, together with its author, until the revolution of 1917. It sold more than 250,000 copies, and the last edition contains almost 4,500 recipes, not counting information and advice on building a house, equipping a kitchen, daily schedules, the science of running a household and entertaining guests, as well as the planning of Lenten and regular meals (there are more than six hundred types of non-Lenten dinners alone!), ordinary and holiday fare for servants and masters, and an estimate of the costs of each type of meal. After the revolution, when cooking had been transformed from an applied art into a theoretical science and Molokhovets's recipes and advice acquired a metaphysical character, her name became synonymous with the fabulous bacchanalia of gluttony that raged on those yellowing pages.

Nowadays, in those Russian families that have kept copies of this old book, no one cooks by it, or only on special occasions, and even then only the simplest dishes. And not just because particular items no longer exist in Russia or are very expensive, or because one has to contend with antiquated measures of weight and volume or the vagueness of instructions like "a hot stove." The very style of life that Molokhovets took for granted vanished irretrievably into the past long ago, values have changed, the pace of life has accelerated, and despite Russians' love of scrumptious, abundant fare, despite their hospitality and their ability to create culinary wonders from a meager assortment of ingredients, people no longer consider a well-laid table to be the crown of creation, and gorging oneself on delicacies has ceased to be the self-sufficient process that it appears in Molokhovets's book.

Russians now open this book to laugh to their heart's content, in order, trembling with holy horror, to immerse themselves in that lost era of culinary titans, maniacs with cast-iron intestines as long as fire hoses, with stomachs of elephantine proportions, with the jaws of the mythical Charybdis, who devoured entire ships and their oarsmen at one sitting.

Where is the creature who rises at dawn and spends two and a half hours roasting chamois for breakfast, or who tosses back a jigger of vodka in the morning and sits down to consume beer soup with sour cream (Rhine wines are served in the middle of breakfast, punch at the end; or the other way around), and, with barely time to recover, again drinks vodka or wine for midday dinner (with hors d'oeuvres: marinated fish, smoked hare, stuffed goose, or pears in honey, ninety versions to choose from), and applies himself to soup with champagne and savory pies (the champagne is *poured in* the soup!), upon which there follows yet another bountiful meat dish, then a heavy desert drenched in sugar and fat?

After that, it's not long until evening tea with five types of bread, veal, ham, beef, hazel grouse, turkey, tongue, hare, four sorts of cheese. This is not counting rolls, different sorts of cookies, babas, jam, oranges, apples, pears, mandarins, dates, plums, and grapes. As if that were not enough, for "tea" one must offer rum, cognac, red wine, cherry syrup, sherbet (a kind of sugary fruit halvah or sweet drink), cream, sugar, and lemon. Plain butter and lemon butter, parmesan butter, butter from hazel grouse, with fried liver, with almonds, walnuts, pistachios. With green cheese. And shredded corned beef. (Molokhovets notes that this "may replace dinner." What? Meaning, it may *not* replace dinner? Here, by the way, one remembers that the subtitle of the book is *Means of Reducing Expenses in the Domestic Household*.) By Molokhovets's reckoning, this evening tea in the spirit of Gargantua is suitable for a friendly conversation that does not go on much past midnight.

In the morning, presumably one starts all over again: suckling pig, breast of mutton, pies, pâtés, stuffed eel. If you happen to be a "vegetarian," then your voracity only grows in the author's view, for after all, neither fried calf's head and feet, nor wild boar roasted on the spit—alas—can be part of your breakfast. Therefore you must eat more frequently, and a bit at a time, for example: morning tea (including cream, butter, eggs), *then* breakfast (main dish plus tea or coffee with babas, cookies, rolls), then a dinner (Russian dinner is in the middle of the day, about three o'clock) of *four* dishes, of which the last two are in fact, sweet—and two hours after dinner, more food (after all, you're hungry again, aren't you?)—and in the evening, tea resembling the one described above, only vegetarian.

Molokhovets notes specifically that her recipes and advice are calculated for a family with a normal appetite, of average means and modest budget. But she sees the plainest, most ordinary "fourth-rate" dinner as a feast of four dishes. (December, Dinner No. II: Wallachian white soup, cold salmon, capercaillie with salad, boiled custard with caramel syrup.) The fanciest diners consist of eleven courses, or even more, for in these cases two soups are served, and the endless small meat pies and cheeses after dessert are not even counted, just mentioned in small print, like something that goes without saying. On these grand occasions wines, vodka, and liqueurs are changed seven times, and the contemporary Russian reader, leafing through the thousand-page folio in horror, begins to guess why Chekhov's early comic stories sometimes end with the words: "Then he was seized by an apoplectic fit and died."

Chekhov, Gogol, Bunin, Saltykov-Shchedrin, and countless memoirists have devoted no small number of pages to descriptions of oblivious gorging, a process that literally becomes orgiastic, virtually a sexual activity. Russian literature's reserve in regard to eroticism and carnal love is compensated for many times over by the lengthy unbridled epic poems devoted to the joys of the stomach. It suffices to read Chekhov's story "The Siren" or Gogol's "Old World Landowners" to believe in the "economy" of Molokhovets's meals and in the ordinariness of her household.

From a contemporary point of view, Molokhovets's housewife (actually a cook under the housewife's supervision) prepares not only huge quantities of food but extremely filling meals, to put it kindly: for instance, in order to make babas, a type of sweet cake, you need to beat ninety egg yolks for two hours without stopping. Eggs, cream, butter, sour cream—all are generously poured into doughs, sauces, and soups: a chicken soup for six contains a cup of cream, meat broth, a cup of sour cream. Molokhovets skims the foam and fat from soup, but "for those who like things greasier" she proposes boiling the skimmed fat and pouring it back into the soup. A "manorial table" uses up two pounds of salt a week. Reading Molokhovets's general instructions, one feels oneself a pathetic feeble dwarf: thus for a "small dinner or evening gathering" she proposes a guest list of fifteen to eighteen people, for whom one may prepare, not counting everything else, ninety cups of cranberry drink.

For greater economy a huge number of stores are supposed to be prepared at home: holes must be dug in the cellar for preserving turnips, pike must be dried, nettles planted in order to make threads for repairing stockings, and many, many other things, not to mention well-known preserves and marinades. One should make rose groats, beet coffee, April birch-sap vinegar, chestnut starch, pear mustard, pine-shoot beer, cucumber jam, and violet syrup. There is, it seems, no object on land, air, or sea that does not find itself in frying pans, casseroles, jars, barrels, sacks, and clay pots. Everything is used, and aside from complex but familiar dishes, one encounters on the pages of Molokhovets such exotic items as cornflower mousse, water ice from currant buds, cream custard with mignonette flowers, and boiled fermented milk with silver leaven.

It is, of course, unimaginable, impossible, to run such a household alone or with the help of merely one cook; and in Molokhovets there's no question of this. All the work is done by servants, though the author doesn't say how many. At any rate, the recipes for servants' meals are based on calculations for four persons. The servants certainly don't starve, but when one reads the menu intended for them, angry class feelings begin to seethe in the soul. Thus, for example, a breakfast for these round-the-clock laborers frequently consists solely of milk or yogurt; dinner consists of soup and kasha; and dinner leftovers are proposed for supper. It's amusing, following the diagram for butchering a cow, to note which parts — third- and fourth-rate — are meant for the servants' soup. Here's a recipe for a *holiday* dinner soup: boil beef tripe, add potatoes and second-rate flour. That's it. No greens, no spices, no joy. There's no mention of fruit: common people should eat common things. Here's a Lenten breakfast: smoked herring. Or: grated turnip with Lenten butter on black bread and tea.

One wonders whether it was gratifying after such a breakfast to prepare stores of barberry: "Each pretty branch of barberry, held by the stem, should be dipped in syrup and immediately rolled in very finely crushed and sifted sugar of the best sort," etc. It makes you want to gather in a group and sing revolutionary songs, or join a band of terrorists, or steal. But Molokhovets won't allow stealing: her housewife sits in the china pantry or in a "warm maid's workroom" at a table, and though "because of frail health" she avoids the larder in cold weather, she nonetheless watches keenly to make sure that nothing is carried past her other than what and how much she has earmarked for the table — whether truffles, cream, and pineapple for the masters, or ox lips, legs, and heart for the servants. She is a delicate lady, and "seeing as the butchering of a boar is a rather unpleasant thing and not every mistress will want to be present during it," she is given only a general idea of the process. Even so, it contains details that might horrify our tender housewife: how to cut off the head, boil the lower jaw, sever the legs at the knee . . . She even does a little work herself: "The mistress may occasionally give herself the pleasure of skimming cream or sour cream, or direct the servants to beat the butter in her presence," etc.

All in all, of course, she does concern herself with her retainers: in "Five Plans for Convenient Apartments" (included in one of the Russian editions), she advises building a niche in the wall of a narrow, dead-end, windowless corridor opposite a coatrack for fur coats: there, on a collapsible board instead of a bed, the lackey may sleep. And "when building a house, it is absolutely necessary to hang the gates no less than two *arshins* from the outer wall so that the gatekeeper may sit in this indentation at night and take cover from rain and wind."

One can only guess what thoughts visited the sleeping lackey and sleepless gatekeeper at night. No doubt they were not happy thoughts, but a means had been devised against them as well. First of all: "I find that servants will partially correct themselves, in the moral sense, and that there will be greater cleanliness and order in the kitchen if it is on the same floor with other living quarters." Not only should one keep a constant eye on the servants, but one should have a special common room for prayer, where "the head of the family, daily, by diligent and unanimous prayer, might by his own good example try to instill both in the family and the servants an unlimited love of God, and faith in His impartial justice and His charity towards mankind."

It didn't help. "There is a tsar in the world, and he is merciless; Hunger is his name," wrote the poet Nikolai Nekrasov at the time Molokhovets's books were appearing, edition after edition. Hunger, injustice, envy, and humiliation did their work. Incited by the Bolsheviks, the lackey left his niche, the gatekeeper came out from under the fence; with hands skilled in butchering boar, they dispatched the masters and their households, they burned houses with "five plans for convenient apartments," destroyed hothouses, cut down fruit orchards, and took particular pleasure in plundering wine cellars. Rivers of Muscat de Lunel, Château d'Yquem, and sweet vodka-ratafias flowed into mouths and onto the ground.

The old life and the old cuisine came to an end. The lifestyle to which Molokhovets was accustomed was never resurrected. Today not even many of the very rich eat as she ate.

Joyce Toomre, who translated and published this insane historical monument, has accomplished an enormous task fully on a par with the original author's slave labor. Her extensive preface and her detailed and entertaining notes are marvelous. Her grasp of history, both culinary and otherwise, is excellent, and she knows how to find the example that will vividly convey the cultural context, not just the recipe for a dish. (Thus, for example, you can't help but appreciate the luxurious dinner for twenty-five people that Molokhovets proposes, if you know that a year's worth of study in a women's course four times a week cost less than one such dinner.)

However, Joyce Toomre, by her own acknowledgment, has singled out only one aspect of the book in following her main goal: to give convenient, practical directions to those who would like to prepare Russian dishes themselves. In other words, she decided to return Molokhovets's book to its original use. And to do this, unfortunately she had to sacrifice a great deal: she chose only a quarter of the recipes for translation, discarding entire sections, entire groups of dishes, consciously sacrificing historicity to pragmatic goals. Her decision to destroy *A Gift to Young Housewives* as a historical monument and recreate it in another more convenient format is probably justified by many considerations: a practical book would be more likely to attract both publishers and readers. And in shortening Molokhovets's tiresome wordiness (for some probably unfair reason, I have always imagined Molokhovets as a fat, rather thick-witted, humorless, spiritless glutton), Joyce Toomre didn't allow the useful tips and techniques to entirely disappear but included some of them in the entertaining analysis that precedes the translation. The book is interesting and informative to read in translation; cooking with it is possible if not exactly convenient, and even simply turning the pages and looking at the illustrations is a pleasure. All the same, the living original has collapsed, perished irretrievably. Toomre herself knows the scale of the destruction she's brought about; furthermore, she specifically draws our attention to it. I don't want to be misunderstood—her conscientious, highly qualified work deserves endless respect. She killed with love.

But what can I do, how can I not heave a deep melancholy

sigh, gazing upon the ruins? How to console oneself when, in the place of a sumptuous and absurd, scintillating and senseless edifice, there arises a neat, serviceable little standard house? Where are our *shchi,* cabbage soup, the basis of all Russian cooking? Of seven recipes for *shchi,* there's only one here, and all the others are given in a list, like a memorial plaque ("Here so and so lived and died"). Why has meat *okroshka* been rejected, that classic cold soup made with kvass, served both in the Kremlin and in forgotten weed-infested villages? And cranberry *kissel,* which survived the tsars and Lenin and Gorbachev? Why, of forty-seven types of pirozhki, have only eleven been left; of twelve mousses, two; of fourteen *kissels,* five; of fifteen compotes, three? I want to see all fifty recipes for babas, eighty tarts, 112 puddings! I want to know all 342 ways of preparing fish dishes (there are more, but I've lost count). Why is so little space allotted to buckwheat kasha, which Russians stuff in everything; in blini, in pies, in suckling pig, in soup mixed with sautéed mushrooms? Why have dishes like French julienne soup, Italian soup with macaroni, fried potatoes à la Lyonnaise, rice à la Milanaise, the German dish *Baumkuchen,* and the Finnish drink Limpopo been chosen for translation when they are unusual in Russian cuisine, instead of Guriev pancakes, the Smolensk dish *rezniki,* and other dishes with undistinguished names that are just as typical?

A glutton is quite capable of including all sorts of exotic recipes in her lists. But fish, mushrooms, aspics, pirozhkis, blini, kashas, cabbage soups, and bread-crust kvass are the foundation of the Russian table, i.e., garden and field grasses, river life, things that you can gather or catch. I think that in translation, and given the necessity of shortening a cookbook, the proportionate "imbalances" of the original cuisine should be retained. The principle of *equal* selection of recipes chosen by Joyce Toomre in fact shifts the entire scale and distorts the face of the culture to unrecognizability. This is all too evident thanks to the original list of recipes, which the translator honestly reproduces in one of the addenda—one can see that Russian cuisine is heavily skewed toward certain ingredients and types of dishes like fish, kashas, and aspics. I can't help but feel that it would have done greater justice to the fallen colossus of prerevolutionary Russia to have translated abundance with abundance, gluttony with gluttony, injustice with injustice, and esoterica with esoterica.

This is important not only in and of itself, that is, as an aid to the lover of authentic foreign cuisine, but also in order to avoid distorting the historical and cultural picture, making the exotica of one culture into exotica of quite another type. Otherwise why bother trying, learning the language and immersing oneself in the culture, at all? Breaking bread at the table by its very nature brings people closer together, and as is well known, the way to the heart is through the stomach; but if you stray from the path, you could end up in an entirely unfamiliar place.

The reader who has a special interest in historical cuisine and who wishes to reproduce Russian dishes, especially the American reader, would do well to pay attention not only to the recipes and technology of preparing dishes but also to the most important thing: the manner of their consumption. The taste and distinctive qualities of a national cuisine are dramatically enhanced by the beverages that are meant to accompany it. (Of course, if you wash everything down with Coca-Cola then it really doesn't matter what you eat.) Everyone knows that the primary Russian alcoholic beverage is vodka. But I have yet to meet an American who drinks it properly.

The American manner of drinking vodka—on an empty stomach and either warm or diluted by being "on the rocks"— is as destructive for humans as it is for the product. It's rather like drinking yesterday's champagne from a tea cup. The whole point of vodka lies in the fact that a small jigger is swallowed quickly in one gulp (it's poured from a bottle kept in the freezer), as if one were ingesting fire, and that at the same instant one takes a bite of something very hot or spicy—mushrooms, pickles, marinated pepper, salted fish, scalding borscht, hot sausages in tomato sauce, it doesn't matter what. Virtuosos don't eat but rather sniff black bread (only black!) or the sleeve of an old jacket—but it's hard to recommend the latter in a country with a well-developed system of dry cleaners: it won't produce the same effect. In order to drink vodka properly, one should open the mouth wide and exhale sharply before swallowing, and tears should well up in the eyes. One of the participants will inevitably shake his head and say with a shudder: "That went down well! On to the next round!" The first jigger should hit the nerves, and there's even an old proverb: "The first strikes like a stake, the second dives like a falcon, and the rest flutter around like tiny little birds."

Vodka and *zakuski* (appetizers) are theoretically indivisible. The word *zakuska* denotes specifically food that is eaten with vodka in order to temper its effect on the body. It's ridiculous to drink vodka without *zakuski*. You'll get drunk immediately, especially if you're hungry, and you won't be able to appreciate the dinner to come. It's even more ridiculous to eat *zakuski* without vodka; you'll ruin your appetite, and if you're having a Molokhovets-style dinner, you'll still have need of it. In combination, vodka and *zakuski* stimulate the appetite, cheer the soul, warm you up, and prepare you for a feast.

Come to think of it, a real Russian is always thinking about vodka. In springtime, when he plants cucumber seedlings, he rubs his hands together—a good *zakuska* is growing. In the summer, preparing pickled tomatoes, canning stuffed bell peppers and eggplant caviar, he dreams about the long winter when there's snow on the ground outside the window and a bottle of Stolichnaya on the table. In the fall, everyone, including old women and children, rushes to the forest to gather mushrooms. They rise at four in the morning to make the early train out of the city and travel at least two hours (the nearby suburbs are hopelessly trampled and picked clean by local mushroomers). Not everyone knows how to correctly salt, marinate, dry, boil, and fry mushrooms, but even people who don't eat them (and they are few) go picking. Well-marinated mushrooms are a host's pride, the best *zakuska*. But in the end, all of this—the food, the drink, and the *zakuski*—is little more than an excuse to indulge in the most cherished Russian tradition of all: the endless "kitchen conversations" about world politics, the Tatar yoke, the fate of Russia, and the enigmas of the Russian soul.

1993

In the Ruins of Communism

Review of *Lenin's Tomb: The Last Days of the Soviet Empire,* by David
Remnick (Random House, 1993)

DECEMBER 1992. A long time ago, or perhaps not very
long ago at all. (Khasbulatov is still speaker of the Parliament.) I arrive in Russia after a long absence, and every
friend thinks it his or her duty to enlighten me about politics.
Regretting my profound ignorance but still fond of me, my
friends patiently explain, as if talking to someone who is color-
blind, the various shades of the political spectrum. Here we have
the dark, violet-red conservative region, where fascists, Communists, and extreme nationalists gather; these vipers and vermin
want to reunite the Soviet Union and herd free peoples behind
the barbed wire of the empire and forbid free trade, free sex, and
free speech. They are the bad guys. And here is the bright, shin-
ing, blue-green realm where radicals, progressives, and reformers romp. They want to liberate prices, republics, peoples, criminals, and anyone who wants liberation. They are the good guys.

The good guys demand freedom of speech for their enemies
and insist that the greatest misfortune of liberalism in Russia is
the closing of some fascist newspaper calling for the assassina-
tion of Russian liberals (with the addresses of the particular lib-

erals provided for convenience). I asked whether I might not choose some reasonable centrist party with a realistic program as the object of my sympathies, and it was patiently explained to me that no, I couldn't, and here's why . . . and there ensued a complicated explanation with details comprehensible only to someone who hasn't slept for twenty-four hours and follows all the microscopic, maddeningly swift changes in the program, the motives and the actions of that particular party. And the other reason is . . . and there followed an even more complex explanation of what one or another step of these unpleasant centrists would lead to.

One friend, a poet, even read me a poem that he had written setting forth the political situation in popular form, which included an assessment of the past and a prognosis for the future, but mostly made fun of one of the centrist parties. The verse was supposed to shame dunces such as myself who sit in America for a whole year at a time and, on returning to Russia, don't recognize a thing: "Who's that? And who's *that?* What's that, our *president?*" It was three o'clock in the morning, and my eighteen-year-old son and I were a little tired of this Russian ritual, I mean sitting up till the wee hours talking poetry and politics. (No one makes you do it, of course. You just hate to waste time sleeping. The day is for errands, the night is for eternity.)

"Let's take a walk and get some fresh air," I suggested. "We can get some more cognac," the poet agreed. We set out. Night-time Petersburg was deserted. Vasilevsky Island — the unrealized dream of Peter the Great, who planned to turn this bit of swampland into a Venice, or at least an Amsterdam, by cutting it into dozens of canals — was steeped in gloom and frozen silence. My friend quoted Brodsky: "Neither country nor church-yard do I wish to choose / To Vasilevsky Island I'll return to die." "God forbid!" my son and I responded, almost in unison. "Better he should never return, better he should live," said the poet, an admirer of Brodsky. We walked along the streets that were not fated to become canals, regretting this as always and trying to remember why, 280 years ago, the tsar's plans hadn't worked. Either the architects had incorrectly measured the width of the canals, or more likely the bureaucrats had pilfered and the treasury was empty. The usual Russian problem: grandiose ideas and then thievery; exalted dreams and then incompetence.

"If there were canals, they would have trashed them anyway," my son noted.

"Why?"

"Because a Russian walking across a bridge can't resist spitting or throwing something over."

"That's true," we conceded, "and that's why Russians are unconquerable."

That December night the island was scary. The avenue along which we walked was torn up, as if the late emperor (who loved to work with his hands) had finally risen from the grave himself to cut the first canal. Heaps of clay along both sides of the trench, pushed back to the walls of the buildings, had frozen and hardened. You could easily fall and break your leg. And the buildings themselves were in frightening condition. One was blackened by a recent fire, another had no roof, another looked like the Colosseum, I mean a ruin, and on the balconies of some buildings, as if in a surrealist painting, trees had sprouted and grown, and the balconies themselves hung threateningly, ripped by powerful roots.

Finally we got to the place (it was called a "night bar-shop," God knows why) where you could buy cognac. On a corner, at knee level, behind a tiny grilled window, a red light bulb burned. The poet got down on all fours and knocked. The window opened almost immediately. Through the crack you could see a tiny space and a young bearded face in a fur hat, and beyond him, in the half-dark, you could just make out a stack of crates.

"Is there any cognac?"

"Yes."

"Not poisoned?"

"No, people drink it, they're still alive."

"OK."

Cognac and money changed hands. The bills passed through easily, but the bottle took some doing.

Around the corner the huge, icy Neva River lay and breathed cold; and beyond it, weakly illuminated, still-luxurious buildings, the tall, snow-covered trees of gardens, and the high gold cupola of St. Isaac's Cathedral stood in silence. The three of us, kneeling and squatting with bottle in hand, thickly swaddled against the frost, must have looked something like a rowdy Flemish genre scene trapped in a Canaletto.

"Lord, what have they done to the empire!" I said, looking around.

"Who?" asked the poet.

At home we poured the cognac and drank to Gorbachev. Ask me why — I don't know.

A year and a month later, in January 1994, I am there again, and again we toast Gorbachev. Not because anybody wants him back; I've never met anyone who did. But in many houses, when toasting friends and the fact that we are alive and well, people drink to Gorbachev and no one protests, no one puts down a glass in indignation. They drink to Gorbachev the way they drink to lost youth, to first love (even if it ended in betrayal), to spring, hope, the dawn, the beginning of a journey, whatever. They drink to him because he didn't drink, or because he pretended not to drink. Because life was good then. Because he unclenched his fist and let go of Eastern Europe and eased our collective conscience. People drink to his southern accent and to his bad grammar. And to humiliation. After all, he lost. We don't like winners, we like losers, because that's what we are, each and every one of us. We kill tsars, then we dig up their graves and, sobbing, kiss their white bones.

In January 1994, no one talks about politics and no one explains anything, no matter how much I ask. No one understands anything. No one believes in anyone or anything. "Yel-tsin has only four months to live, you'll see. He'll die of cirrhosis of the liver. He's only capable of working four hours a week," they tell me. The repetition of the number four bothers me; I want more variety. "And then what?" "Who the hell knows. The abyss." The government? "They're bastards." The Parliament? "You can see for yourself." "And your friend, the progressive millionaire," I ask my poet friend, "on whom you placed such high hopes?" "Oh, he's an asshole like the rest of them." "And this one? That one? The other one?" "Idiots, crooks, bastards." "Who are you voting for now?" "I don't know. I don't care." But the poet's verse has clearly gotten better. Isn't that the most important thing?

Petersburg is thickly covered with commerce, with kiosks in which almost everything is sold. The prices are incredible, much higher than European ones. (The primary goods are alcohol, cigarettes, chocolate, and Tampax.) There is no longer any need to crawl along excavated streets to a "night bar" and knock on a frozen window. You can buy four kinds of Absolut vodka (no guarantee of authenticity) around the clock, as well as Glenlivet and cognac (according to the papers, 100 percent fake) and Makarov, Suvorov, Lev Tolstoy, and Rasputin vodkas. The sales-woman yawns and says: "You know perfectly well it's all the same. They bottle it in Poland and we paste on the labels."

"Lev Tolstoy and Rasputin are the same?" exclaimed my friend. "What is this, relativism, deconstructivism, postmod-ernism?"

"If you don't like it, don't buy it," says the saleswoman. "No one's forcing you." Nectarines are $5 per pound. Cheese runs up to $13. A liter of juice is $2. A Petersburg University professor makes $25 per month. (You don't have to eat, no one is forcing you!) But there are happy surprises, too: a medicine that I bought in America for $50 turned out to be so cheap in Russia that I bought fifteen jars and paid only five cents for it. (I should have bought thirty jars.)

Moscow isn't much different from Petersburg, except that there is more snow, less crime, cleaner water, and the buildings are better heated. You have the impression that everyone is buying, selling, investing, exchanging, pricing everything. My apartment in Moscow is on the ground floor next to a store, so I am subject to many uninvited incursions. Across the landing, in rooms that two years ago were a warehouse for the "Democratic Russia" party bookstore, they now store goods of some kind. I open the door and the guys who work there shamelessly stare into my apartment: "What office is that?" As if there is no longer any such thing as an apartment. At eight in the morning, the doorbell rings; a foreigner has got the wrong door: "Please, Dresdner Bank." Don't tell me my crumbling two-story building, which will soon be razed by bulldozers, can be mistaken for the Dresdner Bank. What is he, blind?

You can't help recalling the humane Gorbachev era, the simplicity of the mores—no parties, no banks, no commerce. Back then, the people who mistakenly rang my doorbell wanted something entirely different. A provincial fellow banged on my door with two fists, loudly demanding that I let his wife in to pee. "Have a conscience!" he cried, "the woman wants to urinate." Thieves who had just broken into the church next door offered to sell me icons. An Estonian magazine thought that I was the office of an English newspaper and sent a letter proposing critical pieces on the Russian oppressors; all the English paper had to do was commission them, and they would be pleased to write anything on any conditions.

In January of this year, by contrast, anything and everything is for sale, or is advertised in the stores, in the streets, in the kiosks, in the subway: a hornless goat and a construction crane; lemon tree saplings; a Cossack calendar that informs you that there exists a "secret Cossack fellowship," something like a mystical order, with unusual occult powers accessible only to Slavs, as "scientists" have shown; kiwis; horoscopes; "Amaretto di Saronno," manufactured, as is well known, in a Moscow suburb; expired margarine; expired olives; expired Milky Way bars; real Marlboros and fake Marlboros; fascist newspapers; dozens of new literary journals; matches with a picture of biceps and the word "Bodibilding"; used slippers; Volvos; roses; avocado face creme (expired); six kinds of matzoh; hard currency; and Chinese weight-losing cream. In the bakeries, they were selling a cake called "The Heart of a Croat," whatever that meant, and the new "commercial stores" had pretty names like Curare Supermarket.

The metro in Moscow, which has lost its shine, its luster, and its cleanliness, had nine fires last year because rats chewed through the cables. A joyous female voice continuously offers vacations in the United Arab Emirates to the crowd of tired Muscovites that descends into the warm, stinking underground pit. People listen, patient and aloof: they're used to it, just as they're used to their harmless idiot neighbor. A friend of mine was amazed to discover that her fourteen-year-old son didn't know when the October Revolution took place (no one bothered to tell him). My niece, who's about the same age, went off to the Mausoleum to look at Lenin "before they throw him out." "Well," I asked, "what did you think?" "Junk," she said. "There's nothing to see. He's all yellow and dried up." In the eyes of this child, the Mausoleum, which is the Kaaba of communism, was no more distinctive than a regular kiosk selling expired goods. The founder of the Soviet state, the sacred corpse and destroyer of Russia, its culture, its people, its peasants and intellectuals, its incalculable treasures, its cities, its religion, this figure was no more valuable than a hornless goat or stinky Marlboros made in Chişinău. How swiftly the past buries its dead!

Books on Russia tend to date quickly, but David Remnick's book, which has received much proper praise, is not likely to suffer this fate. It tells the story of a remarkable four-year period in Russian history—the years of agony, upheaval, confusion, and hope at the fall of communism. Such times are unique. To have witnessed them is a coup for a journalist, and to read an account of this important period is a captivating and educational experience. In Russia, or rather the Soviet Union, those four years were seen as a perpetual spring, partly because Gorbachev came to power in March, and partly because in our climate the arrival of spring is drawn out and difficult: warm days alternate with freezing ones, it sometimes seems that summer will not come this year, and then suddenly you think that all the trees will be heavy with fruit tomorrow. What a windfall for cheap symbolism.

How many bombastic, emotional articles were written, how many bad but touching poems! Every event seemed momentous. I remember one friend, a journalist, who would enthusiastically assure me after every democratic demonstration, "It was a Bloodless February Revolution!" "It was a Bloodless March Revolution!" and so on. How Russians loved Estonians, just because Estonians didn't love Russians. How horrified we were after the demonstrators were shot in Tbilisi. What a furor there was after the Congress of People's Deputies booed Sakharov and refused to let him speak. How readers devoured everything in print, how the subscriptions to magazines and journals soared. The circulation of *Novy mir,* which began publishing Solzhenitsyn after a quarter of a century of silence, zoomed up to 3 million! And how everyone awaited the arrival of Solzhenitsyn himself. (Now subscriptions to *Novy mir* have fallen to 50,000 and will probably fall further, and other journals survive solely on the sponsorship of George Soros, and Solzhenitsyn's books, bundled in twine, collect dust on hawkers' tables in the underground subway passages, where no one buys them, and Solzhenitsyn is finally about to arrive, though nobody is waiting for him anymore.)

No less important is that Remnick's book reads like a documentary detective novel, almost like a work of fiction, in which the author himself plays an important role. At the end of this 500-page account, readers are left with the grateful feeling that they have been led through the labyrinth of Russian names, events, and cataclysms by a charming and witty guide, not an odious, mercenary cicerone. Happily, Remnick avoided the standard squeamish genre of "Russia Through the Eyes of a Foreigner," which has been practiced for centuries: Now that I have returned successfully, am rested and drinking coffee in my spotless study, the time has come to tell you, dear friends, of the horrors of my journey through Muscovy and Tartary and so on.

I should note that the most active practitioners of this genre, for the last twenty years or so, have been Russian émigrés who turned themselves into instant "foreigners" as soon as they crossed the border and were filled with a three-penny snobbery about their former homeland, as if they had been only victims and not active participants in the absurdities of Soviet life. The best example of this is the New York–based émigré newspaper *Novoe russkoe slovo,* but a recent, typical, nauseating example may be found, and I choose at random, in the journal *Slavic Review,* fall 1993: "Many of us have spent more than one excruciating night in Soviet restaurants eating what we thought was bad food while badly dressed people danced badly to bad music." And further: "Western intellectuals, myself included, have been dismayed by the Russian public's laserlike ability to zero in on the very worst of the wretched refuse of capitalism's teeming pop culture shore. Karate films, heavy metal music, professional wrestling — you name it; they like it."

I take particular pleasure in noting that Remnick is devoid of this cultural racism. He doesn't make idiotic generalizations, he doesn't attribute implausible intentions and motivations to his subjects, he doesn't lie, he doesn't confuse; nor does he assume the pose of an aristocrat who, wearied by the people's foolishness, extends the local peasant two limp fingers from his lace cuffs. He doesn't try to rise above his characters or above his readers. With a sort of boyish pleasure, Remnick plunges into the lively chaos of a fast-changing society and draws vivid portraits of our heroes, monsters, and cranks (the three functions are often combined in one person).

Remnick's objective is the unearthing of truth, and his book opens with a genuine, entirely unmetaphoric unearthing: soldiers opening a mass grave of victims of the Stalinist regime—executed Polish officers—near Kalinin. Digging of another kind, in archives, is carried on by a remarkable schoolboy (later a university student) called Dmitri Yurasov, who in childhood single-handedly established the truth about hundreds of thousands of those who perished in the camps. The truth, or rather the thousands of truths, in multiple versions, are discovered by journalists, historians, writers, and just ordinary people. Remnick himself participates in these quests, sometimes successfully, sometimes not, finding and collecting individual pieces of the dispersed mosaic of the past. Sometimes the witnesses lie, heaping new myths on the mountain of old ones that have already been exposed. Sometimes they simply shut up. That was the tactic of Kaganovich, the last dinosaur of the Stalinist regime. Locked in his apartment, once an all-powerful satrap and now a pensioner and a champion domino player in his neighborhood, he kept his silence.

"Reporting is often foolish work, but there was something especially shaming about knocking endlessly on a tyrant's door," Remnick writes. He kept knocking on Kaganovich's door for four years but managed to see the stubborn old man only in his coffin. On the other hand, almost comically horrified with himself, he drank *chacha,* or Georgian moonshine, with Stalin's son, and they drank to the executioner's memory. He ate pot roast and potatoes with an old Stalin supporter named Korniyenkova, who was desolate because Stalin made one mistake: he died too soon. He dined with the famous Stalinist Nina Andreeva and notes that Russian reactionaries "were fine cooks."

That, by the way, is a remarkably accurate observation. Remnick doesn't linger over this amusing detail, but I have observed that Russian liberals are often horrible cooks; and they are as proud of their bad cooking as they are of their bad service (cracked plates, different-size cups, and so on). This stems, surely, from the traditional poverty of the Russian intelligentsia, from its revolutionary asceticism, from the shame that democratically inclined citizens feel about their own advantages when they reflect on those who have nothing to eat at all. The cooking of Russian liberals is a kind of guilty homage to the old cliché "poor but honest." What might seem like a harmless caprice, however, has a terrible consequence. The ascetic liberal doesn't respect the desire of other people for order and comfort, and thus his ideas of reform are completely alienated from human needs. He dreams of the spirit moving upon the face of the waters, but at the same time he wants the earth below to be without form and void.

As a writer, Remnick was lucky. Just as his tour of duty ended, the August coup took place, resulting in the so-called "victory of democratic forces." It's hard to imagine a better gift for a journalist. What's dinner without dessert? Still, leafing through *Lenin's Tomb*, you can't help asking: Well, and if the *putsch* hadn't happened, what would this book look like? If events had just continued to whirl like colors in a kaleidoscope, without the growing tension, and if life had just kept on getting "better and better" despite all sorts of minor unpleasantness, could the author have found the necessary mortar to hold his structure together? Wouldn't the entire book have collapsed into a series of portraits and adventures?

It is an unfair question, but I ask it in order to answer it in Remnick's favor. And the question isn't provoked simply by idle curiosity. The joys of August 1991 are long in the past; former friends have become enemies; the siege of the "White House" was horrible, and it divided the already broken ranks of the intelligentsia; Yeltsin is inept; the democrats are irresponsible; Zhirinovsky won a surprising amount of support in the elections; the people are angry and foolish; the authorities are corrupt from top to bottom; the new constitution is dangerous. And the future is obscure. To divine it, you must search the past for clues.

◆ ◆ ◆

Does it hold any clues? Of course it does. And so Remnick's book is still pertinent, because the characters and the processes that it describes are not colored retrospectively by the "happy ending" of August. Remnick resisted the temptation of a happy ending. (It must have been very tempting, too: you have a group of old-regime villains, a new generation with an awakening consciousness, ideas of "democracy" taking root, the winds of change, McDonald's, everything will be fine . . .) Reading Remnick's book, you feel it was possible to predict the election of December 1993, though the abyss separating the two periods is enormous. Remnick conveys clearly, for example, how the features of nationalism could be discerned in the thick dust of collapsing "communism." Unfortunately, the rise of nationalism is a natural process. If the empire is doomed to fall apart, then what can possibly emerge from its ruins, except hundreds of nationalistic formations? Democracy? Not a chance. If the empire had been capable of transforming itself into a democratic state, then why would it have needed to collapse?

No, Remnick doesn't know the future, but the future seeps through his text. Even the photographs reveal much more than their captions lead you to expect, and the clues are not only in the expressions on people's faces. In one photograph, we see an angry old woman holding a poster and threatening someone with her fist. The caption reads: "Here a woman in Vilnius, the Lithuanian capital, joins in an anti-Moscow demonstration." Fine, as far as it goes. But the poster is disturbing: it depicts a troika of horses with unpleasant human faces identified by some names. One "horse" is a caricature of a Russian with a Russian name; another is a caricature of a Jew with a Jewish name. Over the troika is a star; it looks something like a Soviet star, but it has six points. The poster's message is clear: "Down with Jews and Communists, down with foreigners, they are to blame for all the woes of our people." And in another photograph, a woman holds her sick son's passport and a jar of water. The "healer," Kashpirovsky, promises to "charge" both the water and the passport with "healing energy." Around her is a crowd of equally unfortunate and gullible women.

These are very meaningful photographs, if they are projected into the future. They depict the constituency of Zhirinovsky and those like him. The old woman holding a fascist poster in the first photograph may not understand that it is fascist. She probably thinks that she is fighting for independence. In fact, she is fighting for ethnic "purity." The growing nationalism of the republics will inevitably provoke a corresponding wave of Russian nationalism in response. The women in the second photograph have been reduced to a despair so great that only a sorcerer, they seem to feel, can relieve it. The frightful state of health care and the unavailability of basic medicines opened the gates wide for charlatanism. Traditional superstitions, beliefs in witch doctors and miracle healers, the explosion of religion and religiosity: everything blended together.

They are waiting, these women, for help from Kashpirovsky. But they need wait no longer: Kashpirovsky was elected to the Parliament on Zhirinovsky's ticket, Zhirinovsky sits in the Parliament, and a crowd of yet-unknown charlatans has ridden their coattails to power. In *Lenin's Tomb* there is a chapter on Kashpirovsky, a sketch of Zhirinovsky, and portraits of the people and the groups that voted for them in December 1993, though the author met them in 1988 to 1990. These people don't know what awaits them. They don't know what their own political views are. Some of them don't even know if they have any views at all. Their feelings are tumultuous; they are in the grip of emotion, shocked by all the new information. And every day brings them more unpleasantness and more humiliation. Remnick's book is filled with their voices.

If a person is told daily that everything is very bad, he may be able to take it; but if it is drummed into him that he himself is bad, that he always was bad and he always will be bad and that this is irremediable, then he will revolt. For years Russian intellectuals have painstakingly explained to "simple people" (at least to those willing to listen) that, in essence, they are historically unreliable. "So what should I do?" said the simple man, depressed. "Well, we don't know," yawned the intellectuals, and left to give lectures abroad. And the intellectuals who didn't go abroad express themselves in such incomprehensible language that they barely understand one another.

Gorbachev was obscure and unintelligible; I have yet to meet anyone capable of paraphrasing even the broad outlines of one of his speeches. Yeltsin is mysterious and vague, he tries the patience of his audience. Gaidar was especially menacing: he promised that everything would be very difficult and that this was a matter of science. Zhirinovsky, by contrast, appeared clear, precise, smooth, straightforward. To many people, alas, he seemed like a close friend, someone who took the needs of a tormented population to heart.

Zhirinovsky used television adeptly, buying up a great deal of air time — it's not clear who gave him the money — and from the screen he told Russian women, young and old, that he loved, understood, and pitied them, and from the same screen he presented them a symbolic gift: roses and candy. Like all cheap gestures, it worked. He told homosexuals that he understood their problems. (Nobody else thought to do this.) He promised drunkards vodka. He made brilliant use of the Russians' traditional fear of the "Asiatic threat," real or invented. He spoke in Turkish to a nebulously defined "Muslim" population and, as he explained to surprised Russian viewers, he ordered them to keep quiet, or else. This must have made a strong impression. Language, after all, is power; and the old Soviet bosses didn't even speak Russian very well. And the democrats who give interviews on CNN, which is broadcast in Moscow, may speak a little English, but they come off badly next to the Westerners, who always seem like the winners anyway.

During the years when Remnick was in the Soviet Union, during those years when the process of unearthing the truth was in full swing and everyone was excited about all the discoveries, the common feeling was that thousands of little truths would come together into one large truth, and that this primary truth would be something convincing, sublime, salutary, and that it would set everything to rights and all would be good and just. Many imagined that communism was the main obstacle on the path to this Truth. It was convenient to attribute all problems and all tragedies to communism. After August, however, this naive view was shaken. One can continue to use the word "communism" as a code word, but it doesn't clarify anything. After seventy-five years of Soviet power, the word "communism" means its opposite. "Communism" means reaction. Our "Communists" are closest in their views to America's extreme conservatives: I love to listen to an ultraconservative radio program from Lynchburg, Virginia, because it reminds me of the darkest days of my Brezhnev youth. You can't hear anything like it in Russia anymore. The only noticeable difference is the attitude toward private property. Russian Communists don't want to allow private property for a very simple reason: they know that they're not likely to get any. They would like to continue to make use of government property as their own, so they support the idea of government property.

The word "communism" has become a term of abuse, and Zhirinovsky made good use of it. In his campaign he emphasized the fact that all of his rivals had been Communists and that he had never joined the Party. To be sure, his rivals may well have been members of the Party at one time, which doesn't mean anything; but they were not necessarily Communists by conviction. And anyway none of this would prevent Zhirinovsky from joining with them, if he finds it expedient, and forming an absolute majority in the new Russian Parliament.

Well, I think, I'll wake up tomorrow and there will be yet another psychopathic dictator in Russia. But somehow I'm not frightened by this possibility. I should be frightened; but a number of circumstances inspire optimism. For a start, Zhirinovsky is more of a psychopath than even a dictator needs to be. He promised the "complete destruction" of Germany because they didn't give him a visa; he promised to use the Russian navy to blockade Japan's ports if it doesn't sign the peace treaty. Moreover, Russians are lazy, and so far, thank God, not nearly as nationalistic as they are often portrayed. And if Yeltsin fired tanks at one Parliament, why couldn't he do the same with a second, a third or even a fourth? If, of course, he lives that long.

The really important point is that Russia is never what we would like it to be, and none of its inhabitants has ever been happy with it. "Don't worry, friends," Mark Zakharov, the director of a Moscow theater, said recently in an open letter to his compatriots. "Fascism won't fly. In Russia nothing flies. Communism didn't, capitalism didn't, and fascism won't." Russia lives some life of its own, a strange, fantastical life where the pitiful and the paltry mix with the great, where paradoxes are the norm and harmony is attainable only in verse, where life breaks through in any form it can — in birches on collapsing balconies, in proletarian Amaretto made from stolen alcohol, in Brodsky's almost-thirty-year-old poems at three in the morning on a half-dead but immortal island that was built, according to legend, on human bones, by a mad emperor.

1994

Yeltsin and Russia Lose

Review of *The Struggle for Russia,* by Boris Yeltsin, translated by Catherine A. Fitzpatrick (Times Books/Belka Publishing Company, 1994)

When I was chairman of the Russian Supreme Soviet I got into a very stupid accident in the center of town. . . . That particular morning traffic was very heavy—eight lanes—so there wasn't even a lane or a slot for us. A GAI [state traffic police] officer halted traffic but since we were without our escort car, not all the drivers ahead of us noted immediately that the officer had raised his stick, a sign for them to stop. We should have braked and waited for everyone else to stop. But the driver looked at me, and I automatically gave him a hand signal to go forward. He stepped on the gas and we passed a large van heading toward where there seemed to be a clearing ahead. Suddenly there was a terrible crash! And then a ferocious pain in my head.

This episode from Boris Yeltsin's new memoirs is a good illustration of what power means in Russia. The chauffeur, instead of doing his job, turns to his boss for instructions, and the boss *automatically* waves his hand—onward!—never doubting his supreme rightness.

It was thus—with a wave of the hand—that Yeltsin demolished a huge country in December 1991, for as he himself now informs us, "I felt in my heart that such major decisions had to be taken easily." Two years later, the frightful consequences of this demolition led him, the legally elected president, to order tanks to fire on the legally elected Parliament in the center of Moscow. Why did this happen? According to Yeltsin, it's quite simple: because "I was undergoing an agonizing process of decision making, and that is why our vehicle of state did not roll along the highway in a straight line but knocked down telephone poles and ran into a ditch."

Somehow there are far too many automotive metaphors in this hastily written autobiography. An automobile often equals power in Russia, and often power actually depends on cars. On the eve of one November 7 in the 1970s, when Yeltsin was still Party boss in Sverdlovsk, his chauffeur drove off a country road and got stuck in a ditch. But Yeltsin was scheduled to appear on the platform at ten o'clock the next morning to wave to the masses who would be demonstrating their joy at the anniversary of the October Revolution. And "if I, the chief city official, did not appear at the November 7 celebration, the main national holiday, if I was not seen on the dais viewing the parade, it would be a catastrophe. This simply couldn't happen. People would think that either I had died or had been removed from office."

In order to remain in power, Yeltsin walked all night, crossing plowed fields and stumbling in the snow in fifteen-degree weather, repeating to himself: "The main thing [is] never to sit down, then you don't get tired . . . just *never* sit down." By morning he had come to a village where the entire population, simple people without aspirations to power, were "dead drunk. No matter what door we knocked on, the residents were passed out cold." Yeltsin managed to get to the tribune on time: he made a phone call and sent for a helicopter. The authorities were saved.

A car is also a symbol of power, sometimes in the most vulgar way. At a meeting of the leaders of the Soviet republics, they would usually try to put my car (the limousine of the president of Russia) first in line at the entrance. But one evening my automobile ended up at the end of the line of government limousines. My security people sprang forward in alarm, made an incredible U-turn, digging up the Novo-Ogaryovo lawn in the process, and finally put the car back at the head of the line — Russia first!

Woe to him who forgets his place and tries to grab more than his rank allows.

I began to notice that features in Burbulis's character [Yeltsin's closest adviser] which previously had seemed incidental to me were in fact related to his whole system of behavior and relationships with other people. Burbulis was the first of the new Russian nomenklatura who came to power after the August coup to order a government limousine [a ZIL] for himself. . . . I think he experienced a special thrill when the escort car raced ahead of his ZIL, its lights blinking and siren screeching.

Cars make such an impression that on the road to power one has to use cunning tactics to win simple hearts and minds. "When I was a deputy in the Supreme Soviet, I had turned down the perks of a chauffeured car and a dacha. I also rejected the special hospitals and registered at my neighborhood clinic." Yes, at that time he traveled demonstratively around Moscow on a trolley — a popular mode of transport. And what do you think? It helped! A successful election — and here he is, chairman of the Presidium of the Supreme Soviet of Russia. Now we can start over again and take back the car, the dacha, and the other privileges, and, in Yeltsin's words, fight for them.

Sukhanov [an aide] said in amazement, "Look Boris Nikolayevich, what an office we've seized!" I have seen many an office in my life but I got a pleasant tingle from the soft modern sheen, all the shininess and comfort. "Well, what next?" I thought. "After all, we haven't just seized the office. We've seized an entire Russia."

Precisely! So, what next? Instead of *The Struggle for Russia,* Yeltsin's book could rightly have been called, less pretentiously and more frankly, *The Struggle for Power.* In Russian, to be fair, it's titled, with a certain false modesty, *Notes of the President.* The president. How that word must caress the ear of all those Party secretaries who for years were omnipotent bosses on their own turf—in republics, oblasts, cities—but metamorphosed into humble, trembling lackeys in Moscow, in the Kremlin, where the Big Boss sat. How they clung to their positions, keeping a keen watch: is anyone intriguing against them? Is anyone undermining them? How anxiously they kept score: has anyone got a car above his position? A dacha above his rank? The Party's power was great but fragile. One call from Moscow—"Get rid of him!"—and you'd be gone.

But who can get rid of a president? Who would dare to wave his hand and dismiss the people's chosen man? The people elected the president, the people, *the people!* You're against *the people?* Beat him up!

A president can be gotten rid of only by destroying his country, his house, his people. Yeltsin understood this. And he acted accordingly. His whole book is a confused, inconsistent, incoherent, evasive, but ultimately understandable and even partly truthful story about how he, Yeltsin, rose up against Gorbachev, did battle with him, vanquished him, ravaged his kingdom, and deprived him of EVERYTHING.

And became Gorbachev himself. And lost.

It began with an insult, a grievous male insult. In late 1987, after criticizing Gorbachev's policies at a plenary session of the central committee, Yeltsin fell into disfavor and tumbled from the summit he had attained with such difficulty. (As you may remember: "The main thing was never to sit down . . . just *never* sit down.") He was already the first secretary of Moscow, a candidate member of the Politburo—there was almost nowhere higher to go—and in February 1988 he was brought down to the pitiful post of first deputy chairman of the State Construction Trust. One might think: you're a construction man by profession, and you love Russia so much—build something useful and calm down. But this is the logic of ordinary people. Yeltsin, by his own account, would spend hours in his new office watching the Kremlin telephone. Would it ring?

> A feeling of dead silence and emptiness surrounded me. I will never forget those moments of anticipation . . . Few people know what torture it is to sit in the dread silence of an office, in a complete vacuum, subconsciously waiting for something. For this telephone with the state seal to ring. Or not. As I whiled away the long hours in the Gosstroi office, I finally figured out my relations with Gorbachev . . . I have never intended to fight with him personally . . . but why hide it—the motivations for many of my actions were imbedded in our conflict.

That he "never intended to fight with him personally" isn't true, of course. Anyone in his place would have been mortally offended: in the late 1980s, Gorbachev subjected Yeltsin to public humiliation. On television, which had only recently been allowed to broadcast intimate political events previously hidden from human eyes, the program showed the whole astonished country how Yeltsin—that big, handsome, worthy man, who boldly spoke his mind and was immediately punished for it—tried not to lower his head while Party swine, big and small alike, mocked him, shouted, and literally made faces at him as he left the hall. The herd trampled someone who was already down. Everyone could see—close up, on the television screen —the fake sympathy and poorly hidden triumph on Gorbachev's face.

The world of the Party was a world of wolves. We have never sympathized with the wounded bloodsuckers from the upper echelons—their traumas are part of their job description. But even a boss has human features; he is also a living creature; he, too, hurts. When the fallen Yeltsin walked down the aisle—into

hell, down into the depths, as he thought—his every step transformed him into a human being for the viewer. The foul Party
scales fell from him, he shed his tail, horns, and hooves, and humiliated human virtue began to shine through his features. In
the eyes of many, he exited that revolting kangaroo court as
someone purified, beloved.

Russians—I remind readers for the umpteenth time—are not
Europeans and especially not Americans. Whoever fails to take
this into account will always miscalculate and then wonder in
amazement where he went wrong. Americans love winners. In
Russia, we love losers. In America, those who have a successful
career, make money, or attain a high position are respected. In
Russia, we respect those who have been beaten and robbed, who
crawl on all fours, their faces streaked with blood. And there are
reasons for this. Russian people came to love Yeltsin because
they saw themselves in him: downtrodden, flogged, unjustly
punished, and cheated. It's in people's blood, in the popular
memory: you come to the master with a request, crumpling
your cap in your hands, shifting from one foot to the other, and
he, in a bad mood since morning, orders the servants to kick
you off the porch and set the dogs on you. Sooner or later, what
do you do? You torch the master's house and the kennel into the
bargain—and the greenhouse, and the stable, and the granary.
Then you share the loot with your brother bandits. And the
divvy can't be managed without a few knocked-out teeth and
blackened eyes, of course.

Crowds of clean, well-dressed Americans rushed to catch a
glimpse of the clean, handsome, tan Gorbachev with his snow-
white smile. Someone even suggested he run for president of the
United States, and if that weren't possible, then for governor of
Florida. And meanwhile, in Moscow there were demonstrations
in support of Yeltsin, and my God, what crowds these were—I
once happened to be in the maelstrom of one such crowd in the
spring of 1990 and was transfixed with pity and horror. These

were not the usual fake demonstrators with paper flowers and dressed-up children, pretending to be in a state of happiness, not the ones that Yeltsin was once afraid to be late for as he wandered across the snowy Siberian plains. No, these were real people, in all their poverty, misery, and raggedness. They were unshaven, with ashen faces, bad teeth, dressed in shabby clothes. The democratic intelligentsia had never in its memory seen or heard anything like this, the genuine voice of the people. And for the first time, with mixed feelings of excitement and alarm, we saw that "the people," in whose name so much is done, had emerged as a real political power. "Yeltsin! Yeltsin!" the crowd shouted. One woman, spinning in ecstasy on her own axis, howled: "Yel-tsiiiiin! He eats like usssss! He drinks, like usssss! He's just like usssss!"

Whether Francis Fukuyama likes it or not, history — at least in Russia — hasn't stopped. As long as the central myths are alive, the ones that form the backbone of a given culture, history continues — and repeats itself. The myth of a people's tsar, ataman, defender, protector, was played out once again at that time in the squares, streets, and eventually, by a narrow margin, in the Parliament when Yeltsin was elected speaker, and in the country when he was elected president in June 1991.

Yeltsin rode a wave of popular love to the crest of Russia. But what was Russia at the time? One of the republics, no more. Remember how they gathered in Novo-Ogaryovo, watching like schoolboys to see whose car would be first in line! How that must have irked President Yeltsin, so much so that he decided to recount the silly episode in his book. Further on, he writes, significantly: "Perhaps from the outside, such a collection of 'presidents' who in fact had no real power appeared somewhat ridiculous." This is the whole point. He wasn't fighting for Russia — he had the country in his pocket — he was fighting for real power. And in order to obtain this power, he had to take Gorbachev's place. Become president of the USSR. But he knew that it wouldn't work. All those toy "presidents" of other republics — actually first Party secretaries — nipping at his heels and scenting prey wouldn't let him. They finally had the prospect of unlimited rule at home. They wouldn't have to account to "Moscow," to crawl on their bellies, to send tithes: rugs, diamonds, cognac, money, porcelain vases of human height with portraits of the Great Russian Boss (who regardless of his hair and eye color always ended up with Central Asian features and dark, dark eyes). Yeltsin would have to share with his fellow bandits, especially since this would allow him to seem a great democrat, and pronounce those sweet words: sovereignty, independence, equal rights.

In February 1991, Yeltsin was dying to speak on television and Gorbachev wouldn't let him. (Now, in his book, Yeltsin justifies himself: "Each day, the television broadcasters were scaring the public with the specter of the Soviet Union's collapse and civil war. The position of the Russian republic leadership was portrayed as purely destructive and negative. . . . That was why I was feeling an enormous need to explain myself, to tell the people that reform of the USSR did not yet mean its collapse.") The tension grew. Many people understood that the conflict between these two strong personalities did in fact threaten the country with collapse — and with unforeseeable consequences. Friends, colleagues, and democrats tried to convince Yeltsin to make peace with Gorby, not to inflame an already overheated atmosphere. Naive creatures! They had not been humiliated before the eyes of the entire country. They hadn't sat for hours in the silence, staring at a silent telephone. They hadn't fallen from such dizzying heights as he. When he finally got to speak on television, Yeltsin went for broke: "That was when I got an idea. You're afraid of Yeltsin? Well, then, you'll get that very Yeltsin you fear!" He publicly proposed that Gorbachev resign, and proposed dismantling the central government and giving the republics their freedom.

This attack made an extremely unfavorable impression on

many. Yeltsin knew this. But it was already too late to stop him: he wanted blood. And he understood that the beautiful word "freedom" intoxicated people and enhanced whoever pronounced it. He didn't feel like thinking about what would follow this "freedom": collapse, poverty, the explosion of nationalistic hostilities, a sea of blood, civil wars, millions of refugees. This would all take place outside the borders of Russia anyway, in the "republics." And all those Armenians-Azerbaijanis-Georgians-Abkhazians-Ossetians-Chechens-Pamirans-Tajiks and such — well, they aren't Russian, are they? Let those fresh-baked president–Party secretaries deal with them. They aren't Václav Havels and he knows this, but what does he care? For Russia the most important thing is tranquillity. That's how Yeltsin ends his book, with the hypocritical sentence "The chief goal of this restless president is Russia's tranquillity."

The August 1991 coup was truly a gift for Yeltsin. He was the popular hero who defended the "White House," Russia, and democracy. "Papa, you have defended democracy!" his daughter said to him. How pleasant this sounded. That's right, my child! Let's not forget to write this down in the book. The coup plotters were cowards and behaved stupidly; Gorbachev, as always, was evasive and managed to weasel his way out of things. His role in the coup is not clear even now. But what is clear is that he lost power and Yeltsin did what he wanted. He pushed Gorbachev aside, quickly dismantled the country with the Belovezhsky Woods deal,[1] cast off responsibility for all the complex and tortuous conflicts beyond the borders of the Russian Republic, and ascended to the throne. Yeltsin equated Russia with himself, and, for him, to "seize" a comfortable office meant, as we have seen, to "seize" Russia. The limited mind of Sverdlovsk Party boss Yeltsin was incapable of understanding the priorities, needs, meaning, responsibility, and history of the Russian state. What about the historically outrageous concession of the Crimea and the Russian south to Gauleiter Leonid Kravchuk?

And the Black Sea fleet, which Russia is buying from itself? And the twenty-five million Russians living in their own country and waking up one morning to find themselves unwelcome "foreigners"? And the so-called foreigners waking up in Russia as God knows what? The Berlin Wall collapsed, but Yeltsin erected dozens of new walls in his own country.

Everything was done with such haste that the terms of Russian citizenship weren't thought through, which gave nationalists everywhere the opportunity to divide people by blood, by ethnicity, to declare yesterday's neighbors foreigners, to institute ethnic purges, and to attack "aliens." The explosion of nationalistic feelings among ethnic Russians who were now locked in the other former Soviet republics, and the strengthening of Zhirinovsky's position, are direct and natural consequences of the way this division was carried out. After all, it's one thing to defend Russian *citizens* and quite another to defend ethnic *Russians*.[2] (Truth be told, neither enjoys any defense.) For this reason, the American administration's recent pronouncements to the effect that in view of the growth of nationalism in Russia it is necessary to support Yeltsin sound to my mind like the mumblings of a sleepwalker.

God did not grant this volleyball player a statesmanlike mind. His little passions are utterly human, grandfatherly, domestic. Thus, he complains that he isn't as free now as he used to be: he flies in a helicopter and sees a pretty stream below. Oy, let's land and sit awhile, the President begs. You can't, Boris Nikolayevich, what about the nuclear button? You are responsible for it now, his guards say, shaking their heads. He decided to choose himself a vice-president, so he thought for a while and he thought some more and came up with someone: Rutskoi. A handsome face, mustache, the women like him, and he'll sit quietly and keep to himself. But after a while Rutskoi starts permitting himself to make comments: "He would come into my office, give me a horrified look, and say: 'B.N., where did you get those shoes? You shouldn't be wearing shoes like that; you're the president!'" It started with shoes. Then the vice-president went on to criticize his suits, then it snowballed and got worse and worse until in the end he had to send the tanks after Rutskoi, who was sitting in the White House, and send him off to prison. (Gogol did a good job of describing such conflicts long ago in "The Story of How Ivan Ivanovich Quarreled with Ivan Niki-forovich.") Of course, the reasons for this enmity must have been, and were, deeper, but Yeltsin doesn't write about them in his book. He does, however, write about Rutskoi's criticism of his shoes and suits.

Was it possible to avoid the collapse of the country without amputating living flesh? Many people think not. Yeltsin's answer to this question is: *yes!*

> There were various ways to achieve this [the preservation of the Soviet Union]. We could fight for elections for the president of the USSR throughout all the republics. We could declare the Russian parliament the legal heir of the dissolved Soviet legislature. We could persuade Gorbachev to make me acting president, and so on. That path was barred to me. Psychologically, I could not take Gorbachev's place. Just as he could not take mine.

One is truly flabbergasted by such self-satisfied blindness. Not a shadow of a thought about the country, its people. Only Me and Him. Yeltsin and Gorbachev. Who will beat whom?

If the Russian empire was fated to fall apart by itself—and the fall of an empire is always a painful and complex process—so be it. The lines of collapse would perhaps have formed more naturally, the border conflicts, perhaps, would have been less harsh, had it happened differently. One would like to think that it might have been possible to avoid several wars altogether. Even if this is a naive hope, many people shared it. Including some deputies in the Parliament. And the arbitrary actions of the newly elected "president" in the Belovezhsky Woods split the fledgling Russian state and set the Parliament and the president at odds.

There's no denying it: the Russian Parliament was horrible in many respects. Capricious, unintelligent, hysterical, corrupt, ignorant, belligerent—for that matter, the flesh of the flesh of its people, which it was called on to represent. When Yeltsin decided to implement economic reforms, the Parliament opposed and obstructed him whenever it could. This was a very difficult period for the president: all of his concessions caused the Parliament to foam at the mouth and demand even greater concessions. And here Yeltsin's inadequacy and ineptitude in governing became obvious. Continue reforms or not? Hand his ministers over to be torn apart by the Parliament or not? If so, who and how many? (He handed them over.) Why these ministers and not others? Is it possible to continue reforms if you destroy the reform team? He doesn't explain any of this. He himself didn't know what he wanted (other than peace, respect, volleyball, tennis, comfortable offices, the bathhouse, and that "everything be all right").

Having rushed to "seize" Russia, he didn't know what to do with it. He started disappearing at critical moments, avoiding important meetings and trips, he didn't answer the telephone, even when Clinton called him twice. He used to think that power was simply pleasurable. It's no accident that melancholy thoughts of peace, repose, and a pension filter through the text of his book, reaching their apogee in this envious paragraph which is not, however, in the American edition of the book:

> In America there's a good tradition. When a president steps down, the Congress makes a decision—to build the former president a house anyplace he wants. And he is allowed to keep the presidential library.

Not only does Yeltsin reveal his rosy ignorance of American "traditions" but he clearly sees Western presidents as being rather like tsars, only temporary. (I wonder whether, somewhere in the depths of Yeltsin's subconscious, he is remembering the last house of the last Russian tsar, given to Nikolai II by the Bolsheviks, which Yeltsin himself had blown up on orders from

Moscow.) In any event, I rather think that if an American president willfully decided to get rid of California, Nevada, Florida, Georgia, Alabama, Texas, the two Virginias, both Carolinas, Maryland, and Pennsylvania, the grateful American people wouldn't build him anything more than a hut in Alaska, at best, and wouldn't give him any sled dogs either.

Yeltsin's final battle with the Parliament is the largest and murkiest part of his "autobiography." Everything having to do with it is lies and innuendos. Yeltsin seems to suppose that if he writes a lot of words, they will somehow arrange themselves into an acceptable explanation. But this doesn't happen. In the center, once again, is Yeltsin himself. He thinks. He thinks again. A decision begins to take shape in his thick head. He's sick and tired, damn it, of these people's stubbornness. He thinks again. He "considers it premature" to do something. Then he has a brainstorm: do this. The motives of his political actions are not clarified or explained to the reader, they rustle somewhere in the murk of his sluggish and possibly vodka-soaked brain. You can hear the thudding pulse of his wounded provincial ego. And every night, seized by insomnia, he paces the room and thinks —O irony!—about Gorbachev. About Gorbachev's wife. He compares her to his wife. His wife is better, of course. The main thing is that Gorbachev, they say, had to answer to Raisa, that he spilled his guts to her and thus relieved the stress of office, sought (and received) support, and therefore—ha ha—he was a henpecked husband! The insomniac Yeltsin is pleased with this thought. *He* isn't like this, oh no. His wife has only to peep, "Borya—" and he sharply reprimands her: "Leave me alone!" So there!

We are, of course, happy and interested to know that Yeltsin's wife obeys him, thank you. But the problem is that his former friends, the democrats, don't obey Yeltsin. The Parliament doesn't obey. The government, the Central Bank, the vice president, don't obey him. And, most importantly, the army doesn't obey him. But why, why? Could it really be (O horror!) that he isn't right?

No, he's always right. He knows this for sure. He decided this. Why? Because he's the president, that's why! And he "would like to believe . . . that the majority of Russians realize . . . the only definite guarantor of calm is the president himself." And no one is going to tell *him* what shoes to wear!

October 1993. Yeltsin orders Parliament to dissolve: he is sick of it, honestly. Some of the deputies, of course, don't want to. The White House is transformed into a weapons depot. According to reports Yeltsin receives, it has been seized by armed groups. Yeltsin surrounds the building with unarmed militia, apparently counting on the militia to fight off murderers with smiles and olive branches, but the armed mob breaks out of control, and here they are, killing policemen, attacking the television station, seizing the mayor's office. Where is the army? Get the army over here! The army is digging potatoes, the president is told — it would be inexpedient to take them out of the fields. The head of the armed forces, Pavel Grachev, assures him: Yes, it's coming, the army is coming. It's very close, just wait. The head of GAI calls and says: It's not true, there's no one here, the troops have stopped on the edge of Moscow and don't want to go any farther.

Frankly, this sounds like a mutiny.

Everyone witnessed the bloodletting on the streets of Moscow that followed the dangerous weeklong standoff. Moscow, as the newspapers wrote, "lost its virginity": nothing like this had happened in the capital since 1918. We still don't know what really happened, how powerless Yeltsin really was during this time, why the rebelling army finally came to his aid after all, what concessions the military bargained for while holding the population hostage. And Yeltsin's "autobiography" clarifies *nothing*. Rumors still circulate, but they are beyond the borders of this book.

A few weeks ago PBS showed a film about Russia. It was titled imaginatively, of course, *The Struggle for Russia*. (No relation to Yeltsin's book.) In it, Yeltsin's former press secretary, Pavel Voshchanov, speaks with bitter irony about the fact that in his view, when Yeltsin looks in the mirror these days, he sees Gorbachev. In mirror image, Yeltsin's development and fate reflect Gorbachev's: the love of the populace, disappointment, the attempt to hold on to power, spilt blood, oblivion. As if in a frightening fairy tale, he has turned into the person with whom he struggled to the death.

And, in the Russian tradition, I feel sorry for the loser. For Russia.

1994

TRANSLATOR'S NOTES

1. The nature preserve in Belarus where Yeltsin, Leonid Kravchuk of the Ukraine, and Stanislav Shushkevich of Belarus signed an accord on cooperation that in fact spelled the end of the USSR.
2. The words are, respectively, *rossiiskie grazhdane* and *russkie*. The Russian language has two words that translate as "Russian" in English, but *rossiiskii* means "pertaining to Russia" or "on the territory of Russia," while *russkii* means ethnically Russian or Russian-language. This distinction is important and is carefully maintained by Russian politicians, since Russia is a multi-ethnic country; it is, however, frequently lost in Western discussion of the Russian political scene.

The Past According to
Alexander Solzhenitsyn

Review of *"The Russian Question" at the End of the Twentieth Century*,
by Aleksandr Solzhenitsyn, translated and annotated by Yermolai Solzhenitsyn (Pantheon Books, 1994)

WHAT A STRANGE spectacle it is: Alexander Solzhenitsyn's biweekly broadcasts on Russian television. In the
late evening, when the long Moscow daylight begins
to fade and the construction dust settles, the writer pours out a
stream of banalities, platitudes, and exclamations ("It's a nightmare!" "This is terrible!" "Disgraceful!") in his brisk, hearty fal-
setto, flapping his arms about, stretching them toward the television camera, lifting them to the ceiling, or even covering his
face as if he can no longer bear the thought of so much horror.
He condemns everything that comes to hand. And in his own
way, he is absolutely right—like any elderly pensioner who sits
on a bench in the courtyard to take the fresh air before bed, vent
the irritation accumulated over decades, and grumble against
life, which hasn't listened to him. There really is a lot of dis-
gracefulness around. It's news to no one.

Solzhenitsyn fumes for fifteen minutes twice a month, on
Mondays, beginning at about 9:45 P.M. It's a good time: the hard
day is behind. The Mercedes have run their red lights, carrying

rich "new Russians" to night clubs. Professional beggars have unglued their artificial sores, unfastened their gangrenous legs, and stowed their daily take. Homeless people are laying out their bedding under warm pipes in basements. Children have gone to bed, young men are on the phone flirting with girl-friends, parents have already had dinner, shut and drawn the seven bolts of their steel doors, and are yawning. It's time to relax. What's on the other channels? A music video, a new variety show, a retro-variety show, a film, and the program *Reporter,* which offers "the story of an eyewitness to the eruption of the famous Krakatoa volcano in Indonesia." Didn't the monster erupt in 1883 — can that really be it? The terrifying wave of lava washed away the neighboring islands, and in the aftermath volcanic dust hung about in the atmosphere for decades, creating the fantastical crimson sunsets that so inspired the Symbolists and others. "It was stifling, the sunsets were fiendish, insufferable, crimson. We remembered them all till the end of our days," Akhmatova wrote. But maybe they mean the eruption of 1952? That would be more recent and perhaps more important news than what the Nobel laureate rushes to tell us: he rails indignantly about the injustices of trade union organization in the USSR in the 1920s.

"A disgrace," the writer chastises from the screen. Cleaning ladies sweeping the halls of hotels stop for a moment to listen, leaning on their brooms. They willingly agree: "That's right, a disgrace! Here I am, working three jobs, too, and bread has gone up again! That Luzhkov [the mayor of Moscow] should be put in prison along with the rest of them! It's that democratic mafia!" The writer doesn't hear them, nor do they hear him.

They say that deaf people live longer. Solzhenitsyn looks surprisingly young: fresh, ruddy, few wrinkles, glittering eyes — more vivacious than many fifty-year-olds. Watching him, you would never say that this man spent long years in the camps, hungry and cold, that he had been critically ill (according to him, with cancer), that he was persecuted for years. It's also true that fate was unusually gracious to him, granting him world-wide fame, tons of money, twenty years of peace in Vermont, a faithful, beloved wife, healthy and talented sons. The writer's entire appearance serves as a wonderful advertisement for the benefits of voluntary solitude in the country. Vegetables. Fresh air. Volleyball with the children. Measured labor. No outsiders. A high fence.

This seems to be his modus operandi: admit no outsiders. At any rate, he eventually drove away the guests who were at first invited to appear on his program: other people's opinions obviously irritated him. He found the monologue genre more convenient, more familiar. The broadcast is taped, no viewers' phone calls threaten him. You can't ask him any questions, there's no one to object, the subjects are removed from the present day or are abstract, the exhortations are so vague ("People should be honest") and the threats so nebulous ("If we don't all stick together, we'll perish") that some people, I know for a fact, turn off the sound and simply watch the gesticulations, the supple movements of the spine and the facial expressions, as if the "conscience of the Russian land" were giving an aerobics lesson.

Rumor has it not only that he doesn't receive any money for his appearances but that he paid a significant sum for many months in advance, buying air time for himself (and generously giving us, myself included, a taste of this baffling fog). That's what they say, although I wasn't able to confirm it, and who would have shown me the receipt anyway? I feel rather sorry for him: the old man tries, he prepares, he believes. (How sternly he admonished himself in the BBC film about his return to the motherland: "a strong, thoughtful facial expression" just before stepping out of the airplane.) The old man shouts soundlessly, waves his arms about in the dark, tears his hair, and flies like an incorporeal spirit in a swirl of electrons through the indifferent ether to beat against my television screen, begging to be let out with his moldy prophecies, while I cruelly watch the series *Bel-*

lissima with one eye, and with the other read a summary of the day's events, and with a third (well, yes, we're in Russia) scan a literary journal, and keep a fourth and all the others on the stove to make sure the meat doesn't burn.

Solzhenitsyn always knows precisely what should be done and how. He is truly disappointed that no one asked his advice when the world was created. He would have done a better job of calculating the electrons' orbits than the Lord God, he would have introduced sensible corrections in the table of chemical elements, he would have twisted the double helix in the opposite direction. For convenience's sake his starting point is that Russia is currently without form, and void (and corrupt and immoral, and the WHOLE country, except for the writer himself, has forgotten the Russian language), and that the Divine Spirit moves upon the face of the waters, thinking about where it would be handiest to start, and this is where Solzhenitsyn with his advice and his elbowing is needed, this is where he's indispensable.

In his earlier essay *Rebuilding Russia,* published in Russia in 1990,[1] Solzhenitsyn proposed his version of how to carve up the USSR. Or, more precisely, how to carve off pieces. At the time, separatist ideas were quickly gaining ground. Under the slogan of democracy and the pretext of freedom, any misanthrope or racist who couldn't stand his neighbors demanded that they be divorced from him, or best of all—that they be beaten and expelled. Solzhenitsyn proposed a Russo-centric version of separatism: keep Russia, the Ukraine, Belorussia, and part of Kazakhstan (historically Russian territory) together, and kick everyone else out, whether they like it or not. The Russian population of the other republics should be moved to Russia. In other words, save your own kind and let others figure things out for themselves. And let reality—present and past—adjust to this cruel plan.

Until you take a globe in hand, you're surprised: why does an airplane flying from America to Europe pass almost over the

North Pole? Solzhenitsyn doesn't want to deal with the real globe, his earth is flat and the people inhabiting it are simple. In the garden of his imagination, Ukrainians stroll arm in arm with Russians, casting a leery eye at Armenians and banishing Tajiks with a switch. This is how things seemed to him from the depths of 1989.

By the time Solzhenitsyn wrote *The Russian Question* (March 1994), the Soviet empire had already fallen apart, not by itself but as a result of Yeltsin's haste to seize power from Gorbachev (see Yeltsin's autobiography, *The Struggle for Russia* [Times Books, 1994], where he writes about this himself).

In passing I should note a curious paradox: people who are unhappy with the collapse of the USSR, and there are more and more of them all the time since almost everyone suffered from it, accuse not Yeltsin, who signed the Belovezhsky agreement in December 1991, but Gorbachev, who tried to save the empire at any cost and lost his power for precisely this reason. I'm not just talking about taxi drivers who once dreamed of hanging Gorbachev because the sugar they counted on for making moonshine had disappeared. This strange aberration of vision is characteristic of the most democratic democrats as well. I have to admit that I can't comprehend it.

Here's a typical conversation in a Moscow kitchen. I say: "As a result of Yeltsin's actions, hundreds of thousands of people of all nationalities have already died in ethnic conflicts." My interlocutor only shrugs his shoulders: "Yes, what can you do, the fools keep on killing each other." "But under Gorbachev," I continue, "we all raised a hue and cry when eight people died in Tbilisi during a demonstration—" "Not eight but eighteen. Eighteen!" my friend sternly replies. "What's the difference?" I say. "There's an enormous difference! Enormous!" (This insane arithmetic has its analogy in other countries, of course: come on, tell me how many peaceful inhabitants of Iraq perished while the Americans, with very few human losses, tried, not even successfully, to kill Saddam Hussein? You don't count the other guy's losses, right? That's the way the world works, isn't it?) If I ask straight out, "Aren't we Russians to blame for the fact that, for instance, the Georgians and Abkhazians have killed so many of each other's citizens," I immediately hear: "It's time for you to get rid of that imperial consciousness!" My progressive interlocutor has already done so, and the price is other people's blood.

Actually, this digression bears directly on Solzhenitsyn's text and my rejection of his views. Solzhenitsyn also helped to bring about the collapse of the USSR: "To maintain a great empire means to drive your own people to extinction. Wherefore this motley amalgam? That Russians may lose their inimitable countenance?" Solzhenitsyn's ideas, according to Vladimir Lukin, former Russian ambassador to the United States, made quite an impression on Yeltsin (Lukin was the go-between for their contacts). Of course, not all his ideas. Democracy and parliamentarianism Yeltsin understood in his own inimitable fashion: he sent tanks against the Parliament. The idea he took to heart was "Kick them all out!"

Under Gorbachev, the metaphor of "a civilized divorce" was popular among democrats whenever the possible secession of one or another republic was discussed. But such a divorce is feasible only when each of the spouses has somewhere to go and means of support. Is the American reader capable of appreciating the true significance of this metaphor in the Russian setting? In Russian families, in contrast to American ones, three generations often live in one small apartment and it is not unusual during a divorce for the wife to kick her husband and his elderly mother out on the street. But what is the old lady guilty of? It was precisely that kind of divorce, to continue the metaphor, that Solzhenitsyn proposed and still proposes. If in *Rebuilding Russia* he only considered the divorce process, however, then in *The Russian Question* he goes on to bemoan the jointly acquired children and reproaches the mother-in-law.

The Russian Question is a deliberately tendentious, quasi-historical tract written to show that the Russian tsars behaved incorrectly for the last three hundred years of their rule. They didn't concern themselves with the country's internal affairs, the morality and well-being of their subjects. Instead they carried out needless wars, seizing territories that were detrimental to the people's morality. They grabbed too much—and there's your empire and all the woes that stem from it. From the first pages, the reader wants to ask: Well, and before that? And before that? Were the seizures justified before the Romanovs took over? Sometimes, Solzhenitsyn admits, even the Romanovs grabbed the right stuff. Thus, "the Polish war conducted by Alexis[2] was both necessary and just, for he was recapturing historically Russian lands usurped by the Poles." One might ask: What are "historically Russian lands"? Those which were won in battle a long time ago? Where does one draw the line? Solzhenitsyn knows perfectly well that the Russian people are a mixture of different tribes, but this mixture arose in part as a result of wars, seizures, and appropriations. He writes: "A multitude of tribes blended with the Russian ethnicity," and this is true, but he fails to mention that the Russian "ethnicity" itself is heterogeneous in the extreme. He avoids this delicate, complex problem.

However, beginning with the first years of the Romanov dynasty, everything is clear to him. Tsar Alexis Mikhailovich "brutally and criminally" waged war on his own people when he carried out church reform (the Schism). Peter the Great was "a mediocre, if not savage, mind": he opened a window to Europe, broke through to the Baltic and Black seas, built Petersburg (a "demented idea"), and did not establish the order of succession. Anna Ioannovna carried out "foolish, unsuccessful wars"; her military commander, Münnich, "with an infamous lack of skill . . . stormed Ochakov (1737) from the least advantageous direction, neglecting an easy approach." Although in the Empress Elizabeth "true, the Russian national feeling was alive," still she "unforgivably threw Russia into European quarrels and dubious ventures, so alien to us." Peter III was "a nonentity, a man of meagre and shallow mind, whose development stalled at a child-like level." Enough. What follows is a lot of cursing, we'll skip it.

Then comes Catherine the Great . . . but here history and politics grow so complex that Solzhenitsyn slows his tongue-twister pace and slightly restrains his oaths, offering us an essay on European diplomacy and military campaigns that is so impenetrable that if the reader is not a specialist in eighteenth-century history he cannot follow the simultaneous machinations of Poland, Turkey, England, France, Austria, Greece, Prussia, Sweden, and Denmark. And don't forget Moldavia, Walachia, some pieces of northern Bukovina, western Belorussia, Zabrze, Volynia, Podolia, Holland, Spain, Sicily. Not to mention four Russo-Turkish wars in the eighteenth century, four in the nineteenth; the division of Poland, the Reichenbach Congress, the Treaty of Kuchuk-Kainarji; the victory near Focsani (Romania), the shameful peace with Prussia, Frederick, Khan Krym-Girei . . . Mercy!

The text becomes unbearably dense, comparable only to the poem about everything in the world simultaneously that the mad poet writes in Borges's story "Aleph." And there are still lots of tsars to go: Paul, two Nicholases, three Alexanders. And that's only Russia. How many will succeed one another over the course of two hundred years in motley Europe, which is forever battling and redrawing its borders! Solzhenitsyn is too well prepared for his history exam; as they say, wake him up in the middle of the night and he'll mutter: "One example was, to use Klyuchevsky's assessment, the 'most absurd' treaty with Austria in 1782: to form a non-existent 'Dacia' out of Moldavia, Walachia and Bessarabia, to place Serbia and Bosnia under Vienna, and to give Morea, Crete and Cyprus to Venice."[3]

So, did they found Dacia or not? And to whom did Morea previously belong? And where is it? Did Venice rule Cyprus, and if so, for how long, and most important — why should I care?

The Russian Question is an essay. The style is eclectic: it's an encyclopedia encrusted with sarcasms, oaths, bitter invective;

the author alternately kicks the reigning personage and conde-scendingly praises him. First he arrogantly inquires: "Even had he taken Poland, would Frederick ever have dared to invade the enormous expanses of Russia?" (Why not? Others "dared": Genghis Khan, Charles XII, Napoléon, Hitler . . . Russia had done its own daring and invaded others as well. That's how his-tory went, without asking Solzhenitsyn.)

Having trudged through almost a hundred pages of this briar patch, once you break free from dates and names, you can begin to see the main point. Solzhenitsyn's fundamental re-proach to our clumsy, myriad lords is that they are bad, improv-ident imperialists. And he himself is provident; that's the whole difference. That wasn't the way to make war, those weren't the people to hang out with, to believe. If they had listened to him, everything would have been different. For instance, at the end of the eighteenth century: "Russia reached a natural southern boundary: the Black Sea (including the Crimea) and the Dniestr River (in much the same way as she had already reached the Arctic and Pacific Oceans). We should have known to stop at that." (What could they do? Solzhenitsyn hadn't been born yet, there was no one to give advice.)

Strange logic! Solzhenitsyn has just condemned the idea of the campaign to extend Russia to the Indian Ocean, but he ap-proves of its reaching the Pacific. He's happy that Russia has en-trenched itself on the Black Sea, but unhappy about the idea of seizing the Bosphorus Straits, the idea of aiding brother Slavs suffering under Turkish dominion. He's also unhappy about the scheme to free the Greeks, fellow Orthodox believers, from those very same Turks. None of our business! The Bashkirs re-volted in 1735: that's what should have been dealt with, and no setting out for India. He doesn't consider himself an imperialist, but allow me to say that he's worse, he's more egotistical than any imperialist. Whatever, in his opinion, is good for Russians, he justifies. Whatever is disadvantageous—down with it! Ac-cording to him, with the division of Poland (1772), Russia "regained her long-lost Belorussia"; a bit further along (1829), "we secured independence for the Greeks . . . again, the interests of others." In my view, this is so extraordinarily cynical that the Greeks and the Belorussians should both be dumbfounded. Despite the various insanities of the Russian tsars, in comparison to Solzhenitsyn they at least appear to have possessed some romantic caprice, some style; in our writer we see only the rigid calculation of a shrewd peasant who won't give a piece of bread to a beggar because he needs every crust for his hogs.

Even Soviet imperialism in its post-Stalinist version seems softer, more humane, clearly more democratic than Solzhenitsyn's version. Here is his approach to the Chechen problem (before the beginning of the war): "Was it not equally our duty to manage an evacuation of Russians from Chechnya, where they are mocked, where plunder, violence, and death threaten them at all times?" As if Russians don't steal from Russians, or Chechens from Chechens—if they are thieves; as if Russians don't live peaceably side by side with Chechens in Chechnya and in Russia if they are normal people! And how cynical is the writer's sarcasm:

> And we? We have over these years hospitably found room in Russia for forty thousand Meskhetian Turks, burned out from Central Asia and rejected by Georgians from their indigenous home; for Armenians fleeing Azerbaijan; everywhere for Chechens, of course, even though they declared their independence from us; and even for Tajiks, who have a country of their own. [Etc.]

Well, he's logical, consistent: Solzhenitsyn doesn't want outsiders on television, or in his Vermont retreat, or in our country. And "we," bad, hospitable people that we are, want them.

So, I might ask, perhaps "we" aren't as bad as it suits the writer to portray us. "We must build a *moral* Russia, or none at all—it would not then matter anyhow." Perhaps this is our morality? "We must preserve and nourish all the good seeds which miraculously have not been trampled down in Russia."

Perhaps our hospitality, which Solzhenitsyn condemns, is one of those seeds? I'd like to think that our inept people, for all its vices, is kinder than this uninvited counselor.

Solzhenitsyn is not entirely alone, of course. He has his own unique support group, consisting largely—to his credit—of extremely worthy people. As a rule, these are older, decent, conscientious citizens who are concerned with moral issues and are deeply troubled by the political and cultural crisis that Russia is now living through. At one time or another all of them took to heart Solzhenitsyn's moral imperative "to live not by lies." They have tried hard to follow it, with only one exception, which is that they lie—steadfastly and continually—in matters concerning their Teacher and Prophet. For them, his every thought is a revelation, his every work of fiction a tour de force.

This is really a form of religious fanaticism. A person may be reasonable, generous, tolerant, even attain a certain inner freedom, but if he is, let's say, a single-minded Christian believer, Christ's actions in the Bible and textual inconsistencies in the Gospels are not open to discussion. And truly: it's wonderful that the Lord took humanity's sins upon Himself, and out of love for the people, let Himself be crucified. But was it absolutely necessary to run an entire herd of swine off the cliff just to destroy the demons? And were the demons really so weak that they perished together with the vulgar swine?

It's wonderful that Solzhenitsyn, putting his own life in danger, brought together and interpreted the Russian tragedy of the twentieth century in the *Gulag Archipelago;* that he created a monument to the millions of innocent people who perished in the camps, and thereby awakened the conscience of an entire generation. But does this mean that the homegrown recipes for saving Russia in *Rebuilding Russia* (what to do in the future) and *The Russian Question* (what should have been done in the past) are equally magnificent? These recipes can, in essence, be reduced to a single primitive operation: the destruction of the demons by herding the swine—non-Russians, foreigners, adherents of a different faith. *A Day in the Life of Ivan Denisovich* is an excellent story, but does it follow that the helpless, poorly cobbled snippets and snarls of text that were recently published as two new stories by Solzhenitsyn are masterpieces?[4] The writer's admirers affirm that this is the case—Yes! Yes! Yes! Masterpieces! It is painful to read articles by respected literary critics who try to prove that a jumble of words published under Solzhenitsyn's name is brilliant, and insist that if you perceive neither sense nor style in them then it is you who are blind, deaf, and understand nothing of literature. It is not the text that is extolled but the author, may his name live in glory throughout the ages, Amen.

For those who enjoy observing the spectacle of life, this is but another play on the theme of *sic transit gloria mundi*. And the brighter *gloria* shines, the sadder it is to note her *transit*. Saddest and most instructive of all is to see how little time it takes to rise and fall, how people reside on the ruins of their former world stature, how the last few disciples, who swore to tell the truth, shamefully lie to themselves and their Teacher. This only confirms the old maxim that love is more powerful than truth, and faith dearer than facts. One cannot help but respect the loyalty of these sectarians: like many before them, they wander barefoot along the dusty roads, beating drums and proclaiming that the Truth has been found—while life, in its noisy complexity and cunning, flows in the other direction and drowns out their feeble chant.

Next Monday evening there's another "get together with Solzhenitsyn." Whom will he rebuke this time? Will anyone listen? Competing with him on another channel of our modest television, there'll be a "report from India—universe-building as discussed by the well-known guru Osh."

So they did get all the way to the Indian Ocean after all, the scoundrels. They didn't listen to the old man.

1995

NOTES

1. Published in *Komsomolskaya pravda* on September 18, 1990, and in *Literaturnaya gazeta* on September 19, 1990.
2. The tsars and tsaritsas to whom Solzhenitsyn refers in this and following sections are: Alexis (reigned 1645–76); Peter I, the Great (1682–1725); Anna (1730–40); Elizabeth (1741–62); Peter III (1762); Catherine the Great (1762–96); Paul (1796–1801); Alexander I (1801–25); Nicholas I (1825–55); Alexander II (1855–81); Alexander III (1881–94); and Nicholas II (1894–1917).
3. Solzhenitsyn uses the old word "Morea," which means as little to the average Russian reader as it does to the American. The American publishers have taken pity on their readers and used the contemporary name "Peloponnesus."
4. Published in *Novy mir,* May 1995.

On Joseph Brodsky

W HEN THE LAST things are taken out of a house, a strange, resonant echo settles in, your voice bounces off the walls and returns to you. There's the din of loneliness, a draft of emptiness, a loss of orientation, and a nauseating sense of freedom: everything's allowed and nothing matters, there's no response other than the weakly rhymed tap of your own footsteps. This is how Russian literature feels now: just four years short of millennium's end, it has lost the greatest poet of the second half of the twentieth century and can expect no other. Joseph Brodsky has left us, and our house is empty. He left Russia itself over two decades ago, became an American citizen, loved America, wrote essays and poems in English. But Russia is a tenacious country: try as you may to break free, she will hold you to the last.

In Russia, when a person dies, the custom is to drape the mirrors in the house with black muslin — an old custom whose meaning has been forgotten or distorted. As a child I heard that this was done so that the deceased, who is said to wander his house for nine days saying his farewells to friends and family, won't be frightened when he can't find his reflection in the mirror. During his unjustly short but endlessly rich life, Joseph was reflected in so many people, destinies, books, and cities that during these sad days when he walks unseen among us, one wants to drape mourning veils over all the mirrors he loved: the great rivers washing the shores of Manhattan, the Bosphorus, the canals of Amsterdam, the waters of Venice, which he sang, the arterial net of Petersburg (a hundred islands—how many rivers?), the city of his birth, beloved and cruel, the prototype of all future cities.

There, still a boy, he was judged for being a poet and by definition a loafer. It seems that he was the only writer in Russia to whom they applied that recently invented, barbaric law— which punished for the lack of desire to make money. Of course, that was not the point—with their animal instinct they already sensed full well just *who* stood before them. They dismissed all the documents recording the kopecks Joseph received for translating poetry.

"Who appointed you a poet?" they screamed at him.

"I thought . . . I thought it was God."

All right then. Prison, exile.

> Neither country nor churchyard will I choose
> I'll return to Vasilevsky Island to die,

he promised in a youthful poem.

> In the dark I won't find your deep blue façade
> I'll fall on the asphalt between the crossed lines.

I think that the reason he didn't want to return to Russia even for a day was so that this incautious prophecy would not come to be. A student of—among others—Akhmatova and Tsvetaeva, he knew their poetic superstitiousness, knew the conversation they had during their one and only meeting. "How could you write that? Don't you know that a poet's words always come true?" one of them reproached. "And how could you write that?" the other was amazed. And what they foretold did indeed come to pass.

I met him in 1988 during a short trip to the United States, and when I got back to Moscow I was immediately invited to an evening devoted to Brodsky. An old friend read his poetry, then there was a performance of some music that was dedicated to him. It was almost impossible to get close to the concert hall, passersby were grabbed and begged to sell "just one extra ticket." The hall was guarded by mounted police—you might have thought that a rock concert was in the offing. To my utter horror, I suddenly realized that they were counting on me: I was the first person they knew who had seen the poet after so many years of exile. What could I say? What can you say about a man with whom you've spent a mere two hours? I resisted, but they pushed me onto the stage. I felt like a complete idiot. Yes, I had seen Brodsky. Yes, alive. He's sick. He smokes. We drank coffee. There was no sugar in the house. (The audience grew agitated: are the Americans neglecting *our* poet? Why didn't he have any sugar?) Well, what else? Well, Baryshnikov dropped by, brought some firewood, they lit a fire. (More agitation in the hall: is *our* poet freezing to death over there?) What floor does he live on? What does he eat? What is he writing? Does he write by hand or use a typewriter? What books does he have? Does he know that we love him? Will he come? Will he come? Will he come?

"Joseph, will you come to Russia?"

"Probably. I don't know. Maybe. Not this year. I should go. I won't go. No one needs me there."

"Don't be coy! They won't leave you alone. They'll carry you through the streets—airplane and all. There'll be such a crowd they'll break through customs at Sheremetevo airport and carry you to Moscow in their arms. Or to Petersburg. On a white horse, if you like."

"That's precisely why I don't want to. And I don't need anyone there."

"It's not true! What about all those little old ladies of the intelligentsia, your readers, all the librarians, museum staff, pensioners, communal apartment dwellers who are afraid to go out into the communal kitchen with their chipped teakettle? The ones who stand in the back rows at philharmonic concerts, next to the columns, where the tickets are cheaper? Don't you want to let them get a look at you from afar, your real readers? Why are you punishing them?"

It was an unfair blow. Tactless and unfair. He either joked his way out of it — "I'd rather go see my favorite Dutch," "I love Italians, I'll go to Italy," "The Poles are wonderful. They've invited me" — or would grow angry: "They wouldn't let me go to my father's funeral! My mother died without me — I asked — and they refused!"

Did he want to go home? I think that at the beginning, at least, he wanted to very much, but he couldn't. He was afraid of the past, of memories, reminders, unearthed graves, was afraid of his weakness, afraid of destroying what he had done with his past in his poetry, afraid of looking back at the past — like Orpheus looked back at Eurydice — and losing it forever. He couldn't fail to understand that his true reader was there, he knew that he was a Russian poet, although he convinced himself — and himself alone — that he was an English-language poet. He has a poem about a hawk ("A Hawk's Cry in Autumn") in the hills of Massachusetts who flies so high that the rush of rising air won't let him descend back to earth, and the hawk perishes there, at those heights, where there are neither birds nor people nor any air to breathe.

So could he have returned? Why did I and others bother him with all these questions about returning? We wanted him to feel, to know how much he was loved — we ourselves loved him so much! And I still don't know whether he wanted all this convincing or whether it troubled his troubled heart. "Joseph, you are invited to speak at the college. February or September?" "February, of course. September — I should live so long." And tearing yet another filter off yet another cigarette, he'd tell another grisly joke. "The husband says to his wife: 'The doctor told me that this is the end. I won't live till morning. Let's drink champagne and make love one last time.' His wife replies: 'That's all very well and fine for you — you don't have to get up in the morning!'"

Did we have to treat him like a "sick person" — talk about

the weather and walk on tiptoe? When he came to speak at Skidmore, he arrived exhausted from the three-hour drive, white as sheet—in a kind of condition that makes you want to call 911. But he drank a glass of wine, smoked half a pack of cigarettes, made brilliant conversation, read his poems, and then more poems, poems, poems—smoked and recited by heart both his own and others' poems, smoked some more, and read some more. By that time, his audience had grown pale from his un-American smoke, and he was in top form—his cheeks grew rosy, his eyes sparkled, and he read on and on. And when by all reckoning he should have gone to bed with a nitroglycerin tablet under his tongue, he wanted to talk and went off to the hospitable hosts, the publishers of *Salmagundi,* Bob and Peggy Boyers. And he talked and drank and smoked and laughed, and at midnight, when his hosts had paled and my husband and I drove him back to the guest house, his energy surged as ours waned. "What charming people, but I think we exhausted them. *So now* we can really talk!" ("Really," i.e., the Russian way.) And we sat up till three in the morning in the empty living room of the guest house, talking about everything—because Joseph was interested in everything. We rummaged in the drawers in search of a corkscrew for another bottle of red wine, filling the quiet American lodging with clouds of forbidden smoke; we combed the kitchen in search of leftover food from the reception ("We should have hidden the lo mein. And there was some delicious chicken left; we should have stolen it.") When we finally said good-bye, my husband and I were barely alive and Joseph was still going strong.

He had an extraordinary tenderness for all his Petersburg friends, generously extolling their virtues, some of which they did not possess. When it came to human loyalty, you couldn't trust his assessments—everyone was a genius, a Mozart, one of the best poets of the twentieth century. Quite in keeping with the Russian tradition, for him a human bond was higher than justice, and love higher than truth. Young writers and poets from Russia inundated him with their manuscripts — whenever I would leave Moscow for the United States my poetic acquaintances would bring their collections and stick them in my suitcase: "It isn't very heavy. The main thing is, show it to Brodsky. Just ask him to read it. I don't need anything else — just let him read it!" And he read and remembered, and told people that the poems were good, and gave interviews praising the fortunate, and they kept sending their publications. And their heads turned; some said things like: "Really, there are two genuine poets in Russia: Brodsky and myself." He created the false impression of a kind of old patriarch — but if only a certain young writer whom I won't name could have heard how Brodsky groaned and moaned after obediently reading a story whose plot was built around delight in moral sordidness. "Well, all right, I realize that after *this* one can continue writing. But how can he go on living?"

He didn't go to Russia. But Russia came to him. Everyone came to convince themselves that he really and truly existed, that he was alive and writing — this strange Russian poet who did not want to set foot on Russian soil. He was published in Russian in newspapers, magazines, single volumes, multiple volumes; he was quoted, referred to, studied, and published as he wished and as he didn't; he was picked apart, used, and turned into a myth. Once a poll was held on a Moscow street: "What are your hopes for the future in connection with the parliamentary elections?" A carpenter answered: "I could care less about the Parliament and politics. I just want to live a private life, like Brodsky."

He wanted to live and not to die — neither on Vasilevsky Island nor on the island of Manhattan. He was happy, he had a family he loved, poetry, friends, readers, students. He wanted to run away from his doctors to Mount Holyoke, where he taught — then, he thought, they couldn't catch him. He wanted to elude his own prophecy: "I will fall on the asphalt between the

crossed lines." He fell on the floor of his study on another island, under the crossed Russian-American lines of an émigré's
double fate.

> And two girls—sisters from unlived years
> running out on the island, wave to the boy.

And indeed he left two girls behind—his wife and daughter.

"Do you know, Joseph, if you don't want to come back with
a lot of fanfare, no white horses and excited crowds, why don't
you just go to Petersburg incognito?"

"Incognito?" Suddenly he wasn't angry and didn't joke but
listened very attentively.

"Yes, you know, paste on a mustache or something. Just
don't tell anyone—not a soul. You'll go, get on a trolley, ride
down Nevsky Prospect, walk along the streets—free and unrec-
ognized. There's a crowd, everyone's always pushing and jos-
tling. You'll buy some ice cream. Who'll recognize you? If you
feel like it, you'll call your friends from a phone booth—you
can say you're calling from America; or if you like you can just
knock on a friend's door: 'Here I am. Just dropped by. I missed
you.'"

Here I was, talking, joking, and suddenly I noticed that he
wasn't laughing—there was a sort of childlike expression of
helplessness on his face, a strange sort of dreaminess. His eyes
seemed to be looking through objects, through the edges of
things—on to the other side of time. He sat quietly, and I felt
awkward, as if I were barging in where I wasn't invited. To dispel
the feeling, I said in a pathetically hearty voice: "It's a wonderful
idea, isn't it?"

He looked through me and murmured: "Wonderful. Wonderful."

1996

Russia's Resurrection

Review of *Resurrection: The Struggle for a New Russia,* by David Remnick
(Random House, 1997)

S T. PETERSBURG, 1997. My mother (eighty-one years old)
travels all the way across town to pick up her orphaned
grandson's social security payment: you can receive the
payment only in person and only on a certain day of the month.
She is greeted by a sign: "No money." "And when will there be?"
"Drop by and you'll find out." She goes back into the metro,
where a voice over the PA system entices her with the prospect
of a vacation in the United Arab Emirates. She rides the metro
for free: she's retired. On the other hand, she hasn't gotten her
pension in two months. A friend of hers doesn't get her salary.
But this friend rented her apartment to an Englishman for $100
a month.

True, the Englishman broke the toilet, made $60 worth of
telephone calls to London, and tried to leave without paying:
supposedly he only had one large bill and the banks were closed
so he couldn't get change. But my mother's friend won out, she
was physically stronger: a healthy fifty-year-old woman. And she
runs fast: not long ago she managed to run away from a ticket
inspector on the bus. The problem is that she had a face lift

($500), and now the ticket inspectors don't believe she's fifty-five and eligible for a pensioner's card (hers is in fact fake), which allows her to travel for free.

True, these ticket inspectors are often fake themselves: they counterfeit ticket inspectors' ID cards but are actually regular citizens, con artists who make a living by fining other con artists. Still, running away from them along the ice- and snow-covered streets isn't easy, so on leaving the house, my mother's friend puts on heavy dark glasses and an old lady's hat, hunches over, and gets into her act. I watch her out the window and notice that there isn't a single balcony left on the building across the street, which used to be so beautiful. Instead there are yawning patches of bare brick. What's going on? "Very simple," I'm told. "Not long ago a balcony fell off a building in Petersburg and killed a passerby. The municipal authorities have no money for repairs, so they ordered all the existing balconies to be torn down."

In the newspapers they write that one of the city bosses stole a million dollars from the municipal treasury and renovated his own apartment, but he can't be arrested because he has parliamentary immunity; they write that Petersburg is counting on becoming the site of the next Olympic games (it won't); that a particular firm is offering the services of sorcerers who "will erase the previous inhabitants of your apartment from your memory." With irritable curiosity they await the arrival of the heir to the Russian throne, that fat child from France, with his fat mother and fat grandmother. The tsar, they say, will live in his own house (without balconies?), paid for by our democratic government. (They must not have called in the sorcerers, for the memory of the monarchy hasn't quite been erased.) All this is St. Petersburg, the former capital of the empire, the divorced wife. But even here there are signs of the new, a kind of liveliness in business: an aide proudly tells a new young doctor come to work in the hospital: "And here's our prestigious ward: all directors of companies, businessmen with bullet wounds . . ."

Petersburg is poor, Moscow is richer. Anyone who hasn't been in Moscow for the last five years wouldn't recognize the center: it's clean, the store windows sparkle, and although the prices seem inaccessible, the shops and restaurants are full. In the metro at night — by my own observation — 90 percent of the women are wearing expensive furs. There's a woman in a simpler coat who sings ballads in a good operatic voice: alms fly into her box. Mayor Luzhkov, who everyone thinks is a crook and yet whom everyone loves, is fixing up the city according to his own taste. The new architecture is eclectic: a mix of 1910s moderne with huge spacious windows and forged gates; and on the roofs, fairy-tale towers top almost all of the rebuilt buildings.

No concrete utilitarianism here — just the dreams and fantasies of people who made their fortune yesterday and haven't read anything but children's books. All in all — it's pretty. Snobs don't like the new buildings, but Moscow was so thoroughly destroyed by pompous Stalinist architecture, then by the desolate boxes of the 1960s and dead, barnlike factories wedged into its very heart, that it has long since lost any style, and these new fantastic creations cannot ruin it. The only thing that can is the rebuilt Cathedral of Christ the Savior — a hideous huge remake with an abnormally large "head" that makes it seem rather short-legged. The cupola can be seen from afar, and it's rather frightening, as if King Kong had suddenly appeared above the rooftops. A quarter of a billion dollars was reportedly spent on it, and the protests of those who feel sorry for Moscow and begrudge the money are already pointless. The cathedral is considered a "symbol," and it is indeed: of senseless luxury in the midst of poverty, of despotism, of vainglory, of antidemocracy.

In his new book, David Remnick continues the themes of his previous book, *Lenin's Tomb*, but his task is more narrowly defined: if in the first book he was dealing with the Soviet Union on the eve of its disintegration, then in the new book Remnick's theme is Russia collecting herself among the ruins, stealing, hoping, losing hope, and yet trying to figure out just who she is and where, therefore, she should go. The task is narrower but no less difficult, because Russia has not managed to deal with any of the questions that faced the USSR, but new ones have already arisen.

As in his previous book, Remnick interviews a lot of different people: Gorbachev, Solzhenitsyn, Yeltsin's entourage, businessmen, journalists, simple people. They all have different pictures of the new world, which they try to describe to him with varying degrees of conscientiousness. Many have not yet fully formed their vision of this world, or when they have, it's unrelated to reality.

This is hardly surprising: reality itself is changing with fantastic speed and no single person can encompass it. The motley spectrum of opinions — usually strongly colored with emotions, expressively formulated, cynical, disillusioned, mad, idealistic — creates a lively account, and since Remnick is an extraordinarily good writer with a vivid sense of the comic and a wonderful dramatic sense, this book, even more than the first, reads like an entertaining novel in the spirit of Gogol.

How can one fail to think of Gogol, when the characters of contemporary history appear to have come straight from the pages of his books? Describing the 1991 meeting at Belovezhsky Woods in Belarus (which Leonid Kravchuk and Stanislav Shushkevich attended as "presidents" of Ukraine and Belarus, and where Yeltsin autocratically decided the fate of the Soviet Union), Remnick quotes a participant:

> Yeltsin was so drunk he fell out of his chair just at the moment that Shushkevich opened the door and let in Burbulis, Kozyrev, and the others. Everyone began to come into the room and found this spectacular scene of Shushkevich and Kravchuk dragging this enormous body to the couch. . . . Yeltsin's chair stayed empty. Finally Kravchuk took his chair and assumed the responsibility of chairman.

In his memoir *The Struggle for Russia,* Yeltsin described it this way: "I well remember how a sensation of freedom and lightness suddenly came over me," etc. Anyone who has ever gotten drunk will recognize this sudden feeling of lightness and freedom—it usually sets in after about the second shot of vodka, after which, if you continue drinking, you may start breaking dishes, furniture, whole countries if you are given the chance. Smart drinking companions (friends don't let friends drink and . . .) could have stopped him, but Yeltsin's weren't smart enough. "To get a sense of how improvised this period of history was, to understand the lack of sophistication involved," Remnick writes,

> one need only know that on the night before he left Moscow for Minsk, Kozyrev [then Minister of Foreign Affairs] went to the Savoy Hotel not far from the KGB headquarters and met with an old friend, Allan Weinstein, head of the Washington-based Democracy Project and the author of a book on the Alger Hiss case.
>
> "Allan," Kozyrev said, "what is the difference between a commonwealth, a federation, and an association?"

This entire get-together took place, as planned, outside Minsk, since the participants were afraid that Gorbachev, who didn't want the country to fall apart, would interfere in some way and start something (just like teenagers get together to drink out of town at the country house since the city apartment is occupied by a strict father who won't allow it).

At the same time that this boisterous party of ambitious ignoramuses was deciding on their own how to divide up the country, another group, Remnick tells us, was meeting in a dacha outside Moscow (they weren't afraid of Gorby). This was a group of so-called *vory v zakone,* or thieves-in-law, the biggest mafiosi, heads of organized crime who had controlled numerous markets—from airports to cigarettes—for decades. (N.B.: the translation of this term is literally correct, but somewhat confusing. The term refers to a self-appointed category of criminals who have sworn to break forever with society and to live by special criminal "laws" or vows that are particularly cruel, barbaric, and merciless; by no means every thief or mafioso attains the status of a "thief-in-law.")

The mafiosi got together in order to discuss a serious problem: how to run the shadow economy in the new situation, when the country was threatened by changing borders and thus a concomitant redistribution of markets. Remnick doesn't have much information about this meeting, which isn't surprising given the nature of the group. He only gives one figure—$60 billion, which by some accounts was the income of the shadow economy for 1991 alone. However, despite the absence of detail, it's hard for me to imagine that these gangsters, before their meeting, made hasty inquiries of informed friends: "What is the difference between wholesale and retail prices?" or "What is cash?" It's also hard to imagine that these criminals, people both practical and professional, would have acted like Yeltsin and given Kravchuk not just the whole Ukraine but the entire Crimea—in fact all of southern Russia, together with the Black Sea fleet and the Black Sea itself.

This territory—the Crimea—has no relationship to Ukraine. Russia won it at war in the eighteenth century, and Khrushchev illegally transferred it to Ukraine in 1954, as Vladimir Lukin, a historian, member of Parliament, and former Russian ambassador to Washington, once confirmed to me in a conversation. The signing of the agreement on the transfer took place *before* the then Supreme Soviet voted its formal agreement, which violated even "despised" Soviet laws. There was an attempt to discuss this with Yeltsin, but he didn't want to hold things up; he was in a hurry to spite Gorbachev.

Previously the criminals had controlled the country, distributing their influence according to region, ethnic group, and economic sectors; now they were faced with the complex task of coordinating all these factors and working in changed circumstances. Actually, this is precisely what Yeltsin and his "colleagues" were supposed to do, but it's one thing to wave to a thrilled crowd from atop a tank, and another to think.

In the end, everything the politicians did turned out badly; everything the criminals did turned out just fine. True, the mafia bosses have killed off a few of their colleagues since then, but haven't the politicians had their political deaths as well? (Neither Kravchuk nor Shushkevich is president any longer, and there's hardly anyone left from Yeltsin's entourage either.) All in all, one can't help thinking that it might have been better if in 1991 the politicians and criminals had joined forces and not wasted time fighting each other. After all, they have become indistinguishable. Our politicians are completely corrupt, and the criminals have the real power anyway. "There is no border between the legal and the illegal," Mikhail Leontiev, economics correspondent of the newspaper *Sevodnya,* told Remnick.

In a general sense, no one in Russia today is honest. The laws contradict each other, as Remnick shows, and if they didn't contradict each other they'd be impossible to enforce. How is one supposed to pay taxes if one isn't paid a salary? Why pay for the bus or subway to get to work if it costs $30 a month and your salary (which you don't receive) is $60 a month? The law forbids (even now!) possession of foreign currency, but there are official exchange booths on every corner. And who makes the laws? The Parliament? We know how they vote, we've seen it on television: one deputy votes simultaneously for five, reaching out with hands, elbows, and nose to hit all the accessible buttons. He votes "for his comrades who asked him." After indignant protests from the public it was stopped—no, not the practice, they just stopped showing it on television. Taxes hold at a figure of about 90 percent, but sometimes they exceed income. Everyone understands that this is ridiculous, but nothing changes. At the same time, according to the press, the tithe that racketeers collect from businessmen is about 25 to 30 percent. So who is the thief here?

◆ ◆ ◆

Remnick is a satirist of Gogolian persuasion: he combines the grotesque with the lyrical, and this works particularly well when he describes two men for whom he apparently has a certain weakness: Solzhenitsyn and Gorbachev. These two extremely dissimilar figures do, in fact, have something in common: grandiose achievements in the past that remain unappreciated; a tendency to a global — if mistaken — view of things; a tendency to pontificate; a certain naive view of the frightful tangle of Russian problems; and an overbearing self-assurance, which has ruined both of them. Not least of all, they have both been personally lucky: by all the rules of the game, each in his own way should have perished, but neither did, and therefore they are not tragic figures (unlike Sakharov, for instance); each lives well, is successful, and is trying to express his own truth, which no one wants to hear. Both of them missed their opportunity to play a big role in the life of Russia: they waited too long, sat it out, their timing was off.

I only half agree with Remnick: of the two, I sympathize only with Gorbachev, a man whose achievements, in my view, are enormous, and whose potential as a politician has not been exhausted. As far as Solzhenitsyn is concerned, though his life and work are themselves an immense subject, I am primarily amazed and disappointed by his lack of humility and by his limitations as a writer. To spend eighteen years in the depths of Vermont to write *The Red Wheel,* a huge, boring novel that tries to explain the reasons for the Russian Revolution — and this is at the end of the twentieth century when the world has moved so far away from 1917! When the literature of the twentieth century (even his own *Ivan Denisovich*) has proved that a vivid statement of two to five pages or less can be worth an enormous, heavy tome!

Real life, as we can see from Remnick's account, has passed this obsessive man by, and he has passed life by: to spend eighteen years in America and not even be curious about what happens outside the walls of your voluntary prison! (Although it does seem that he went to the store occasionally: somewhere he recommends getting rid of the colorful magazines set out in supermarkets near the cashier and replacing them with philosophical brochures "for workers.") To see nothing in Western culture but "manure"! For a writer to remain hidden behind a fence! For a politician, teacher, prophet not to race to Russia during the most gripping moment of her history—in August 1991! (Here my store of exclamation points is exhausted.) And his reward: they don't even tell jokes about him. By Russian standards, that's oblivion.

Gorbachev is another story. True, no one will vote for him—but I know a lot of people who said, "I won't vote for him because I know he doesn't have a chance, but I like him better than that vulgar drunk Boris. What can you do? Life teaches us to be realists!" I know people who, having spent their last rubles on a bottle of vodka for a holiday, will sit around a traditional Moscow kitchen, criticizing everything and everyone, complaining about their life, and then will say: "Now—let's drink to Gorbachev!" And everyone present will drink to Gorbachev. I do, too. Gorbachev—in our cynical time—has become the hero of jokes, almost a holy fool, a ridiculous clown who, despite everything, mumbles on about his own ideas, keeps on talking. You listen closely—maybe he's speaking the truth; but the truth is too much for life, we just steal, brothers, steal! Gorbachev has become the hero of rock-folklore, his voice, phrasing, image is included in songs, because he seems nice, inoffensive, safe—valuable qualities in a harsh time of nightly murders and rampant crime. This is probably not how he would like to go down in history. But the gods laugh at people, fate hands out the wrong gifts, not always what we ask for. And yet, and yet . . .

One of the sad things about political games is the wordplay, the volleyball of concepts whose meaning seems real to the players: "imperialism," "nationalism," "democracy" . . . In the Russian context, such words seem particularly empty, just pretty candy wrappers. In politics, "death" isn't something one talks about, one doesn't imagine real live people. It sounds lovely: "Let us turn our backs on imperialistic thinking. Let every country settle its own ethnic problems." Everyone immediately applauds, smiles, and hands out the flowers. And the next morning they start shooting. No one will say the truth, for instance: "We decided the following. We're sick and tired of you, and as Solzhenitsyn writes, you should be cut off definitively, with no turning back. Tomorrow morning your neighbors—who are just as unpleasant as you are—will start killing you, stabbing pregnant women, throwing children out windows, setting homes on fire. And you will do the same. It's not our affair any more. Yesterday we thought of you as 'one of us,' we drove you to poverty, humiliated you, exported all your goods, dried up all your lakes, and defiled your land. Today we were told that this wasn't nice. So starting tomorrow we aren't responsible for you."

This is basically what has happened, and if we know from Remnick and others more than we care to about the horrors of the war in Chechnya (because it took place "in Russia"), we hear much less about the carnage in Tajikistan, where one half of the population is taking care of its "ethnic" problems by systematically slaughtering the other half; we hear almost nothing of the mutual butchery of Georgians and Abkhazians, or of the complete lack of human rights in Turkmenistan or Uzbekistan—it's someone else's head, so it doesn't ache as much. And to me it seems the height of hypocrisy that the Russian government is condemned (rightly) for the war in Chechnya but no one holds it accountable for the wars and blood being spilled outside Russia's borders, on the territory of the former Soviet Union. After all, there are all kinds of ways to kill people—not only by bombing the city of Grozny.

When we are told that we should "rid ourselves of imperialistic thinking" as fast as possible, what is really being proposed is that we relieve our conscience of responsibility for the tens of thousands of deaths that have been a direct consequence of the meeting near Minsk. Not everyone can manage such an easygoing attitude. The widespread nostalgia of the Russian population is hardly surprising. Many are amazed at the number of people voting for Communists, and at the enduring love for symbols and signs of the past. Thus, for instance, after the popular wave of returning the old, prerevolutionary names to Russian cities and towns, we now witness the reverse process: recently I found out that the city of Kirov (named after the Communist leader murdered by Stalin in 1934) voted against returning to its old name Viatka. Ninety-eight percent of the population wanted to retain the name Kirov! Those who are surprised by this ask: "Do you really want the return of communism: prisons, torture, arrests, hunger, the Iron Curtain?" The answer is: "No, we want communism: i.e., cheap food, unrestricted passage through the country, peaceful towns, and on the streets, girls in summer dresses and not people armed with Kalashnikovs."

The truth is that communism was both of these things, and some people saw only its dark side, while others, more simple, were content with the rosy side. When it's dark ahead, you feel like turning back: memory obligingly illumines only the bright spots. When people nostalgically recall the peaceful, stagnant 1970s, flourishing Georgia, safe Tajikistan; when they prefer this and people tell them that they are imperialists—what should they think? I myself, a person who hardly harbors any sympathy for communism, also enjoy recalling 1980, when I worked in a publishing house and Vladislav Ardzinba, the current president of Abkhazia, published a book with us and the only person he was afraid of was an editor named Natasha—a fierce woman who made him rewrite his footnotes three times. Back then his hands were covered in ink; now they're covered in Georgian blood and he is called a nationalist. And what am I, an imperialist? Does it really matter? Let's drink to Gorbachev, but not to Solzhenitsyn.

Recently Americans have not shown much interest in what is

going on in Russia. The press reflects — or perhaps initiates? — this oblivion. David Remnick, a wonderful connoisseur of Russian reality and a tireless traveler of her political labyrinths, recognizes the danger in this attitude, and in his new book he warns against the indifference that has gripped the American press and American society: "This is a serious mistake, for the process of creating a new country — a country that will undoubtedly reassert itself in every sense in the twenty-first century — is at least as interesting, as essential, as the process of erosion and collapse."

Let's hope that his appeal will be heard.

1997

Dreams of Russia,
Dreams of France

Review of *Dreams of My Russian Summers,* by Andreï Makine, translated
from the French by Geoffrey Strachan (Arcade, 1997)

R USSIAN LITERATURE may take pride in a strange success: Andreï Makine, a Russian of indeterminate French
origin, was awarded two of the most prestigious literary
prizes for a book written in French, in France, and about France
—a book which is nonetheless quintessentially Russian. In our
time, it seems you have to be born Russian and spend thirty
years of your life in Russia, a country where cruelty and reverie
form a paradoxical unity (this, of course, is a cliché, but like all
clichés, it's true) in order to hallucinate with such power and
passion, in order to create a fabulous country—a nonexistent
France—from words and dreams.

On first glance (but only on first), this France is the subject
of Makine's book. The author created a stir in 1995: he was the
only French writer (and he wasn't even French, for that matter!)
to have ever been awarded the country's two highest literary
awards for one and the same book: the Prix Goncourt and the
Prix Médicis, as well as the "Lycée Goncourt," which is awarded
by students. How the prizes were awarded is a detective story in
its own right: Makine's books were rejected by French publish-

ers; the writer lived in poverty, half-starving, slept at night in a cemetery crypt, wrote his books sitting on park benches. Finally, driven to despair, he passed off one of his original French-language books as a translation from the Russian—and only then was any attention paid to it. Nonetheless, fame eluded him, and Makine came up against unexpected difficulties. For example, the publisher of his second book demanded to see the original Russian, which, of course, didn't exist, and Makine was obliged to quickly translate his own work into Russian. Finally, the author's third novel—the subject of this review—was noticed by Gallimard, published, and it collected all the honors imaginable. A foreigner! *L'Étranger!*

Russian vanity is, of course, flattered by this very pleasant scandal.

Dreams of France are an old Russian tradition. A Frenchman doesn't dream of France for obvious reasons: he lives there. Other foreigners, if they dream, are pragmatic: you can save your money and take a trip. The Russian, locked up for decades behind the Iron Curtain (in a country constructed from dozens of other countries and yet unified), in a country where not even all its cities are open to its own citizens, and sometimes are not even marked on the map, a country of secrets and taboos, locked doors and underground secret railways, a country of fences and suspicious glances—the Russian has developed a capacity for reverie unlike anyone else's. The climate, the regime, and the huge distances facilitate lethargy and dreams. There, beyond the horizon, beyond the undulating steppe or the forests of fir trees, beyond the endless snowy expanses, far, far away, there is, of course, the marvelous country of Paris: not so much France as Paris. There they have boulevards and fashion, artists and lovers, cheese and poetry, gallantry and wit, culture and philosophy, and above all a language unbelievably beautiful and melodious. It was not by chance that throughout the nineteenth century French was for Russia the language of education, a mark of belonging to the upper classes; it was not by chance that after the catastrophe of 1917, millions of Russians sought sanctuary in France. Later, after the fall of the Iron Curtain, practical Russians left for America, idealists for France. "Well, what is Paris like?" I asked a poet friend in 1987 who had just spent a week in Paris for the first time in his life. "It's exactly what we think it is" was the answer. (This doesn't mean that we are right in what we think about Paris. It just means that Paris corresponds to all dreams of it, that it disappoints no expectation.)

The almost nameless narrator (his name—Alyosha—appears only once, and even then nearly at the end of the book), whose biography in many ways runs parallel to the author's, spends every summer of his childhood in a small Russian town, almost a village, on the steppe, with his French grandmother. He and his sister, who also is not named in the book, sit on the flower-entwined balcony every day, in the shadow of a lamp with a turquoise shade, and, dreamy and relatively obedient children that they are, listen entranced to their grandmother's stories of France (Paris and its environs) at the time of the Belle Époque and the beginning of our century—in French. The narrator is not a child but a grown man, recalling his childhood in complex, adult language much influenced by Proust, whose presence in the narrative is noted both by the epigraph that opens the book and by references to Marcel himself, who plays tennis in Neuilly-sur-Seine.

The nameless children, strangely indifferent to their nameless parents, spend every summer in a nonexistent world: there are none of the childhood games, friends, fights, or childhood dramas we all know. Their toys: a memorial collection of Grandmother's pebbles, each of which has a name—for instance, Verdun is an iron-colored shard given to Grandmother by an officer in World War I. The children's living space is the balcony and, only occasionally, the courtyard, which is alien to them, inhabited by frightened babushkas and filled with the shouts of a local drunkard. The warm breath of the Volga steppes, the fragrance of flowers, the rustle of brittle newspaper clippings that Grandmother retrieves from her trunk, the music of the French language, of French poems, yellowed photographs of a bygone time—this is their enchanted country. Each evening, when Grandmother sits down on the balcony, eternally mending the same lace blouse, and the children fall silent at her feet, harking to the murmur of foreign speech, the world is transformed: the melodious sounds of French have the power to evoke visual hallucinations.

> It was above the line of the horizon that we discerned a pale reflection—it was like the sparkle of little waves on the surface of a river. Incredulous, we peered into the darkness that surged over our flying balcony. Yes, far away on the steppe there shone an expanse of water, rising, spreading the bitter cold of the great rains. The sheet seemed to be lightening steadily, with a dull, wintry glow.
>
> Now we saw emerging from this fantastic tide the black masses of apartment blocks, the spires of cathedrals, the posts of street lamps—a city! Gigantic, harmonious despite the waters that flooded its avenues, a ghost city was emerging before our eyes.

A mirage of the steppe? No, it's the magic power of a child's imagination at work—the boy hasn't noticed that Grandmother has been telling the story of the Paris flood of 1910 to the quiet children for some time.

The children, entranced, read the menu of a dinner given by the president of France in honor of the arrival of the Russian tsar Nicholas II in 1896—unheard-of, incomprehensible dishes, engaging not so much for their promise of gastronomic delight (what could the children know of this?) as for the very sound of the words, magical formulas that grant access to an enchanted kingdom of red *bartavelles*—rock partridges—and ortolans. And later, for the narrator-adolescent, these magical words will be the mysterious consolation of a hidden knowledge, when the crude Soviet crowd pushes him and his sister out of a line for prosaic oranges, which were in short supply anyway. Well, so the young people didn't get any oranges, they were injured and humiliated, but they have what no one can buy or take away— *bartavelles* and ortolans, the keys to an enchanted country!

> As I looked at her pale face with the winter sky reflected in her eyes, I felt my lungs fill with an entirely new air—that of Cherbourg—with the smell of salt mist, of wet pebbles on the beach, and the echoing cries of seagulls over the endless ocean.

The Paris flood, and the arrival in France of Nicholas II, and the death in 1899 of the French president François-Félix Faure in the embrace of his lover are unrelated events joined by no chronological thread other than the make-believe one of narrative. But these are the events around which the universe of the dreamy narrator turns. And the center of this universe is the grandmother, Charlotte Lemonnier. How did she end up in Russia? Her father, a Frenchman, worked as a doctor in a Siberian city before the October revolution—a fairly common situation: Russia has always been home to lots of foreigners. After the death of Charlotte's father, her mother didn't want, or wasn't able, to return to France (there were some family problems; here the narrator obscures things), and, weak-willed and alone, she became a morphine addict. Each year, Charlotte's mother traveled to France with her daughter, and the girl found herself in a completely different world utterly unlike that of the impoverished Siberian town. One fine day, the mother decided to remain in her native France after all and, leaving her daughter in Neuilly, returned to Russia for her things. It was 1914, World War I had begun. Charlotte next saw her mother in 1921, when she went off to look for her; she didn't immediately recognize the old woman when she found her hunched over a pile of kindling in the courtyard. Charlotte returned to Russia—and fell into a trap. Russia's doors slammed shut and she never saw France again. From then on France became a myth. Grandmother Charlotte transmits this myth to her grandchildren.

Charlotte's Russian life is terrifying, and along with a knowledge of France, the grandson learns the truth about the horrors of Russian history as well: the brutality, the prisons, cruelty, concentration camps, early deaths, lawlessness. As the novel's action moves forward and the narrator matures, France and Russia become intertwined in a fantastical pattern of irreconcilable elements. He himself is both Russian and French. If in childhood he is more French, a dreamer, a visionary, then, in maturing, he becomes more and more Russian: his reverie alienates him from his surroundings, his knowledge and tales of France provoke bewilderment and ridicule; he is ultimately ashamed of his awkward situation among his peers. But every summer he returns to his grandmother, to the almost irreal balcony entwined with flowers, hanging over the steppe, in the last house on the edge of the inhabited world, to listen once again to the stories of things that exist nowhere. Is it imaginary France that draws him, or his grandmother as the incarnation of that France?

Grandmother is also a beauty (descriptions of her face and figure recur frequently); grandmother is a sorceress (she survives the most terrible circumstances — war, hunger, a march on foot across half of Russia); grandmother is an animal tamer (she calms a threatening drunk; an exhausted peasant woman turns to her to rest and, overcoming the class and ethnic hostility that one might have expected, lies down on the floor of grandmother's apartment, arms outstretched — a strange scene that can only be understood symbolically, not as a real event). Grandmother is also a poisoner: she permanently infected the boy with a dangerous reverie, she split his consciousness, so that he feels French among Russians, an eccentric, an outcast, forever and endlessly other. The narrator comes to revolt against Grandmother: his parents (faceless, nameless) are dying during his adolescence. How dare she outlive them! Why is she stronger?

He no longer wants to be French, he protests. The more horrible the truths he learns about Russian life as he grows older, the more Russian he feels. He develops a strange adoration for this barbaric, wild, cruel country. Charlotte turns out to be stronger than his revolt against her, she is stronger than everyone in this story. She lives through the death of her mother, husband, and daughter—just as, her horrified grandson finds out, she lived through a rape. As a result of this rape, she gave birth to a son by the Uzbek rapist. The narrator's uncle is an intelligent, quiet boy with noticeably Eastern features.

And at some point in the story we notice the strangest thing of all: the grandmother—is Russia herself. Raped (by a criminal), loving (her husband), tormented by her adopted country and incapable of leaving it (and not wanting to), accepting both her children equally—the offspring of her beloved husband and of her rapist—she refuses to die. She carries with her throughout her life a dream of France like a fairy tale told of some far-off, imaginary, nonexistent place. The grandmother incarnates everything in Russian fate: filth, love, dreams, absolution, patience, saintliness, torment. The narrator (at the end of the novel) manages to escape to France and tries to become a writer there. He wants to finally bring Charlotte to Paris—when he receives word that she has died.

A year after her death, the narrator receives a letter from her. Yes, there is a certain "mystery" element in the novel, a turn of the plot I don't want to write about, so as not to ruin the reader's pleasure.

Makine's book is deeply, densely symbolic, even allegorical. There are wonderful scenes built on allegories. Thus, the adolescent narrator, tormented by awakening sexual curiosity, sees a prostitute bringing two clients to an old boat, and the boy, amazed by the secrets of adult behavior, watches through different portholes. Through one he sees the crude physiological details of fornication, the mechanical movement of bodies (the participants couple in a kneeling position); and through the other window he sees the indifferent face of the prostitute, touched with the boredom of the everyday—she even scrapes the polish off her nails. He looks through the first window again, and then through the second.

The sense of two layers of a single existence being cut off, divided, disconnected (everything depends on which window you look through) is symbolized in this and other scenes, although this is its most graphic expression. Having grasped the author's symbolic device, one can see an analogous conflict (a simultaneous merging and disengaging) in almost any scene, passage, character, or turn in the plot. Once you discern this, the prose becomes much more meaningful, the reader's interest more justified, and those parts of the narrative that might have seemed tedious are suddenly presented in a new, engaging light. The flow of the narrative on the surface seems too monotonous at times, and the action too slow: it spins in one place, as if it didn't have the strength to break away from Charlotte's gravitational pull. That is, in fact, what's going on: Charlotte is Russia—the mysterious captured princess at the center of the writer's universe.

As far as I know, none of the reviewers of this book has noticed this obvious and profound meaning, has bothered to dip below the surface of the book's glinting, moiré, very French, very "stylized" surface. Hence the mistakes and perplexed questions of a largely favorable press. One reviewer regrets that the image of the sister wasn't developed further (although all the rest of the characters in the book are deliberately blurred, fragmentary, functioning mostly as "furniture"), another imagines that the Volga steppes are in the Ukraine, and many stubbornly call the book "Dreams of My Siberian Summers," latching onto the word "Siberia," which is often repeated but has little to do with the narrator's childhood—Siberia was where Grandmother spent her childhood, but the narrator lived in European Russia! This mistake is produced by the reviewers' own reveries, for they generally have as vague an idea of Russian geography as the narrator of this book has of the geography of France.

Most of those writing about *Dreams of My Russian Summers* agree that it is a love story. This is, of course, true, but the love in it is stranger and more profound than an ordinary love for a woman: it is the inexplicable, unshared, tortuous love for Russia and, perhaps, for what is traditionally considered Russia's "feminine" being. People run away from a love like this, as did the writer. They try to save themselves, they fail; they curse, write, and sing about it; finally they receive awards in their invented, overseas kingdom.

1997

History in Photographs

Review of *The Commissar Vanishes: The Falsification of Photographs and Art in Stalin's Russia,* by David King (Metropolitan Books, 1997), and *Eyewitness to History: The Photographs of Yevgeny Khaldei,* with a biographical essay by Alexander Nakhimovsky and Alice Nakhimovsky (Aperture, 1997)

AT ONE TIME or another every kid draws a mustache or eyeglasses on a portrait in a history textbook. Men are usually decorated with beads, earrings, fluffy curls, bow-tie lips, a deep, ample décolletage, and, space permitting, a crinoline. Women are provided with a five-day beard, scars, a pirate eyepatch, and a burning cigarette stuck between their teeth. My history book looked more like an illustration of the Venetian carnival than a text. This long-forgotten, thirty-year-old pleasure held nothing insidious: as I see it now, awakening sexual curiosity and awareness of the difference between the sexes drew a thirteen-year-old child into a creative game. It was all dressing up, theater, carnivalizing, the testing of borders, changing social roles.

At that age we have an easygoing attitude toward ourselves: we're perfectly happy to be photographed with our tongues sticking out or our eyes crossed. As we grow older, our relationship to our own image is more often characterized by alarm and suspicion: How fat I look there! Hide that photograph! Eventually some of us turn to direct interference with the past. (Why is this photo cropped? And whose arm is around your shoulders? Oh, that's an old friend. We had a fight, I got mad and cut him out of the picture.) And at some point in life, we realize that certain photographs (our own photos!) could be compromising evidence. We wish they had never existed. And in those shots we allow to exist, we may ask the photographer to remove the bags under our eyes and the shadow under our noses.

All this is the harmless mischief of private life. Who are we, after all? Just people. But what if we were tyrants with limitless power?

David King's album of photographs opens with a large, three-quarter, color portrait of Stalin by the artist Andreyev in 1922, that is, while Lenin was still alive. This very realistic portrait is at once strangely competent and inept: the artist seems to have trouble with the contours, part of the forehead seems dead, the hair glued on, the proportion of the head is wrong. But the skin, the wrinkles, the heavy Caucasus beard, which seems literally to crawl across the face like a shadow and thicken into blackness at the nose, are ably drawn. There's no sense of flattery in the portrait, other than perhaps a bit of politeness vis-à-vis the bosses.

Here Stalin looks older than his forty-two years. He's not yet in power, but in the expression of his eyes and mouth you can read hidden expectations and caution. Did the future dictator like this portrait? The reproduction has preserved the surprising comments of the "marvelous Georgian" (as Lenin called Stalin): "This ear speaks of the artist's discomfort with anatomy." And again: "The ear cries out, shouts against anatomy." And the ear itself (an ordinary, unremarkable ear) is marked by a fat red cross!

This extraordinary illustration, strategically placed at the very beginning of the album, sets the ominous tone for 192 pages of photographs, abundant historical notes, and the grim humor of the text. The album is devoted to the way in which, throughout the Soviet period but particularly under Stalin, history in its photographic incarnation was changed, distorted, corrected, and cleaned up to the point of unrecognizability. It shows how people disappeared from photographs one by one in accordance with political necessity, leaving a hole in space, a seemingly inexplicable gap in a crowded row of colleagues.

The empty space once occupied by the disappeared person is filled either with a whitish smoke, or a black spot, or sometimes a sudden outgrowth of bushes or an unexpected antique column. Sometimes the disappeared seem to clutch at those remaining; they don't want to fade into nonexistence. And then an attentive gaze, aided by a magnifying glass, can make out here and there either an aborted shoulder (like a slight swelling on the neck of a figure left in the picture), or a knee (sticking out of the folds of someone else's clothes), or a strange luminescence where someone once stood. And do we need to explain that the people scratched out of the photographs were just as ruthlessly and tracelessly scratched out of life, were destroyed in the Gulag, transformed into "camp dust," in the expression of the era's executioners? Do we need to remind the reader that their wives, children, and parents were also turned to dust?

David King has done a remarkable, meticulous job gathering a huge photographic archive of the Soviet period consisting of originals and their many, diverse reincarnations. *The Commissar Vanishes* contains only a part of this archive. That the falsification of photographs under Stalin (and later, too) was an inevitable and well-established practice is a well-known fact, but when you see with your own eyes the scale and tendencies of this falsification, you are struck dumb. Trotsky never existed, nor did Zinoviev and Kamenev; they didn't participate in anything; Sverdlov never had a brother named Zinovy; Bazarov, Avanesov, Balabanov, Khalatov, Mekhonoshin, Karakhan, Radek, Bukharin, Lashevich, Zorin, Roi, Belenkii, Petrovsky,

Smirnov, Rykov, Bubnov, Skrypnik, Antipov, Tomsky, Rudzu-tak, Peters, Yenukidze—all of them never existed. If some of these names are unfamiliar, you may well wonder why.

The double-headed eagle on the front of the Bolshoi Theater disappears, as does a crowd of rich peasants, entire regiments of soldiers, a crowd of thousands (glued in their place are tens of thousands bursting with revolutionary enthusiasm). Lenin didn't spend the last two years of his life paralyzed, smiling the smile of a holy fool, but was active and healthy until his last breath. Stalin was always at his side on important trips, always present when important decisions were made; they basically worked as equals. But what are we talking about? It was Stalin who directed the revolution and the building of the Soviet state, while Lenin just added the final touches. Like an awkward schoolboy or a loving parent, he listened to Stalin's wise advice with interest and admiration and was constantly amazed at the perspicacity of the Georgian genius. It's not surprising that a passerby pointing his finger disappears from one completely innocent photograph; he seemed to be showing Stalin the right direction, but Stalin will find the road himself, thank you very much. (Are you still alive, passerby?)

People staring as the Politburo crosses the garbage-strewn expanses of Red Square disappear. The garbage disappears as well (page 125). Nature itself becomes cleaner (after all, the Leader is passing by), is swathed in a veil of pink fog, an unseen light pours from somewhere behind Stalin's back, the tyrant's face glows, grows younger, his hair darkens and smoothes out, his shoulders widen, the wrinkles disappear, he grows in height and stature, as if bathed in magic milk from the source of eternal youth (pages 146, 150, 167).

At the same time, there is a series of portraits in which he seems to become not older (he acquires a slight, noble dusting of gray hair) but endlessly wiser, with a hint of exhaustion in the eyes (after all, he broke the back of Fascism and seized half of Europe with his own two hands) (page 173). Finally, by his seventieth birthday he is incorporeal, immortal, and enlightened, like the Buddha. In the crossed rays of spotlights, his image shines in the nocturnal Moscow sky, endlessly magnificent, in a general's cap and epaulets against the heavy December clouds (page 175).

Looking at the photographs and fantastical drawings that Stalin approved (where he is wise and glowing, the most important person present), and comparing them with the originals (where he is small and cunning, pockmarked and swarthy, lost in the crowd), you can't help but wonder about the portrait with the crossed-out ear. What was it about that ear? Why such rage, such sarcasm (he shouts and yells), such poison? The aged, rough skin, the cautious look directed inward, the darkness pouring across the face — are these mere trifles? Yet the ear, which people are not likely to notice, provoked not one but two sarcastic comments. He doesn't understand anatomy. Shouldn't the artist be shot? Stalin doesn't yet have the power to do this. But soon he will.

Ears are curious things. First of all, we don't know our own ears, we don't really even see them in the mirror unless we make a special effort. Second, we don't control our ears. Unlike our eyes and mouth and hair, we can't change them with cosmetics or mustaches or beards. Third, it's thought that the form of the ear is just as unique and individual as fingerprints, and there are branches of criminology that study ears from this particular point of view. Fourth, there's a proverb whose meaning can be summarized as: You can recognize an animal by his ears, his ears give him away (a wolf or a donkey). King Midas has donkey's ears! There is, in particular, a Georgian (!) fairy tale about a king whose ears turned into a donkey's — long hairy animal ears — and the king hides them under a scarf. A barber accidentally learns the king's secret and is tormented by the desire to tell the whole world about it, but he is bound by fear and an oath. In the end, he shouts out the truth into a hollow reed; then a shepherd passes by, makes a flute out of the reed, plays it, and the flute cries out to the whole world: The king has donkey's ears! One imagines that Stalin, with the instinct of a born tyrant, smelled an as yet unspecified danger of exposure with some animal sense, and sounded the alarm.

Soon he started destroying people by the millions. People turned out to be secret enemies and were eliminated; one was supposed to curse them and applaud. Why pretend that those destroyed never existed if everyone remembers that they did? Why, instead of simply settling accounts with vanquished enemies and collecting their skulls, was it necessary to make believe that the enemies had never really existed? It seems to me that besides the obvious reasons (the desire to attribute all good to oneself, elevate oneself to the status of God, and so on), the tyrant's dark soul was troubled by mystical, irrational notions as well. There is an old rule of magic: evocation calls forth epiphanies, that is, speaking a name brings forth the spirit, the demon, the divinity; thus, God's name must not be spoken in vain; thus, religious people speak of the devil indirectly, using nicknames; thus, in many languages the names of frightening creatures (bears, wolves, snakes) are constantly replaced with euphemisms, and they, in turn, with new euphemisms. This is the source of the ban on depicting God, and the source of blasphemy when God's image is destroyed or distorted; this explains the jealous destruction of icons after the 1917 revolution, and their equally jealous conservation. Hence the hatred with which early Christians hammered away at the marble faces of pagan sculptures. The motivation here is not that "this never was" but that "this will never again be," a purge not so much of the past as of the future. Which makes it even more frightening.

This partly explains, as David King relates, why the libraries were purged not only of books by and about Trotsky but of anti-Trotskyite literature as well: titles like *Trotskyists: Enemies of the People* or *Trotskyist-Bukharinist Bandits* (page 10) simply disappeared. In this respect, the most extraordinary material in David King's book is perhaps the six pages (pages 128–133) showing people in jackets, shirts, ties, but without faces; instead we see squares and circles of blackness. The artist Alexander Rodchenko painted over the pages of a book that he himself had designed; the figures in the book (Party workers) had fallen into disgrace (i.e., they were killed by the NKVD), and therefore the artist (in fear or disgust?) ritually, symbolically, covered their faces and names with darkness.

Armed with a magnifying glass to better see the details, the reader can make amazing discoveries on his own. On pages 46–48, for instance, we see two photographs taken at an interval of perhaps thirty seconds. In one, the collar of a man's coat is white with snow; in the other, it is completely black, as if his personal weather had changed. Comparing the shots, we see that the retouchers forgot to draw the snow on his shoulders, so engaged were they in destroying the figure that formerly stood in the place of this atmospheric miracle. Often, looking for the traces of the photo censor's awkward work, you can't help but react as Stalin did: these hands (legs, jackets, this lighting, furniture, etc.) cry out, shout against the laws of nature! The difference, ironically, is that Stalin was infuriated by a real ear, while we are amused by artificial limbs, the product of unknown masters.

In addition to photographs, a fair amount of art is presented in King's album as well: engravings, oil paintings, rugs, sculptures. The quality is horrible, the subjects are comic. But the laughter sticks in your throat when you remember the scale of the tragedy. This extraordinary combination of tragedy and farce, which evokes strong, mixed emotions, makes King's album a work of art.

But what is art, and specifically, what is the art of documentary photography? And more specifically, what degree of lie is permissible in this border zone where the artist and reality are separated for a moment by the camera lens? Another book, *Eyewitness to History*, is an attempt to comment on this question. It is a small collection of photographs by the Soviet photographer

Yevgeny Khaldei, who worked for the Tass news agency and the newspaper *Pravda* (and who died this October, after the book was published). His photographs of World War II are known worldwide and have been reproduced many times, often anonymously, by the state agency Sovfoto, as the authors of the book's biographical essay inform us. This album leaves a strange impression: it seems that its authors were torn between the idea of an anniversary gift (Khaldei turned eighty in March 1997) and an attempt to undertake an artistic study of his work, with inevitably negative results for the photographer.

If we are to believe the biographers, Khaldei's own life is typical, tragic, and extraordinary. He was born in the Ukraine into a poor Jewish family. His mother died during a pogrom in 1918; the bullet that passed through her body lodged in the body of her year-old son. (Two decades later the Germans destroyed the photographer's entire family: his father, grandparents, and sister.) Khaldei received only four grades of schooling; poverty forced him to go to work. Obviously a gifted artist from birth, he made his first camera himself and took photographs from an early age. He went through the entire war with a camera, capturing extraordinary scenes, some of which he staged himself, such as the famous picture of the Soviet flag being raised over the Reichstag. Despite his significant contribution to Soviet art, he lost his job twice, in 1948 and 1976, during anti-Semitic government campaigns.

Khaldei's best photographs are definitely from the war period. Some of them in this book have never before been published, for reasons of censorship, and undoubtedly have both artistic and documentary interest. This justifies the album. The shots taken before and after the war seem to belong to an entirely different person and are among the worst examples of Socialist Realism. Understanding this, and constantly justifying themselves, the book's editors seem to be trying to lessen the photographer's guilt by reproducing these pictures at a very small size, as if to say: no, no, this never existed! (But they did exist, didn't they? Yes, they did, but they were verrrrry small!)

These efforts and excuses are pointless: Khaldei's prewar photographs are marvelous in their own way and deserve decent reproduction. Looking at the extraordinary cover of lies thrown over the revolting truth of socialism, the viewer sees several dimensions of reality simultaneously: the artist's talent; the totalitarian coercion to which he was subject; and the truth that filters through the lie. The decision to publish inconvenient photographs at matchbox size reminds us of the work of the anonymous retouchers in King's album.

Khaldei's postwar photographs are truly awful. Here the compilers of the album, inspired no doubt by political correctness, permitted themselves to stand tall: after all, these are portraits of Rostropovich, Shostakovich, Akhmatova, Marshal Zhukov! The correct choice of subject matter is meant to justify the photographer, although these saccharine, official, dead, staged frames seem to have been done not by the lively Khaldei of the wartime storm but by his corpse, a Party zombie with no soul and empty eyes. Rostropovich, pretending to hold his bow (page 90), is indistinguishable from the fake workers pretending to read *Pravda* (page 89) in a photograph where the worker holds a copy of the newspaper but that's not enough for him: he enviously glances over at the copy his comrade is holding!

Congratulating Khaldei on his eightieth birthday, the authors acknowledge with some embarrassment that it never occurred to the photographer to do uncommissioned work, that he was never drawn to capturing real problems, though life presented them in abundance. For this reason, the concluding words of the biographical essay, "a man of rare soul," leave the reader somewhat perplexed. That he had a soul is without doubt; it spread its wings during the war years and, after that, got lost somewhere amid the cheap cardboard and sweet-smelling glue of Soviet props.

The editors' language adds to the awkward impression. "On October 31, they got some wine, salami, and candy, went to the registry, and then celebrated the marriage in Svetlana's room.

Soon after, they had a daughter, Anna, and a son, Leonid. Svet-lana died in 1986." I think this must set a record for short de-scriptions of a human life. Navigation through the album is dif-ficult, since references to page numbers are abundant but the full-bleed pages are unnumbered. The reader soon realizes that his hands are trapped: in order to look at the book the way the authors intended, he must keep all of the fingers of one hand stuck between the pages, try to turn the pages of the resulting fan with the other hand, count aloud at the same time (18, 19, 20, 21), and, losing count, start all over again.

However, I don't want to end the review of such a curious album on a negative note. The patient reader (as well as those endowed by nature with fourteen fingers) will find many amus-ing scenes in the book (and will once again remember King's in-comparable volume). Thus, for instance, on pages 60–61 (I think) one of Khaldei's wonderful photographs is reproduced: a Russian soldier raises the red Soviet banner on the top of the Re-ichstag, at a head-spinning height. An officer holds him by the leg so he won't fall. The officer is wearing a watch. After the photograph was taken and printed, the authors tell us, the cen-sor's careful gaze detected two watches on the officer in the orig-inal photograph, i.e., the officer had stolen at least one of the watches and had obviously been pillaging. The watch had to be scraped off the photograph! And where did the famous red banner come from? It turns out that Khaldei, in preparation for his famous shot, prudently brought three banners from Mos-cow for hanging in strategic places. These banners were sewn by a friend of his, a Moscow tailor, from red tablecloths sto-len, in turn, from Soviet organizations. One guy hangs up a stolen tablecloth, the other holds him with hands wearing sto-len watches! But the stealing doesn't stop here: Comrade Stalin didn't like the fact that the soldier was Ukrainian, and he gave the award to other people — one Russian and one Georgian!

1998

The Price of Eggs

WHEN I OPENED the newspaper on the morning of August 17, I saw the headline "Market Crashes." I'm not an economist and understand nothing of the enigmatic world of money. For me, the word "market" means open-air stands where old ladies from villages near Moscow sell cheap freshly picked mushrooms, garlic, potatoes, and dill, and men from the Caucasus whose teeth are capped in gold for the beauty and prestige of it offer unbelievably expensive peaches and a spicy sauce called *adzhika*—you taste a drop and flames leap out of your mouth. Reading the words "Market Crashes," I imagined dilapidated wooden stands collapsing and velvety peaches rolling across wet asphalt in consort with escaping potatoes.

Nonetheless I stopped in my tracks. No serious newspaper ever covers such trivial events on the front page. I called a friend, an English businessman. "Simon," I said, "they're writing that the market has crashed. Can you explain what this means?" Simon explained the default of the Russian government in paying its debts so professionally and in such detail that I understood virtually nothing. "So what should I do?"

"I'd get my money out of the bank, just in case," said Simon.

I got back on the phone and called all my relatives and friends—people even more naive than I am with respect to financial matters, and ordered them to take their money out of the bank.

"What do you mean?" they asked, clearly reluctant. "We just put it in there."

"No back talk! Simon says. Get your money out."

"Who is Simon?"

"It doesn't matter!" Simon actually saved several people from losing everything—I'm sure he'll be rewarded in the next world. In the first two days of the crisis, it was still possible to withdraw money from your account. We managed to do so. The only problem was what to do with it once we had it.

By the beginning of September, the crisis in Russia had already emptied pockets and store shelves. I dropped in to see a girlfriend and found her small children dressed in tutus and eating black caviar as if it were porridge.

"Have you all gone mad?" I asked.

"Not at all," my friend replied. "It's just that all our regular clothes are dirty and you can't get laundry detergent anywhere. And caviar is cheaper than anything else at the moment. I can't afford cheese anymore, can I?"

And she was absolutely right. The strangeness of the situation was that Russian-produced delicacies had suddenly become "bargains." Caviar didn't get cheaper, of course, but it didn't go up in price either, and psychologically it went down three or four times relative to the ruble-dollar exchange rate. All imported goods, on the other hand, tripled or quadrupled in price. The exchange rate of the dollar jumped up and down, but prices only went up, reaching mind-boggling heights: merchants included the cost of possible future losses in their prices, just in case one fine morning they woke up and the exchange rate, which had been somewhere between ten and eighteen rubles to the dollar, suddenly soared to fifty. There were rumors that this might happen. And why not? The central currency exchange closed several times without setting any rate, and stores simply slammed their doors in despair: the owners didn't know what to think or do. Other shops kept their doors open, but signs next to appealing goods on the shelves read NOT FOR SALE.

Those lucky people who managed to get their last paycheck,

or withdraw their money from the bank before it closed, ran back and forth between stores and exchange booths, trying to figure out what made more sense: should they buy up reserves of salt, sugar, and flour to make it through the winter? Change rubles into dollars, go into hibernation, and wait for better times? Or buy yet another television while it was still possible? But salt, flour, soap, and toilet paper had already been bought up by the poorest, most distrusting and enterprising part of the population. And if you changed all of your rubles into dollars, you could end up in the position of King Midas, who turned everything to gold and died of hunger: after all, the stores don't accept dollars—the dollar is a fiction, a "theoretical unit." Moreover, as soon as it was to your advantage to buy dollars, they were no longer for sale, the exchange booths were closed. They opened up only as soon as using them was no longer advantageous. There was one point at which the dollar cost ten rubles one day, twenty the next, and then dropped back down to ten. In theory, you could have doubled your capital, but I don't know a single soul who did. People were confused, and anyway they didn't have the cash for such operations. But one can just imagine the killing made by the people who planned that dip in the exchange rate.

As for buying a television, or any other sort of expensive item, you had to do that before August 26. As it happened, that was the day I decided to buy myself a new vacuum cleaner. There was a kind of vague anxiety in the air, but I didn't give it any thought. I went to the store and inspected the selection. There were as many vacuum cleaners as you could possibly want. Having discussed their relative merits with the salesperson, I decided to think about it a bit and went to another shop that sold dishes, furniture, and lamps. Everything was expensive and not really necessary. There weren't many customers. Guards in dappled uniforms, carrying automatic weapons and cell phones, stood by the doors. Suddenly, as though a breeze passed through the shop, the doors slammed. Worried faces peered out of the offices, bored cashiers suddenly hopped up from their seats and huddled together, whispering and glancing around. The manager ran through and shouted in a muffled voice, "Close up!" The guards immediately chained the doors. What happened? Terrorists? But terrorists could hardly be out to capture electric teapots and Venetian glass chandeliers.

"What's going on?" I said, rushing up to a guard. He waved his hand and ran off, his army boots thumping. Two more people clattered by. A woman squealed quietly.

"But what's going on?!"

"It's crawling," the manager shouted, running in the opposite direction.

"Who, what's crawling?"

"The exchange rate."

The customers all froze in their tracks, like pillars of salt. Then everyone had the same thought simultaneously. We all ran toward the doors: the people with the automatic machine guns let us out, and I ran to get my vacuum cleaner, knowing full well that it was too late. And sure enough: a small crowd was banging on the glass shop doors in vain. "Let us in!"

"We're on technical break!" came the obtuse answer from the same salesperson who just a half-hour earlier had been sweetly convincing me to buy a French vacuum cleaner assembled in Malaysia.

"We know your breaks! Open up! You don't have the right!" yelled someone in the crowd.

"If you know so much then just shut up," the sweet-talking salesman answered rudely. And he disappeared behind the dark glass.

"Bastards!" people in the crowd muttered.

"But what can they do? They aren't the owners."

"Clinton owns the lot of you now!" a communistic-looking old man suddenly grumbled. "You're all in his pocket!"

"What does Clinton have to do with it?"

"That's what he has to do with it! International Zionism!

Clinton and Soros decided to divide up the world. So he's coming to Moscow to make sure they don't steal everything without him." Everyone ignored the old man, but he continued prophesying to our backs.

"Damn, I didn't buy a TV," one woman laughed.

"What's there to watch, anyway? Just that old Chernomyrdin," a man muttered. "I need to stock up on cigarettes." That's right! I ran to the cigarette stand and bought five packs—all that were left—at the old price. I dreaded to think what the new price would be. Then I ran to the next kiosk—it was already empty. I looked around: all down the long commercial street, people were running up to the shop windows, looking in and trying to figure out whether the store was open for business and whether or not the prices had changed. The door of a cosmetics store opened and a woman struggled out—the huge box filled with French perfumes she was carrying began to fall apart. In a fabric store several saleswomen ran along the hanging swaths of silk and tulle, pointing at them with a roll of paper: this is imported, it's no longer for sale. In the furniture store, they roped off armchairs and beds, in effect turning the place into a museum where you could look but couldn't touch. In the food store, a huge worried line formed for fake Italian macaroni (the pasta has a soapy, mother-of-pearl glint and much the same taste) and fake Uncle Ben's rice (also, I think, made of soap, only very old gray soap; normally Russians don't eat it).

A white wedding limousine stood in the middle of the street with its doors wide open: a bouquet of flowers fluttered on the hood; inside it was empty. The car had obviously broken down, but it looked like the bride and groom, hearing on the radio that "it's crawling," had abandoned the car and rushed off—as they were, in veil and patent leather boots—to the nearest shop to buy up whatever they could get their hands on.

When the storm subsided and the seas receded, the pitiful ruins of the Russian economy stuck out on the bared sandbars as if after a shipwreck. Rare domestically produced objects lay here and there like clumps of matted seaweed and empty crab shells: household soap, old-fashioned clothes, crooked furniture, cheap, smelly cigarettes. Suddenly something we all knew but rarely stopped to consider became painfully apparent: we produce virtually nothing. Over seven years of reform, Russia has not managed to manufacture any noticeable consumer goods. All the abundance to which we have become accustomed in recent years was imported: today it's there, tomorrow it's gone. Everything disappeared: screws, lightbulbs, mops, door handles, chairs, pillows, shampoo, wallpaper, yeast, coffee, computers, blankets, and pencils; they disappeared only to return a bit later at inaccessible prices. But for how long? Amid the dirt and junk, our national pearls shone proudly: Kristall vodka and caviar. There was nothing to do but buy a case of vodka and a mountain of caviar and sit down in front of the TV to watch the Chernomyrdin we'd been promised.

From the newspapers, we knew that he was being promoted by Boris Berezovsky, the shadiest and supposedly most dangerous of the oligarchs. Berezovsky controls the ORT television channel, so this channel presented Chernomyrdin as a young unblemished bride who had been out of view for a time but who resurfaced to bring joy to all our hearts. Chernomyrdin alone, so the message went, knows how to save the country from the terrible crisis created by that stupid boy Sergei Kiriyenko and his band of malicious liberals. Chernomyrdin will feed, clothe, and warm us, he'll take care of the elderly and the homeless, give striking miners their back pay. The miners had been on strike for a long time, blocking railways and causing huge losses to the sickly Russian economy. A large delegation of the miners camped out in front of the "White House," home to the government. They demanded money, demanded that unprofitable mines be reopened, demanded a change of government. They were supported by some of the Communists, Berezovsky's absurdly named newspaper, the *Independent Gazette,* and his television station.

The miners have not received their salaries in over a year, but they aren't the only ones. Their problems need to be solved, but they are the problems of the Russian economy as a whole. Many political analysts think that Berezovsky, who facilitated the collapse of this economy, used the miners' strike to pressure Yeltsin and promote Chernomyrdin. He did this so that Chernomyrdin —a proponent of monetary expansion—would begin to print rubles (which could well have been advantageous to Berezovsky in his shadowy dealings) and would prevent the banking reforms that Kiriyenko was about to enact. If Chernomyrdin became prime minister, and later president, how grateful he would be to Berezovsky.

This outline, this explanation of one part of the scenario of the Russian crisis, proposed by "liberal" analysts, may even be true. It is thought that three people basically control the reins of power in Russia: Yeltsin's daughter Tatyana Dyachenko, a strong-willed woman who knows how to influence her father; Valentin Yumashev, the head of the presidential administration, the ghostwriter of Yeltsin's "autobiography," and the man who filters information and controls access to the Patient; and Berezovsky, a sort of late-twentieth-century Rasputin who deftly pulls the puppet strings in his personal interest. Berezovsky is reported to have a large interest in Aeroflot, whose director is none other than Tatyana's brother-in-law, and Berezovsky was, according to the *New York Times,* "one of Yeltsin's major financial backers during the 1996 presidential elections." His power is said in the press to derive in large part from such close financial relations with the Yeltsin family. *Sic transit:* if Rasputin-1917 held the health of the sick tsarevich in his hands and thus could change ministers in the tsar's government as he fancied, Rasputin-1998 can only advise on the ruling family's fortune. The contemporary magician seems for the moment just as invincible as his precursor, however. Poison and bullets were used against Rasputin—and he briefly survived them. Berezovsky was blown up; a chauffeur and a guard died, torn apart by a bomb, but Berezovsky himself emerged from the wreck slightly burned but intact.

So we sat down in front of the TV screen to watch the caring, wise Chernomyrdin, who was being thrust on us as prime minister with such insistence. The candidate was supposed to talk briefly, then answer telephone calls from viewers. He doesn't know how to speak, but most important, there was nothing to say. He muttered something along the lines of "the situation is very complicated, but I'll manage." The phones started ringing. One man called and said in a calm, insulting tone of voice that we hardly need a prime minister who has already ruled for five years and thus is responsible for everything, including the present crisis, which wasn't created by Kiriyenko, after all. "How do you explain all your monkey business?" the man asked in conclusion.

Strangely enough, Chernomyrdin wasn't prepared for this question: it seems no one had reminded him that there are human beings living in our country and that they may have their own opinions. He paled, and then got mad and sort of sputtered. He didn't answer the question. His eyes started popping out—at which point the moderator quickly went on to the next call. "What about the price of eggs?" an energetic old lady shrilled in a demanding voice to the whole country. "No, you tell me, why were eggs three rubles, and now they're three twenty? Are they imported or something? You said that our Russian goods wouldn't be going up! Well? What kind of nonsense is this, that's what I want to know!"

This was the people's genuine voice, the voice of an angry housewife who couldn't have cared less about the significance of the moment. There's a power vacuum in the country, Yeltsin's comatose, the banks are paralyzed, the Communists are rattling sabers, drunken, hungry soldiers are stealing radioactive materials, the Parliament is about to be dissolved, the president's about to be impeached, the market collapsed, investors are fleeing in panic, newspapers are closing; there's chaos in Indonesia, a crisis in Asia, Wall Street is about to crash . . . But what's it to her? A strong, cantankerous breadwinner, long accustomed to standing in lines, to carrying home heavy bags, to counting every kopeck, screamed at this thieving bull with his mindless lust for power, not as an equal, but the way an enraged mama screams at the neighbor's kid who breaks her window: Just wait till I get my hands on him!!! Chernomyrdin had the opportunity to say something human, at least to smile—to pretend that he is truly concerned about the simple needs of simple people. But he hadn't recovered from the previous call. Suddenly he shouted menacingly, straight into the camera, right at the whole country: "No, this is what I have to say! Monkey business! I have serious business, that's what, not monkey business! That's right! Monkey business. That's what I—Right!" And he sputtered again.

"And the price of eggs?" the moderator reminded him gently. Chernomyrdin's cheek twitched, as if a fly had settled there and he wanted to shake it off.

"The market," he growled. "Everything's going up, so they go up, too."

We ate up the national caviar reserves and stared in amazement at the farce that was unfolding before us. Of course, we had seen and heard the candidate before, but that was when he was swathed in the lead apron of power and X rays couldn't penetrate him. Now, however, naked for all to see, he seemed a stupid, stubborn animal, blinded by a thirst for power and revenge. We—the country—looked on in horror: after all, he could become our next president! He didn't even smile. He did nothing to hide his disgust for us. He was like those fourth-rate goods that suddenly became visible after August 26—ugly, useless, smelling bad, made by an indifferent, clumsy idiot. He himself was just such a piece of goods. And he was the one being forced on us with such persistence.

The Parliament voted against Chernomyrdin twice, and Yeltsin—or what was left of him—was ready to nominate him a third time. Had the Parliament voted against the president's candidate a third time, it would automatically have been dissolved. A vote for impeachment would have been its last act;

and by the way, we know that this demand would likely have been considered unconstitutional. Yeltsin had managed to write such a wonderful constitution that it would be almost impossible to impeach him as long as he's alive. So the Parliament was preparing for collective suicide. New elections would have been called, and for at least three months the country would have remained without even a semblance of government — not even a thoroughly corrupt one.

Hatred and disdain for all the authorities seemed to have reached a boiling point. What awaited us? They say that it was just at this moment that Sergei Yastrzhembsky, Yeltsin's press secretary, known for his extraordinary facility in translating "from the presidential into Russian," managed an audience with the president and convinced the Patient to relinquish Chernomyrdin. The Patient agreed to Evgeny Primakov, who was proposed by Grigory Yavlinsky. Enraged, Berezovsky and Tatyana fired Yastrzhembsky. The rest is known: Primakov became the prime minister, bringing in a moldy group of old apparatchiks: Gerashchenko, Maslyukov, and others.

My sister wanted to buy potato starch. Jars of caviar gazed at her from all the store shelves. Kristall vodka twinkled, reflecting the halogen rainbows of the ceiling lamps. There was no starch to be had. Finally, in a shop on the outskirts of Moscow, she caught sight of the sought-after packets, bought up a supply for the winter, and brought them triumphantly home. She opened one package. A strange gray substance rather like pumice greeted her inside the wrapping. She peered carefully at the label. PACKAGED AUGUST 20, 1981. EXPIRATION: USE WITHIN SIX MONTHS.

Back to premarket innocence?

1998

Snow in St. Petersburg

S T. PETERSBURG has one sea, 101 islands, and endless rivers. There's no point in trying to count them: the sky is the source of the most important river — rain. Rain floods the city's canals; it saturates buildings, gardens, earth, and stones. All summer, it falls in a soft drizzle or in torrents. Occasionally there are small interludes during which the inhabitants of Petersburg raise their eyes and discover magical sunsets in maritime hues — green, gold, and violet — and gaze in astonishment at the beauty of their city: its palaces, arches, columns, spires, and cupolas. Everything is spectral, a watery gold trembling in the air and reflected in the waters. But these flashes of light are brief, and the most lasting impression, the image I have carried with me since childhood, is of a snow-filled black-and-white print.

The snow begins to fall in October. People watch for it impatiently, turning repeatedly to look outside. If only it would come! Everyone is tired of the cold rain that taps stupidly on windows and roofs. The houses are so drenched that they seem about to crumble into sand. But then, just as the gloomy sky sinks even lower, there comes the hope that the boring drum of water from the clouds will finally give way to a flurry of . . . and there it goes: tiny dry grains at first, then an exquisitely carved flake, two, three ornate stars, followed by fat fluffs of snow, then more, more, more—a great store of cotton tumbling down.

Pure bliss! Winter! The sky, lightened of its load, brightens and seems to lift. The grimy cornices, roofs, and windowsills are covered instantly: everything vertical is black, everything horizontal white. The city becomes a sketch of itself, a huge map or blueprint that is slightly worn at the corners and intersections—a stage set, the ideal landscape this city was supposed to be. Children race outdoors and tramp across the thin white layer as if it were a blank sheet of paper, leaving behind clear black footprints. Look a little closer and those comments they've stomped out in the snow will be legible; another minute and the footnotes will arrange themselves into a text, an ode to winter, a hymn to freedom.

But the snow collectors have already started out. Frightening censors, they are led by a crazy machine that looks like a lobster with an escalator on its shoulder. A driver peers out with beady eyes while the machine's claws rake in the snow with circular movements. The snow, so new, fresh, free, and precious, is grabbed by the greedy claws and spat back out onto the escalator. From there, it travels up the lobster's shoulder and, pressed into tight clumps, drops into a dump truck that rides quietly along behind the crustacean. The machine, with its metal plow and whirling claws, scrapes along the ground, baring the asphalt—taking away our gift and leaving only blackness behind. The grownups call it a Vuchetich, after a rich Soviet sculptor, a government favorite, who has covered the country with hideous, skyscraper-high monstrosities. He's probably paid by the meter, which is why his statues are so tall; and he rakes in money as fast as the machine collects snow.

The Vuchetich moves on, but the snow keeps falling in its wake. The city slowly recovers from the theft, replenishes itself, emerges whole, stubborn, unconquered, an etching on white paper, as it was forty years ago, during my childhood—a sublime and indifferent engraving, unaffected by any commentary.

1998

Andrei Platonov's Unusual World

Introduction to *The Fierce and Beautiful World*, by Andrei Platonov, translated by Joseph Barnes (New York Review Books, 2000)

ANDREI PLATONOV is an extraordinary writer, perhaps the most brilliant Russian writer of the twentieth century. Very different from any other writer I know of (in a sense he has no literary predecessors), he is still little known to the Western reader, in part because of the extraordinary difficulty of translating his prose, in part because he is not a "proper" writer; he is "different." Platonov never uses the formal elements of narrative—plot, character, denouement, conclusion—in a conventional way. He continually undermines the reader's expectations in the most bizarre manner. In a Platonov story, the reader encounters a range of sensations for which he has no sensory organ—and this organ may or may not develop in the process of reading.

"Woe to the people into whose language Andrei Platonov can be translated," Joseph Brodsky once said. What does this strange statement mean? The great difficulty of understanding Platonov arises from the fact that he created his own peculiar, unique language using only standard Russian, without recourse to a single neologism.

In the story "Dzhan," for example, a poor young woman says to a man who has given her a great deal of money and many expensive gifts, "I will also soon give you presents. Wealth will soon arrive!" The translator renders the last sentence as "I'll be rich soon," but it means something entirely different. In Platonov's odd usage, wealth "will arrive," "will come," flowing out of the stream of time just as the future, the seasons, and changes "will come," without human intervention, on their own. "Wealth," in Platonov's language and system of sensations, is just as much a part of nature as the wind, spring, earthquakes, fate, time, and death. Even if one were to translate this sentence as "wealth will come," the English-language reader wouldn't sense the striking usage, wouldn't see it as a fragment of Platonov's unusual world.

Similar microdeviations from the norm, dislocations of meaning that suddenly reveal other ways of thinking and feeling, can be found in almost every paragraph of Platonov's prose, if not in every sentence. The unique linguistic shifts in the original are so distinctive that it's possible that there is no adequate way to convey them in English (or French, or German). However, if these sorts of subtleties are lost in translation, other elements remain.

Platonov writes as though no one before him had ever written anything, as if he were the first person to take pen to paper. Things that are normally considered secondary often occupy a central place in his work, while "important" events are shunted off somewhere to the periphery. Characters who have no direct relationship to the narrative arise without evident necessity; at first (and even second) glance their role is unclear, and they disappear without warning. Platonov's protagonist is energetically engaged in some important activity that consumes all his strength; then, a mistaken calculation, a blunder, or a catastrophe destroys the fruits of his activity. He remains undeterred, however, and his life is not destroyed: like an ant, or a bee, he immediately begins to rebuild everything from the beginning, enriched by a new understanding of life, a new relationship to it.

At times it seems that Platonov's work was written by a creature from outer space forced to live among us. In his short novel *The Foundation Pit,* a story of collectivization and the impoverishment it brought, he wrote:

> From the age of twenty-five, Engineer Prushevsky had felt the restraint on his consciousness and the end to any further concept of life, as though a dark wall had arisen right up against his sensate mind. And since then he had been in anguish, moving about right next to that wall, and he comforted himself, thinking that in essence they had achieved the very median, true structure of the substance from which the world and people were combined. All essential science was located in front of the wall of his consciousness, and beyond the wall was only a boring place that there was no point in striving to reach. But still, he was curious—had anyone made it onward beyond the wall?
>
> In the distance, suspended and without salvation, shone a dim star, and it would never be any closer. Prushevsky gazed at it through the murky air, time was passing, and he couldn't decide: "Or should I perish?" Prushevsky couldn't see who would need him enough to definitely keep him going until his still far-off death. Instead of hope he had only patience left, and somewhere beyond the sequence of nights, beyond the gardens that withered, blossomed, and perished anew, beyond encountered and passing people, there existed his time, when he'd have to lie down on his bed, turn his face to the wall, and pass away, without having been able to cry.

Perhaps this is how a mythical beast would write if he were to assume human form—some nocturnal creature who hears with his legs, sees with closed eyes, and can smell a creature of the opposite sex a dozen miles away. He uses words awkwardly, incorrectly, he puts them in the wrong place in the sentence, where they don't go. Most important, he tries to convey some other kind or quality of soul with these words, another sense beyond the five familiar senses.

Andrei Platonov was born in 1899 in a small village not far from the town of Voronezh. He was the oldest son of a large, poor, working-class family, and he went to work at an early age in order to help his ten-member family survive. His parents died while he was still young. He worked as a train mechanic, as an assistant foreman in a foundry, and as a journalist at a provincial newspaper. At the same time he began writing poetry, then prose. His youth coincided with the revolution of 1917 and the civil war that followed. The world as he had known it was destroyed in an overwhelming social cataclysm. The "destruction of the old world" and the "construction of the new world" with one's own hands were popular slogans of the era. If the first part of the agenda—destruction, the creation of chaos—was successful; the second part—construction—was a slow, tortured process.

New people rushed onto the scene, new classes that spoke in new voices. The new ideology basically negated the whole foundation of the known world—economics, psychology, law, education, even the laws of nature. The Bolsheviks promised that the new world built by the hands of the formerly oppressed classes would be one of complete and continuous happiness, an earthly paradise. Moreover, it was supposed that the Bolshevik Party—the priestly caste—had some mystical knowledge of how to achieve this happiness. It is easy to see the influence of these ideas in Platonov's stories. His interpretation of them, however, turned out to be so peculiar and unacceptable that he was quickly pushed to the literary margins, and one can only speculate why Platonov was not arrested in the 1930s and did not share the sad fate of many of his colleagues.

Platonov was hardly alone in his enthusiasm for construction, and his ideas did not spring solely from the new Communist ideology. In Russian circles in those years a certain kind of dreamer was common: a person obsessed with grandiose plans for reshaping life on earth and the world itself. Whether envisaging social changes (the creation of paradise on earth, a society of equality and abundance) or mastery of nature's secrets, the Russian dreamer always thinks big. It won't do to make yourself and your family happy; you inevitably have to do it for all humanity. It's not enough to harness a stream or a horse to work for the common good, one must bridle the sun, the stars, the entire universe.

Characteristic of the Russian dreamer's mentality are impatience, a very particular sort of impracticality, disdain for exactitude, and dismissal of details. How can you worry about details when humanity is faced with an urgent task—for instance, how to achieve instant immortality for all! A Westerner might choose to invent some modest, marvelously conceived gadget that actually works, and then organize mass production of a multitude of identical, marvelous working gadgets. A Russian, on the other hand, consumed by a fever of grandiose, poorly thought out plans, will build something huge, ambitious, and unprecedented—which fails to work. The light bulb that Edison lit is still burning, but in Siberia, one "project of the century" after another is in ruins. Thousands of miles of railroad are rusty and overgrown with weeds: they built the railway and only later realized it had nowhere to go and nothing to transport. The greatness of Russian thought lies not in its precision but in its scale, not in the details but in the strength, not in the realization but in the idea.

It is no accident that many of Platonov's early stories are about the construction of some giant electrical machine that is entirely inconceivable from the point of view of known physics and technology. With the aid of this device, which works off the energy of human will or thought, for example, one can turn the globe upside down, harness the energy of distant stars, knock a small planet into the sea and sink a ship, raise a huge wave in the ocean, or simply grow cucumbers year round. This isn't science fiction—it's an entirely different genre. Platonov's leading characters take charge of such natural forces to their own detriment, and you'll find no normal plot and no moral in these strange texts, only the seething of words and dreams.

In the story "Fro," one of Platonov's best, the subject is, as always, the search for happiness, and here's what the married lovers talk about:

> Fedor listened to Fro, and then he explained to her in detail his own ideas and projects—about the transmission of electric energy without wires, by means of ionized air, about increasing the strength of all metals by processing their ultrasonic waves, about the stratosphere one hundred kilometers up in the sky where there exist special light, heat and electric conditions capable of guaranteeing eternal life to a man—this is why the dreams of the ancient world about heaven may now actually come true—and Fedor promised to think out and to accomplish many other things for Frosya's sake and at the same time for the sake of all the other people in the world.

Needless to say, Platonov does not put this "scientific" nonsense in Fedor's mouth in order to laugh at him. Apparently he himself believes in the possibility of such discoveries—well, if not precisely these, then similar ones. He believes in the power of human thought, which sooner or later will invent something unprecedented—and then happiness will reign, in the form of liberation from the torment of everyday labor. But at the same time he recognizes another kind of happiness as well:

> Frosya listened blissfully to her husband, half opening her already tired mouth. When they finished talking, they threw their arms around each other—they wanted to be happy right away, now, sooner than their future and zealous work would bring results in personal and in general happiness. The heart brooks no delay, it sickens, as if believing in nothing.

The mind believes but the heart doesn't; the mind can be directed toward the future, toward the submission of the universe, but the heart isn't interested; the Communists' plans are grandiose, but what does that matter to the simple human heart?

The central theme running through Platonov's work is the happiness of the mind and the happiness of the heart in their complex interaction; he studies what happiness really is, why and how it appears, where it goes, how to find and hold on to it. Even this theme the writer investigates as though he were not quite a human being but some other kind of creature. As he writes in *The Foundation Pit:*

> The disquieting sounds of sudden music gave feeling to conscience, they offered to preserve the span of life, to pass through the distances of hope to the very end and arrive at it, in order to find there the source of this disturbing song and before death not to cry from the anguish of futility.

And:

> He was more comfortable feeling bereavement on this terrestrial, extinguished star; alien and distant happiness provoked shame and alarm in him.

In 1922, Platonov wrote about himself in a letter to a publisher:

> Besides the fields, the countryside, my mother, and the sound of bells ringing, I also loved — and the longer I live, the more I love — steam engines, machines, shrill whistles, and sweaty work. I believed then that everything is man-made and nothing comes by itself; for a long time I thought they made children somewhere at the factory. . . .
>
> . . . There is some kind of link, some kinship, among burdocks and beggars, singing in the fields, electricity, a locomotive and its whistle, and earthquakes — there is the same birthmark on all of them and on some other things too. . . . Growing grass and working steam engines take the same kind of mechanics.

The world of Platonov's characters is a cosmic world, the world before (or simultaneous with) the appearance of God the Creator; the world of the soul, which seems to exist parallel with the Creator; the world of the spirit, which in some sense (for example in stubbornness and willpower) is equal to the Creator. The universe, as we know it, with its gravitation, molecules, hellish radiation, planets forming from lumps of stardust, and the blinding flash of suns burning at millions of degrees—this universe, according to Platonov, is in a state of constant becoming within each human soul. This is a universe where beast, grass, stone, electricity, and human beings—that is, all things animate and inanimate—are equal and indistinguishable in their foundation: they all exist. They *are*. They are incarnate. Moreover, incarnation continuously and incomprehensibly torments them. "Torment" is a key word for Platonov. Life, existence, being *here* is torment, anguish, albeit a creative, fruitful torment, a heroic anguish. Another key concept is "patience" or "endurance." One must live and be, one must endure. According to Platonov, one must not only endure grief, sorrow, need, and other forms of unpleasantness. One must endure happiness, love, and pleasure.

This is an entirely unique view of being, not merely a unique way of describing it. This is the way an angel of the upper heavenly circle might feel if, by some tragic accident or mistake, he had been born among humans and had not yet forgotten the expanses of the otherworldly universe where he once flew in an inchoate whirl of magnetic fields, particles, and quarks. Life is the joy and torment of incarnation.

Platonov was published little during his lifetime, and the few stories that made it into print elicited invective from official critics. He was known only to a narrow circle of readers. Perhaps this is what saved him from arrest; his novels, *The Foundation Pit* and *Chevengur,* were considered shockingly anti-Soviet and were not published in the USSR until the very beginning of the 1990s. In the account of collectivization in *The Foundation Pit,* people are digging a foundation pit for a huge building in which all the inhabitants of a small town will live. They don't till the fields or sow their crops, they have nothing to eat; but they give themselves over entirely to heady dreams of the bright future that will soon arrive. And since only the poor are deserving of this bright future, everyone who owns anything at all is put on a raft and sent off down the river to the cold winter sea. Those people remaining gradually die of starvation. The theme is the same in *Chevengur:* people destroy everything in the name of an idea, in the name of the future.

The writer achieved fame only posthumously. He died in poverty, from tuberculosis, in 1951. In the last years of his life, he lived in a janitor's room, ironically enough in the building of the Literary Institute. They say that he cleaned the courtyard, sweeping the yellow autumn leaves to one side. Hurrying to their classes in the morning, the students grew accustomed to seeing him and paid no attention to the coughing middle-aged man. Some of them said that this eccentric also wrote stories.

In his youth Platonov wrote: "I know that I am one of the most insignificant of people. You have, no doubt, noticed this, but I also know another thing: the more insignificant a creature is, the more glad it is for life, because it is least deserving of it."

And further on, the mysterious words: "For you, being a man is just a habit—for me it is joy, a holiday."

Whoever he may have been—let us be grateful that such creatures sometimes visit our world.

2000

The Making of Mr. Putin

Review of *First Person: An Astonishingly Frank Self-Portrait*, by Vladimir Putin, with Nataliya Gevorkyan, Natalya Timakova, and Andrei Kolesnikov; translated by Catherine A. Fitzpatrick (Public Affairs, 2000)

A T THIS YEAR'S forum in Davos, the question "Who is Putin?" was put to the members of the Russian delegation. They became confused, looked at one another, and mumbled something incomprehensible. There was laughter in the hall. But indeed, who is he?

For a certain group of Russians—let's call them left liberals —the answer was obvious from the beginning: Putin is a bloody tyrant and a future dictator. This point of view requires no detailed evidence. It is enough that Putin worked in the KGB for many years. For that matter, for this part of the liberal intelligentsia, which has recently supported Grigory Yavlinsky and his Yabloko Party, conclusions are obvious in advance and require no argumentation. In their dogmatism the members of this group are indistinguishable from their opponents. It's no accident that this group is called the "liberal gendarmerie." The opponent of a bad person almost always seems good in their eyes. Black and white are their basic colors.

By the time of the election, left liberals had formed their

judgments from uneven but identically repellent components: Putin worked in the KGB; he is presiding over the war in Chechnya; he hates the Radio Liberty correspondent Andrei Babitsky and called him a traitor. With this, the question of trusting Putin became closed and the left liberals called on everyone to vote for Yavlinsky. (Five percent of the voters did so.) The logic was the following: "We know that we will be defeated, but we will take defeat with our heads proudly raised. We will express our protest against impending dictatorship. We will lose beautifully."

Yavlinsky himself, asked for whom would he cast his vote in the case of a second round of elections—which could only have been between Putin and the Communist candidate, Gennady Zyuganov—answered that he would vote for no one, that both were abhorrent to him. This is exactly the way he behaved during the elections of 1996, when the choice was between Yeltsin and Zyuganov. Yavlinsky didn't like either of them. By acting this way, however, in the name of purity, he helped no one with anything—neither people nor ideas.

The right-wing liberals, headed by Anatoly Chubais, a former deputy prime minister and minister of finance, and Sergei Kiriyenko, who briefly served as one of Yeltsin's prime ministers, supported Putin. Being political pragmatists, they were concerned with real change, the necessity of using all available means in order to get a package of desperately needed liberal reforms through the Duma, including changes in the punitive and unworkable tax laws and, most important, measures providing for the private ownership of land. Both men knew from firsthand experience what real politics and real struggle were like in the endlessly complex and confused Russian situation. Both of them knew what it means to take responsibility and make decisions, with all the consequences, including falling from the heights of power at the caprice of Yeltsin and his circle. Both fell and got back up without wasting time on complaints and pointing to their wounds.

Their position was as follows: it is impossible to demand liberal economic reforms from the president while depriving him of liberal support. If the liberals hold their noses and turn away (Yavlinsky's solution), then less-fastidious and greedier forces, of which there is a bountiful supply in Russia today, will be all too happy to rush to power. Yes, Putin wasn't raised in a democratic garden. But he worked for approximately six years on the democratic team of Anatoly Sobchak, the mayor of St. Petersburg who was one of the first reformers to appear in the post-Gorbachev period. Putin supported Sobchak when he was attacked, at a time when this support was unpopular and even dangerous.

Putin's program is being written by a liberal team including German Gref, Aleksei Kudrin, and other members of the "Petersburg democrats" whose thinking is close to that of Chubais. Putin recently appointed Andrei Illarionov, another liberal economist from St. Petersburg, as his adviser. The right liberals think that there is a chance — let's call it their political calculation — that things will continue this way. In short, it seems that the right liberals are trying to push Putin toward democracy, while the left liberals are throwing rotten tomatoes from behind the fence they have constructed around their idea of democracy. This is the main split in Russia's democratic forces, and it will surely deepen.

Besides the democrats, there is also the rest of the population, which voted for Putin by a clear majority over the Communist Gennady Zyuganov. This can be interpreted as a desire for a "strong hand." But it could also be seen as a welcome sign of society's recuperation. It could mean that almost two thirds of Russia's voters do not want to be pulled backward toward the "bright past" of the Soviet era that Zyuganov's propaganda offers. It is possible that during ten years of reform many people have developed a taste for the new freedoms and opportunities that have appeared in Russia — and this despite mass impoverishment, the painful collapse of the country, the growth of crime, and pervasive corruption. These voters are placing their hopes on the future and not on the past, and in Putin they see someone who they believe will help the country to press forward. Of course, people may have simply wanted something new and unknown.

Yet is it possible to objectively answer the question "Who is Putin?" Or, more aptly, "Who will Putin turn out to be? What can we expect from him?" Watching Putin on television and listening to his speeches, and especially reading the ones that are published, is a waste of time: the texts are written by speechwriters; the video clips are meticulously put together by image-makers; and everything is vetted by the presidential administration.

When we see Putin skiing down a mountain on TV, mixing with the crowd (his bodyguards also pretend to be red-cheeked skiers), or watch him drop by a little restaurant, supposedly to eat blini (Russian crepes), you understand that Putin himself is absent, that you are watching a kind of national fun-house mirror in which the projected fears, hopes, tastes, and customs of the electorate are reflected. He's skiing—so he's young and healthy, no comparison with the old, sick Yeltsin. He's mixing with the crowd—so he's democratic. He's eating blini—so he observes national traditions, especially around Easter—a nod in the direction of the Russian Orthodox Church. Specialists in PR wouldn't allow him to eat, say, sushi and sashimi in public before the elections—that isn't Russian food. What if this faux pas suddenly cost him a couple of million votes?

Thus, for example, the image-makers, preparing Putin's interview on television's Channel One (controlled by the "oligarch" Boris Berezovsky), tried at first to hide the candidate's dog from the voters. Putin's dog—a toy poodle, small, white, fluffy, named Toska—didn't fit the image of the mysterious, steely, decisive, masculine leader that they were trying to create. But the press somehow sniffed the dog out and even published its picture. The dog was forced to come out of hiding (more accurately, Toska suddenly appeared on the screen, dropped on

Putin's lap from somewhere off-camera, obviously thrown into the picture by some assistant). Then came the following conversation:

"Is this your dog?"

"Well, I don't even know whose she is — mine or my children's. We used to have another dog, a ferocious dog. But it died, and so the kids convinced me to get this one." He's disavowing his own dog! — so anti-Putin viewers exclaimed in outrage.

Some light is thrown on Putin's past by the recently published book by and on him, which is really a long interview. Three journalists from the newspaper *Kommersant* (also controlled by Berezovsky) met with the presidential candidate six times (altogether for a period of twenty-four hours). There are many interesting details in the book, but it's clear that the information in it is carefully doled out, with Putin keen to make a good impression on his readers.

What if we try to understand "who Putin is" without relying on those who are molding his image — since we aren't inclined to believe them? I've heard that the training program for U.S. Green Berets includes an exercise in "determining the contents of a box without opening it." Let's try to apply something of the same approach to the freshly elected president of Russia as well. Central to understanding the image of our protagonist is the well-organized and effective Soviet state machine that found, convinced, educated, and defined Putin during his youthful, formative years, which coincided with "developed socialism," that is, the Brezhnev period. At the time, the KGB was the most efficiently functioning part of the Soviet state machine. Its strength was founded on the absence of any control by law, on panic-stricken fear of its omnipotence, and on its immensely detailed information about what was going on in the country and in the heads of its citizens.

Putin, according to his own account, dreamed of joining the

secret service from the age of fifteen, i.e., from an age when ideas about a spy's work are still colored with "romanticism." While still a schoolboy he tried to volunteer for the KGB but was turned down because of his age and was told that they don't take volunteers. First he must receive an education. "What kind?" asked the boy. "Law school." Putin entered law school and waited. Eventually he was approached by the agency. From that moment on, Putin has lived behind a thick curtain of lifetime secrecy; at that moment he entered a secret order about whose inner workings we know very little. This was in the middle of the 1970s.

A few words on this period in Soviet history. The end of the 1960s brought the USSR's invasion of Czechoslovakia and a strategic failure in the space race: after the Americans landed a man on the moon in 1969, it became obvious to the Russians that they would forever be in second place. The beginning of the 1970s saw the flourishing of the "Andropov" approach to the country's internal life. Dissenters were pushed out of the country. If that was not possible, it was easy enough, without resort to any criminal prosecution, to make it impossible for "inconvenient" people to function: careers could be cut short, new works banned from publication, and people forbidden to travel abroad or emigrate for reasons of "state security." And if such measures failed, the psychiatric hospital could be substituted for the labor camps. That the economic system had more or less reached a dead end was largely clear by the middle of the 1970s. At the same time, a colossal military potential was unleashed: the country began to build its most powerful nuclear rocket systems. It was also the period of the greatest hypocrisy in the foreign policy of détente—tensions were created mostly by the USSR itself.

It was at this moment that Putin passed into the sphere of the secret institution. This work requires not only the personal desire to do it, but "positive vetting" by "competent organs." This meant that the candidate must possess a number of qualities that will guarantee lifetime loyalty to the system that considers itself the backbone of the state. When Putin entered the KGB, the candidate had to believe, and not just in words, that the Soviet system was the most just of all, that imperialism was truly enemy number one, that the Communist Party was indeed the vanguard of humanity, that the history of the USSR was a series of victories, and that the unbearable difficulties on the path to these victories were caused by the stubbornness and cunning of its enemies. The regime's foreign and domestic politics had to be seen as optimal strategies, to be protected by all possible means from hostile attack. Not many Soviet citizens were prepared forever to exchange a regular civilian career for the onerous labor and indissoluble obligations of a KGB officer.

Putin made this choice. This means that he was ready to renounce, consciously and for his entire life, any critical reconsideration of the stereotypes of Soviet life. It means as well that he agreed that from then on, even the slightly significant steps he would take in everyday life would have to be cleared with his bosses. He would have to renounce any defense of his "own opinion"—it could harm the cause. He agreed that the "personal" should yield to the "social." Working in the foreign service of the KGB, he had to remember the cardinal rule: don't ruin relations with anyone, no matter how bad, who might come in handy. But at the same time, one must not have any close friendships either: the moral obligations that might arise could conflict with the duties of service. A good worker should be utterly convinced that unquestioning fulfillment of orders facilitates the strengthening of the state that exists.

There is reason to believe that Putin was a good worker. Therefore, in order to understand the internal structure of the positions, convictions, and motivations of our protagonist's behavior, we must understand the system of priorities, preferences, goals, permissible methods, ideology, and human relations within the gigantic Corporation that was the state security system of the USSR and Russia. Putin was an indivisible part and a reliably working component of this system. Understanding the basic perspectives of the Corporation, we will understand better "who Putin is." According to an unspoken tradition, for example, the work of a state security officer abroad was considered more prestigious and professional than work in the KGB "against our own people." (Similarly, regular army officers are more respected than officers of the internal police, who suppress disturbances within the country.)

The late 1970s and 1980s was also a period of the growing senility of the Brezhnev regime and the "five-year plan of flamboyant funerals." The KGB, as the most informed organization in the country, was the first to realize the disastrousness of the gerontocracy's course. It is well known that Gorbachev's rise to power was Andropov's doing. The KGB was looking for, and nominated, a man capable both of reformist thought and of recognizing the limits of permissible change. The KGB would never have chosen a rebel as leader. It needed a man who was able, and wanted, "to change without destroying."

Putin seems to fit at least part of this description. It is true that for most of his career he was not a leader. His work in East Germany between 1985 and 1990 was by KGB standards a bureaucratic job in a relatively predictable, tightly controlled place, nothing like West Germany. The fall of the Berlin Wall meant a change of work and position for Putin; and such an event would necessarily be reflected in the Corporation's strategy. In 1990, Putin became the international liaison assistant to the president of Leningrad State University (LGU) — again not a leader and not a director. But he was a loyal, reliable person in a hotbed of dissent and badly controlled contacts with foreigners.

The state was collapsing; another state was being born. Which state's security should be guarded at this time and place? This decision was not within Putin's jurisdiction. Only the Corporation could answer that. That Putin was working at LGU meant the KGB had sent him, and in fact, as he says in *First Person,* the KGB continued to pay him. During the period of confusion, of shifting loyalties, of free elections, the rise of Yeltsin, the popularity of Sobchak, Putin neither welcomed nor criticized anything; he didn't get distracted, he didn't look for popularity—he wasn't like Oleg Kalugin, the KGB major general who wrote a self-dramatizing memoir and left Russia for the U.S. in 1994. At a time when everyone was in a rush to declare his changed views, Putin remained true to the discipline of the Corporation. One can only think that his unprecedented rise to the position of deputy mayor under Sobchak meant the Corporation trusted him with this high position, anticipating that the inexperienced democrats were likely to botch things up.

Putin has had no experience in concocting slogans or in popularizing ideas formulated during open debate with ideological opponents. He has no experience in speaking at meetings and demonstrations where the audience might be either indifferent or hostile, and where one has to quickly turn the mood in one's own favor with a strong speech. In short, he doesn't have the experience of a politician—he has no record of public success or bitter defeat. Broadly speaking, he has experience in implementing the idea of strengthening the state, which has involved, among other things, implicitly trusting people whom he considers to have authority. In particular, this means that on joining Yeltsin's team, having won Yeltsin's trust and been named his heir, he again found himself in the position of serving a "Corporation," serving an idea, serving a system.

But this time, it's another Corporation—the Russian State Machine. This machine has its own system of priorities, its own view of Russia's development, its own permissible methods, its own strategic friends and enemies. If we can correctly identify the circle of people who control this new Corporation—its brain center—we can find another key to the enigma of Putin. At the moment it appears that the team Putin is putting together is heavily weighted toward advisers and economists from the liberal right—i.e., colleagues of Anatoly Chubais. But it is also widely thought that the oligarch Boris Berezovsky—the sworn enemy of this group, and of Chubais in particular — is currently controlling, or trying to control, most of Putin's important moves.

We still don't know what the real balance of power is in Putin's entourage, and this will become apparent only as events unfold and as Putin appoints his government. Another indication will probably be the May elections for governor of St. Petersburg, a city whose complex politics have great influence on the national scene not only because it is Russia's "second capital" but because many of the government's important players — including Putin himself, Chubais, Sergei Stepashin, Kudrin, Gref, and Illarionov — have ties to that city. It was generally assumed right after Putin's victory on March 26 that one of his priorities would be to see that the current governor, Vladimir Yakovlev, would not be reelected in May. Yakovlev and Putin both served as deputy mayors under Anatoly Sobchak, an outstanding democrat who was at one time thought to have a chance at becoming president of Russia.

In 1996, amid charges of corruption, Sobchak lost the election to Yakovlev, a man who has since become closely associated with the criminal world and who is now accused of being responsible for St. Petersburg's having acquired the title of Russia's "crime capital" (there have been numerous political assassinations in St. Petersburg in recent years). Yakovlev headed the campaign against Sobchak, which was conducted on all fronts, and at the time Putin publicly called Yakovlev a Judas. In the event, Sobchak lost not only the election but his former popularity; he became persona non grata, a persecuted politician and citizen, and was obliged to move to France for several years, out of fear for his life.

For many, Putin's relations with Sobchak remain a mystery. It is usually claimed that Sobchak trusted only spineless flatterers. But this clearly doesn't describe Putin. It is possible that Putin's successful relations with Sobchak were based on the fact that Putin's true bosses were in the Corporation, that Sobchak was only his nominal superior. Gaining Sobchak's trust gave Putin the opportunity of controlling an emotional politician. Thus, in this interpretation, Putin's ability to get along with Sobchak was simply a reflection of his professional competence as an intelligence officer.

If so, however, then another enigma arises. Sobchak's fall was precipitous and devastating to both his local and national reputation. As a tough intelligence officer turned politician, Putin, according to all calculations, should have crossed his former boss off his accounts. Instead, after becoming acting president, Putin unexpectedly brought Sobchak back from "exile" and into his inner circle, making him a trusted official in his election campaign. Before Sobchak suddenly died of a heart attack in late February, it was widely expected that he would be appointed to one of the key posts in the government.

Why such loyalty to Sobchak? The answer lies in the same place—in the system of Putin's values. As a professional who needs to be careful in choosing the most reliable people for important tasks, Putin understood who Sobchak was. Sobchak had evident personal weaknesses, which his opponents have gladly exploited—such as his poor mastery of the details of municipal management and his love of expensive, flamboyant festivals in a city with a broken economy. Nevertheless, he was a man who proved that his political commitments and moral values not only remained steady over the years of perestroika, years of disappointed hopes, but, on the contrary, were strengthened. Putin chose Sobchak, for whom honor and conscience were dearer than public opinion of himself. Only his sudden death prevented Sobchak from resuming their interesting partnership on a national level.

The state for Putin is unified and indivisible; it has its clear interests, which cannot be compromised either in foreign or in domestic policies, no matter how strong the objections of human rights advocates in Russia or abroad. The Chechen rebels don't take Russia's interests into account—so Putin isn't going to take Chechnya's interests into account. The opinion of foreign powers must be taken seriously as long as the interests of foreign powers don't interfere with the government's domestic policies. This would not necessarily preclude a pragmatic response to international protests against conditions in Chechnya. As a nuclear power, Russia should be treated as an equal partner with other nuclear powers and not be ashamed of its small budget. If Russia has renounced the ideas of an Iron Curtain and of personal and party dictatorship, then its leaders have to be consistent. Putin's first political demands were for "the dictatorship of law" and "the defense of the rights of property holders."

At present, Putin's policy is based on the idea of strengthening the state, raising the army's morale, making Russia's incoherent economic reforms consistent with one another, bringing about order in Russia's vertical ruling structures, and taking a pragmatic approach to foreign policy. Who will Putin rely on in his new role, in the role of the director of the new Corporation? It seems to me that the answer is clear: on those forces that genuinely support him, regardless of their political affiliation. And he will respond to their support from the point of view of his understanding of "benefit for the country," and not benefit for individuals or parties. It would be naive, if not silly, to think that Putin's policies can be influenced by accusing him in advance of all possible sins (as the left liberals are doing). And on the contrary, for a Russian who genuinely believes that his economic initiatives will enrich the state and the population, then the only place to seek support for these initiatives now is from Putin (as the right-wing liberals are doing). Now as never before there is a historic chance to carry out systemic reforms in Russia. It would be a great mistake not to try to make use of it.

Putin: We had a dog, true it was a different one, a ferocious dog. Unfortunately, it died, run over by a car. But the kids wanted a little dog, and they finally convinced me. Now, it's not clear whose dog it is more—mine, my wife's, the kids'. The dog just sort of lives here on its own.

Interviewer (jokingly): Like a cat.

Putin (not laughing at the joke, coldly): No, no, don't insult our dog. It doesn't work as a cat. A dog is a dog. We really love it.

No, he's not disavowing his dog. It's just a completely different dog. And he won't let anyone offend it. In his own way he loves this dog. Just as he loved the previous one.

2000

Lies I Lived

MY BROTHER attended Soviet schools in the late 1940s, when the Americans were our enemies. No one had ever seen them, of course. This made them even more terrifying for simple people because, who knows, they might be anywhere, disguised as Soviet citizens in regular clothes. They would reveal all our mysteries, steal the secrets of our might, and, God forbid, become just as strong and unconquerable as we were. That's what my brother was told in school. Above all, it was strictly, *strictly* forbidden to let anyone know what went on in gym classes. The enemy could not be allowed to find out how many sit-ups and push-ups Soviet schoolchildren could do in a row, how fast they could climb up a rope, and whether or not they could do handstands.

When I went to school ten years later, Stalin had died, and the mood was much lighter. But I remembered my brother's stories. Although he laughed at the paranoia of his schoolteachers, at the advanced age of seven I suspected him of a certain youthful frivolousness. I loved my country and wanted us, Soviet schoolchildren, to be strong and healthy. Let those Americans walk around grasping the walls from weakness.

One day the spring I turned eight, I was playing in our courtyard in the sand, building a castle for a rubber hippopotamus. Suddenly an old man and an old woman towered above me. The old woman had fat, swollen legs, and the old man breathed with a slow asthmatic wheeze. "Is this the right way to the Botanical Gardens?" he asked. *There they are,* I thought. *Enemies!*

I answered instantly, brave, very convincing, almost without a tremble in my voice: "No, you're going the wrong way. You need to go back that way."

"Thank you so much," replied the old man. The couple turned slowly and headed back. I sat in the sandbox and watched them go, the hippopotamus clutched in my hands. My heart thumped. I had just done something heroic! I had fended off spies!

The Botanical Gardens were in fact right behind our building. The enemies moseyed along, in no hurry, holding onto each other. The old man frequently stopped to catch his breath, and the old woman stood patiently on her swollen legs, waiting for him to move on.

Something was wrong with this picture. I felt an acute surge of shame. Suddenly, in one overwhelming moment—a moment I shall never forget—the truth was revealed to me. This was knowledge: that comes in an instant, without words; complete knowledge, clear, indisputable, the kind of moral knowledge that requires no questions or explanations, the kind of knowledge that transforms an ape into a human being.

I clearly saw the couple as old people who had lived a long, loving life, had survived a terrible war, gone hungry, suffered illness, been crippled; who had perhaps—in fact, even certainly—lost friends and loved ones in the recently ended massacre of peoples. I saw them descending the steep staircase of their home slowly, step by step, in order to go to the gardens, to sit on a bench, enjoy the young leaves and spring flowers on this warm day, in what might be their last spring. I saw the lies and vileness of my teachers, their paranoia, their ruthlessness, their sadism. I heard the scrape and clank of the cogs in the state propaganda machine, a machine that had forgotten why it was turning. And at that moment, burning with shame, I swore a silent oath: *Never*. But *never* what? I couldn't explain, and no one asked me.

The idiocy of total secrecy led to the opposite result: nothing at all remained secret. For example, most Russian cities had "secret institutes" or "military factories," which were marked on maps with numbers or code names. Everyone knew perfectly well what kinds of factories these were and what was produced there. Most important, they knew how to get onto the factory grounds—not through the official entrance, where passes were meticulously checked and where a sharpshooter sat with a gun, but through a hole in the fence a mere hundred yards from the automatic gates. People climbed through the hole in the fence not to take out secret documents but simply to buy food in the store or cafeteria, for secret institutions were always well stocked. I did the same myself: I used to buy meat patties at some tank factory. No one ever stopped me.

During perestroika the old regime was destroyed, and the system of secrecy along with it. Russians began to remove everything they possibly could from institutes and factories, and to sell everything they stole, including state secrets—actual, not imagined ones. They stole poisons, mercury, uranium, cesium, and vaccines. Even, in one instance, smallpox virus. Years of searches for invented enemies have thus led to the opposite effect: now no one can keep secrets that it might be reasonable to keep or lock up materials that might pose a danger to humanity.

2000

ALSO BY TATYANA TOLSTAYA

THE SLYNX

"Tatyana Tolstaya's first novel...has been hailed as a postmodern literary masterpiece of the same stature as Gogol's *Dead Souls* and Nabokov's *Pale Fire*."
— **Nina Khrushcheva, *Times Literary Supplement***

Tatyana Tolstaya's satirical first novel is set in what remains of Moscow some two hundred years after the "Blast," an event that catapulted Russia back to a blank slate. The current focus of Russian culture is mice—the source of food, clothes, and commerce. Owning books is prohibited by the tyrant, whose scribes plagiarize the old masters, becoming society's only authors. One of those copy clerks, Benedikt, is the narrator of *The Slynx*. He is in love with books as objects but is unable to derive any meaning or moral benefit from them. The Slynx of the title is a ravenous, catlike, imaginary animal that represents unknown dangers to the denizens of this post-civilization. The creature is also Tolstaya's metaphor for lust, cruelty, egotism, ignorance, and moral blindness. ISBN 0-618-12497-7

AVAILABLE IN HARDCOVER FROM

HOUGHTON MIFFLIN COMPANY